A FICTION
OF UNITY

Why Global Business
Strategies Fail

Peter Close

Cover design by Andy Meaden
Edited by Anne Abel Smith

ISBN: 979-8-9897161-0-4 (paperback)
ISBN: 979-8-9897161-1-1 (ebook)

Author's website: www.peterclose.global

Acknowledgements

The world is a better place thanks to people who see the power of mutuality and express this through their shared endeavors. It is not a complex idea. We know the results are reliable. Yet, we discount the strength of the deep currents that pull us off course. My thanks then to those with the perception and the resilience to correct the drift.

This book is based on research and I am grateful to all of the international business leaders who contributed their experiences, insights and ideas. The puzzle pieces that you presented were such a gift. Sometimes they fit together to reveal part of a whole picture. Many times, they did not and you challenged me. So, whether you hold global, regional or local responsibilities, or work in the board room or on the front lines, I hope you enjoy the satisfaction of seeing yourselves, and knowing you were heard, in the pages of this book.

Thank you to my former CHCI compatriots: Tom Booth, Ian Swanson, Lori Ingerman, Nathalie Robert, Denise Schlette, Susan Levy, Michael Tease, Raquel Bouer, Carlos Garcia Cubas, Roberto Muñoz Fernandez, Aurelie Bonnet, Andrew Gibson, Ekaterina Stevlingson, Artur Gano, Maja Stakovska, Amgad Mabrock, Leanne Spratt, Paula Toe, June Zhang and Shirley Qu. Over the years I have held on to your example as positive proof there is a way to make global business strategy sing. I was beyond proud to be *Global Pete* in your company.

Many thanks to my editor Anne Abel Smith. It is a joy to trust in your meticulous process. I must also express my delight in finding Andy Meaden to design the cover.

Finally, love and hugs to Mogies, John and Penny for their intellect, buffoonery and unshakable support.

Contents

Introduction

A Global Vision

What do you imagine for your global company? When you think of all its component parts and their combined potential, what is the picture in your mind? Perhaps, these are some of the attributes that you wish for:

- Leaders equipped to succeed in a world of complex and diverse challenges.
- The agility to focus resources wherever they are needed.
- International differences harnessed as valuable advantages.
- The countries and regions where you operate combined into an interactive and purposeful portfolio.
- Connected stakeholders who believe in the importance of collaboration.
- Colleagues empowered to draw from a collective bank of worldwide expertise.
- Functional and geographical teams working together across borders and without silos.
- Senior executives who are honorable, and admired for their curiosity and empathy.
- Shared decision-making that flows quickly throughout the company.
- Strategy that is clear, actionable, and inspiring.
- Everyone knowing where they fit and what they need to do.

Can such a paragon of organization, leadership, character, and operational behavior exist in a global company? How might we move closer to it? Is anything stopping us? Does everyone want it? Can we agree on the value of the opportunity?

Many global companies share a common vision of integrated performance. Yet, most are much less global than the word suggests. They are certainly global in the sense that you can sum up the value created across their geographic footprint, although that is a better fit for the definition of a worldwide business. "Global," on the other hand, deliberately infers that the business as a whole is something greater than the sum of its geographic parts. It implies that these parts, while separate, operate together with a shared purpose and in some kind of connective harmony that is meaningful and creates more value. That is the whole idea. The separate parts can be similar or they can be different, but the impetus for forming a global company is just that—the superior value created by a single coherent entity.

This simple idea is our North Star. The whole point of a company being global is to unlock superior value above and beyond the sum of its separate geographic businesses. Crucially, this bonus potential only exists when the company's component parts are connected, complementary, and also share a common purpose.

A Global Tension

Yet, as we imagine this harmonious, orderly, and interdependent ideal and contemplate how globally connected our company is today or might become, there is a snake in our garden, a sometimes stealthy but ever-present adversary to our vision. This is our vulnerability—and possibly our downfall—because the separate parts of all global organizations invest incredible energy in becoming more separate.

In many organizations, the scenario plays out this way: While the business is small, individual regions and countries want to benefit from the scale and the capabilities that come with shared resources, collaboration, and interdependence. Yet, the minute they are large enough to achieve meaningful results alone, these countries or regions will change their tune in favor of autonomy and independence, working hard to secede in as many ways as they can.

This is not a high crime. Self-government—the freedom to act or function independently—is a motivation that we all share. However, it chips away at the potential value of our combined global company. When multiple countries or regions begin to secede, the chips become cracks and global unity begins to splinter. Left alone, these cracks become wider and increasingly permanent. The global value that we might have created moves increasingly out of reach.

If you have held a global or regional role, then you have contended with this fragmentation. You have felt the symptoms of a rebellious pressure for increased separateness, autonomy, and independence. On the face of it, this is self-defeating for a global company. Even modest progress against these objectives will degrade performance today and downscale future potential. Yet, not everyone feels this way. And you have seen it: You know what real collaboration looks like. You know how it feels when everyone involved is enthusiastic and when they can't wait to work together, excited by what they will accomplish. Yet, instead, you have been served a diet of feigned alignment and fake commitments as you try to build value across a global matrix that is often misaligned and deliberately opaque.

A Global Solution

This book is a playbook. Or maybe it will be the inspiration for you to create your own playbook because, in the following chapters, we will discuss some of the successes that you may be imagining for your global company and how they may be realized.

If you are new to a global or regional role, or perhaps to a multinational team, then the insights, tools, and practices that you will find here will offer you tremendous advantage. I can't promise that you will find all of the answers, but you will be infinitely better prepared than most of us were when—in the past—we signed on for one of these roles.

If you are charged with developing a global strategy, or if you are part of such a team, then this is a map of the minefield in which you will be treading.

To all of the leaders of international businesses who have felt the symptoms of fragmentation, and to the many who have wrestled with their consequences, I hope that you will feel seen and heard in these pages. If you are a frustrated practitioner, then please know that you are in great company with many compatriot brothers and sisters who will understand the true scale of your achievements and also identify with your disappointments, exasperations, and fuming irritations.

We start the book with two short chapters to set the stage and then move quickly into a second series of chapters that describe several "Forces of Fragmentation." Here we explore and label the major causes behind the dysfunctional symptoms that global companies experience. We will see that each force applies continuous pressure, seeking to disrupt coherence, collaboration, and goodwill. It is a revealing discussion, particularly if we haven't appreciated just how hard it is to be globally integrated and effective.

The next part of the book, "Suffering the Symptoms" details the findings of an in-depth and robust research study that dissects the anatomy of a global company's effectiveness. We will hear from a large number of different stakeholders as they describe their experiences and share their insights. Many of the findings are disappointing and some are shocking. Overall, the report card is very poor.

Now, with a clearer understanding of all of our challenges, we can begin to "Diagnose the Dysfunction." These chapters describe several assessment tools that you can use to detect global dysfunction in your own company. There is also counsel on how to present and use your findings to best effect.

Introduction

Finally, we end the journey with "Positive Principles." These final chapters promise hope for the future by offering road-tested recommendations and advice to help you preempt, avoid, or confront your company's current recipe for global dysfunction.

There is a flow to this book. Each section builds deliberately upon the one before. However, you don't need to stay on this path. Most chapters contain a summary and an itemized list of takeaways. So, if something catches your eye in the Table of Contents, feel free to jump straight to it.

A word of warning though: It is unusual for any single global dysfunction to exist alone. The forces behind them are insidious. They hide from view and often work together. For this reason, I recommend that you spend time exploring the "Forces of Fragmentation" before you try to use any of the assessment tools.

To illustrate the complexity and the depth of the behavioral, attitudinal and organizational challenges that we are dealing with, consider the final fragmenting force that you will find described in the chapter "Global Strategy Theater". Here we discuss the gestalt of the most pervasive findings that have emerged from all of the research. Both quantitative and qualitative work reveal multiple forces that combine to undermine the very idea of a coherent global strategy. When these forces are left unchecked, then a strategy's development, definition, and deployment can become a theatrical production. Imagine the players free to act out their roles but without accountability or commitment to a strategy's implementation and results. As outrageous as this sounds, the research participants reported again and again that—in so many supposedly strategic global companies—they were, to varying degrees, watching or participating in a staged performance.

Let's recommit ourselves to our vision of what is possible. There is no need for us to stay caught up in this ineffectual drama. If, with insight and courage, we strip away the masks and the artifice, we can reverse the fragmentation. Our reward will be an effective global organization where we can lead, collaborate, and unlock our global advantages.

We are long overdue for a bold renovation of the status quo. Let's get to it.

Autobiography

I have spent my career in global, regional, and local business in both operational and strategic roles. I have lived in the UK, Europe, and North America working with different multinational corporations, both public and private. At one time or another, I have held commercial responsibility in every part of the world. Over these 30-plus years, global leadership, strategy, and organizational effectiveness have become my craft and my journey.

I was educated as a post-graduate scientist and, while I can't remember how to solve fourth-order differential equations anymore, I took the scientific method to heart. In international commercial roles, working in a confusing matrix where there seemed to be no rules, I paid attention to what worked or failed and induced hypotheses to explain what happened. Bit by bit, proof by proof, misstep by misstep, I built and refined a set of principles to guide me in global leadership and to improve my effectiveness.

Over the years, I had some great mentors who shared their experiences and the lessons that they had learned. There was also that other kind of mentor—the nightmarish leader whose behavior made it clear which fork in the road you never want to take and the kind of boss you never want to be.

In every organization that I worked with, it was clear that international collaboration was a painful and frequently wasteful struggle. There was always dysfunction, and yet the causes were rarely acknowledged and never addressed. It is amazing when you think about it: These companies were well-respected, they achieved decent results, and their leaders were intelligent people. So, why did they struggle so much with global leadership and collaboration? And, perhaps more importantly, why was the dysfunction allowed to continue? Why was it acceptable for global, regional, and local leaders to maneuver around each other pretending commitment and playing politics? Was this invisible to those at the top? Were they unaware, complicit, or powerless?

After you have watched this go on for a while, you start to wonder if there is a reason why nobody is trying to fix it. Why the inertia? Who benefits from the dysfunction? Indeed, the more you dig into global structure, matrix organizations, effective decision-making, strategy development, operating models, etc., the more a global company starts to look like something that is built with all of the wrong parts. It is not that the parts don't work but rather that they are designed for something other than global strategy and operations.

I resolved to crack this code. I wanted to understand why all the dysfunction happens and also why it persists. So, I started to interview global, regional, and local leaders across a range of multinational companies. As we explored hypotheses and posited more, parts of the puzzle started to take shape. We began to identify common factors, each a harmful headwind to global operations. To dig deeper, I stopped the work, refreshed the hypotheses, and started again. This time I began a much larger research study. Its findings are the incendiary fuel for this book.

Understanding leads to insights, which lead to action. Today, it is my good fortune to assist global leaders, teams and organizations in decoding the complexity of their challenges, to help them re-engineer how they lead, how they develop strategy, and how to prosper.

It is my sincere wish that this book, this playbook, helps you to do the same.

A Fiction of Unity

The Global Stage

1. Global Companies

The motivation to grow a business internationally has amazing consequences—it is a fascinating adventure of opportunity, risk, and reinvention.

However, many of the strengths that make a company successful domestically frequently become disadvantages as it grows geographically. Where once there was mastery of the rules of the game, suddenly the game starts to feel like three-dimensional chess. Where once a strong player could see all of the threats and know all of the possible moves, now the game is much more complex and harder to master, as external and internal challenges multiply. Yet, the rewards can be worth the work. If we can figure out how to win at this multi-dimensional game then it is possible to unlock the kind of growth that is transformational.

In this first chapter, to set the stage for all that is to follow, we will briefly review the complex world of global companies. Our focus will be on their common motivations, objectives, and challenges, how they are built, how they operate, and how their formation histories can influence their outlook.

This information is important context as we start to introduce some of the inherent challenges that are built into the DNA of every global company. As we begin to reckon with the reality of systems and structures that frequently oppose global ambition, it will become clear just how un-global multinational companies can be.

The Global Marketplace

Since World War II, the systematic reduction of international trade barriers has powered the growth of global companies. Starting with the General Agreement on Tariffs and Trade, which in 1995 became the World Trade Organization, our nations' leaders built a multilateral economic system that fueled some of the highest growth rates in international commerce.

Improved geopolitical stability allowed companies to search for competitive advantage and arbitrage across borders. As international supply chains became cheaper and more efficient, companies invested their increased profits and expanded. International trade became the lion's share of global gross domestic product as it grew from 37% in the 1980s to over 60% within the next 20 years. After decades of market and product integration, we achieved a remarkable state of globalization. From consumer goods, electronics, telecoms, and medicine to the automotive industry, even foods and beverages, which traditionally show a strong domestic influence, you would be hard-pressed to name a category of business that has not shown a progressive merging toward a global or regional marketplace.

The convergence of markets and trade is characterized by the interplay of two opposing forces: Independence and interdependence, or—more simply—local and global considerations. Recently, we saw an educational illustration of this when the fragility of the post-pandemic global supply chain caught the world by surprise. In November 2021, the United Nations' Committee for Development Policy (CDP) noted that countries were seeking to reconcile their ecological, social, and economic ambitions through industrial policy—for example, by shielding "strategic" industries from foreign competition. The CDP observed that 'Industrial policy is seeing a revival as governments face the challenge of simultaneously securing economic recovery, addressing the deep inequalities that were magnified by the crisis, securing the transition to a low-carbon economy and adapting to climate change.'[1] What was happening was that, through their policies, countries were attempting to adapt unilaterally in response to tremendous and unprecedented pressures.

Country leaders were acting on a perception of separateness and yet the inescapable fact of our international interdependence opposed this. Just a few months later, in April 2022, Janet Yellen, the United States Secretary of the Treasury, claimed, 'We cannot allow countries to use their market position in key raw materials, technologies, or products to have the power to disrupt our economy or exercise unwanted geopolitical leverage.'[2] The US response is revealing. On the one hand, it shows a dependence on other countries and their policies. On the other, it exposes a point of view that not all countries should have equal sway in this interdependent system. Indeed, this inequity is the Achilles heel of engagement in the global marketplace. For many, there is a steep price for access. Interdependence and compromise, or even disadvantage, are two sides of the same coin.

---

[1] 'Post-pandemic industrial policy: jobs, growth, sustainability and resilience.' Dialogue with members of the UN Committee for Development Policy (CDP), UN DESA and UNIDO on post-pandemic opportunities and challenges in industrial policy. November 2021.

[2] Remarks by Secretary of the Treasury Janet L. Yellen on 'Way Forward for the Global Economy.' US Department of the Treasury. Press release. April 2022.

With its flaws, inequality, and biases, the global marketplace remains. It may evolve, contract, or expand in different sectors, but the two fundamental opportunities that fuel this shared endeavor endure: Greater growth potential and the protection of a diverse geographic portfolio to weather local instabilities.

It is important to appreciate that these two core benefits introduce a fundamental tension. To reach more customers worldwide with your product or service, you want each region and country to be as similar as possible. This keeps your business simple, which makes it more efficient and profitable. However, a geographic portfolio strategy requires meaningful differences between those markets. For protection, we need a diversity of market conditions. It seems that we want the world to be both uniform and inconsistent all at the same time.

The global marketplace offers its participants opportunity, but it is also unequal. Larger players want to take advantage of a connected system that they can dominate. Smaller players want to access this system but fear being steamrolled.

We see the same dynamics reflected in the objectives and tensions within global companies. However, while in the marketplace writ large, competitive forces tend to dampen anomalies and punish eccentric behavior, there is much less constraint on the idiosyncrasies within individual companies. This makes for an exciting and complex milieu. Global business will never be boring.

The Global Opportunity

A global company seeks to grow by increasing its worldwide market penetration.

All international companies are working to do this. This is the opportunity—whether they are starting to build their geographic footprint, or they are already large enough to call themselves regional, multi-regional, or global. Access to new customers builds scale. More scale offers improved margins, better pricing, more ability to self-invest, stronger product performance, and greater market influence. Market differences, for example, in taxation, costs, capital, compensation, or trade regulations—create imbalances, which can become opportunities. This is the potential. It is a self-reinforcing and upward spiral.

Of course, not all markets are equally attractive. However, an international footprint offsets weakness in domestic demand and helps to soften the effects of other macro-national concerns such as political instability or unfavorable changes in regulations. In fact, with a constrained home country, targeted geographic expansion may be the best and only path for a company's growth.

What a global company actually looks like has evolved many times over since the first international corporations took advantage of tariff and protectionist laws back in the 1930s. Today, as barriers to connectivity have largely dissolved, it is so easy for global headquarters, regional and domestic offices, as well as remote workers, to connect and collaborate. Fueled by technology, communications, and ever-increasing market integration, global companies are more connected, more agile, more entrepreneurial, more adaptable, and more international than ever. In fact, some are effectively country-less.

Formation History and Biases

Each multinational company has a unique backstory that not only defines its identity but explains many of its motivations, its structure, and even how it operates.

This globalizing journey describes how the business grew in scale and geographic reach, and how it was shaped by its successes, failures, and other events along the way. Indeed, the impact of good leaders, bad leaders, and their decisions for good or ill, are all stored in the company's memory and DNA as valuable lessons or burdensome baggage.

This journey defines where a company is strong and where it struggles. Its unique collection of experiences, advantages, and limitations informs how the company acts and adapts today. This unique set of prejudices and blind spots will shape how the company approaches challenges and opportunities.

It is impossible to avoid these biases. They are always present and often quite influential. Indeed, many biases not only started strong but have been reinforced continuously. This happens with regularity when a mindset or a behavior benefits a group or a part of the company that has more influence than others. Unchecked, such biases create winners and losers. Indeed, the biases of almost all global companies contribute to geographic imbalances in their focus, strategy, capabilities, and—inevitably—their results.

While understanding the active biases of your competition can be an effective way to gain an advantage, the inverse is also true and your competitors may be watching you. These internal inequities are rarely strengths.

Below, in brief, are a few common examples.

Domestic Bias

A global company that was built in one country and still identifies that country as its home market may struggle to invest in other markets of opportunity. For example, a company that started in the US, where it maintains a global headquarters and where many leaders are also US citizens, will often find it hard to build an objective growth strategy that would prioritize other countries. Companies with this bias can still be slow to adapt even when their international sales exceed that of the home market.

Large Country Bias

A global portfolio of countries only offers the protection of diversity when the countries are managed interdependently with each having a defined role. Ideally, large and established countries that offer less future growth can be the engines that fuel investment in new markets. However, a history of investment in a large country can be a hard habit to break. From a global standpoint, it may be obvious that investing to grow and investing to maintain a business are not the same thing, and that heavy spending to conserve the status quo means less fuel for growth. However, the idea of changing focus and perhaps seeing some softening in the large market's performance often proves to be a high barrier.

Centralized Bias

Many global companies are built with centralized functions where people are physically in one market but are intended to serve several, if not all of them. However, the idealism of this structure often falls prey to bias. A common example is centralized innovation. While on paper, this function should invest according to a global strategy, it is likely to prioritize serving the country or the region where the people are physically located ahead of serving any others. Proximity is powerful. In this example, we might see a focus on new products or services that are relevant for the home country while the needs of other countries come second.

It is not unusual to see the triple threat of domestic, large, and centralized biases all acting together. This is a common scenario for companies originating in the US and it impedes their international growth.

Small Acquisition Bias

Acquisition is a common growth strategy. However, when companies acquire smaller and more agile local competitors in the hope of integrating their capabilities, they run a very real risk of diluting the very qualities, such as speed and adaptability, that made that competitor an attractive acquisition candidate in the first place.

Frequently, the acquiring company will attempt to enforce its operating model on the acquired party. The big fish swallows the small fish. However, this approach is almost guaranteed to create blind spots and dysfunction. Integration is a complex and challenging process. While each case is unique, often the best answer is a new and modified operating model that reflects and accommodates the combination of entities.

Stepping back, it can seem ludicrous that an acquiring company would attempt to add a new organization while simultaneously maintaining the status quo. However, even the language we use, which infers that only one entity is the object of the acquisition, fuels an expectation of inaction by the acquirer.

Cultural Bias

As it is human nature to interpret situations, behaviors, language, and information based on our cultural norms and standards, it is very hard to avoid making assumptions and judgments that create cultural bias. In this situation, company culture is no different from national culture. So, it is easy to understand how company culture can easily become an excuse for our conscious or unconscious biases.

This bias can be hard to navigate—particularly, as we so often promote company culture as having the potential to be a competitive advantage. How are we supposed to know when a bias for certain attitudes and behaviors is valuable or when it is damaging?

There are many examples of negative company cultural bias, such as when culture is used to avoid what is unfamiliar and to promote what is familiar regardless of context. For example, consider that the behavioral style that fuels success in a leadership role is different in different countries. Without the specific knowledge and experience to see this, how can leaders overcome their tendency to prefer similar actors and so build a more effective diverse organization?

A common example of negative cultural bias is the use of company culture to protect the status quo. Consider the widely accepted idea that a new hire has just a few short months to offer objective insight into a company's ways of working before they too "drink the Kool-Aid," which is, of course, a euphemism for embracing cultural bias. What is interesting is how passively we accept its inevitability and that we don't question our complicity.

As another illustration of how these biases nest, consider how the national culture at your company's global headquarters will influence your executive leaders' soft skills, including how decisions are made. Is this an advantage or are certain stakeholders disenfranchised if they do not fit? How is new thinking tolerated? Is diversity of ideas a casualty?

Public Company Bias

The tyranny of quarterly reporting for public companies can create enormous challenges for long-term investment and strategy. This short-term fiscal mindset constrains a global company as it tries to develop its portfolio of markets. After all, its priority is investor return today and not business growth in the future. As a consequence, this hurts the company's ability to enter new markets. Market entry, especially in countries such as China or Brazil, is not quick: The local learning curve will rarely allow for fast returns on investment. This bias has enormous consequences for the freedom to place long-term bets, to future-proof a company, and to make competitive decisions. Meanwhile, a private company has no such accountability.

Capability Bias

Global companies that invest heavily in a specific set of capabilities will often be slow to adapt in markets where these capabilities are not an advantage. While it is entirely appropriate to leverage your company's capabilities as far as they will go, it can become a harmful bias if you don't realize their limitations in supporting new growth. This is very common as there are often meaningful differences between countries and, to quote Marshall Goldsmith, 'What got you here won't get you there.' For example, imagine that a company, which has invested in factories to make canned soup, finds that consumers in countries where they hope to expand prefer their soup in cartons or pouches. Now that company must decide whether it is a canning company or a soup company.

Differences between established and emerging markets will also highlight this bias. For example, a company with a strong ability to serve large retail chains in established markets must set this aside and build more intimate sales capabilities if they are to do business with the small independent retailers that are more common in emerging markets.

Conceptually, this bias is obvious. It is the risk of an overplayed strength. It follows the adage that every problem looks like a nail if all you have is a hammer. Yet where there is a runway for growth, where the global market is not saturated, taking existing capabilities into new markets forms the basis of many growth strategies—and appropriately so. The bias only becomes detrimental when customers have an alternative preferred choice, the cost for your company to adapt is too high, and the speed to do it is too slow.

This short list of biases is by no means exhaustive, but it makes the point. A global growth strategy aims to create a future state. However, the lens through which we plan and execute that future is shaped by the past. So, our perceptions of what is in focus and what is not, what feels comfortable or possible, or what is risky, can all be skewed from objective truth.

So, the next time your chief executive officer (CEO) says, 'Honor the past, build for the future,' schedule some time.

Seeds of Dysfunction

From the outset, the journey to increase global penetration is made difficult by the reality that, without the drama of an acquisition, companies must gradually build their scale and capabilities. Indeed, a global footprint does not appear overnight. It seems appropriate, if not the only choice, to manage this transition incrementally, to handle it step-by-step.

However, problems arise because, when faced with new uncertainties, we tend to seek comfort in what we know and we try to build the future with what worked for us in the past.

As a consequence, it is common practice in international expansion to stick with what was successful domestically and to modify it, a piece at a time, as the business becomes more and more international. So, structure, leaders, and strategy are often chosen or advanced based on domestic experience, existing biases, and familiar criteria, rather than on their ability to unlock growth elsewhere or create competitive advantage in new and less familiar conditions. While this may seem messy, it is predictable normal behavior as the company enters a transitional phase. However, something of a tipping point occurs when new international scale requires an evolution in the roles and ways of working of company leadership.

The journey towards increasingly effective global operations requires ever more high-functioning interdependence between company stakeholders. Yet, there is rarely a scenario in which previously independent stakeholders will readily accept an evolution that dilutes their autonomy and power. Most human beings are simply not made that way. Even when the benefits of interdependence are clear and strong, the more powerful players will look for ways to stay separate to maintain that power. Such ego-driven antics can be bewildering, particularly as it is often so obvious that personal and business objectives have become divergent. It is not unusual, therefore, to see a refresh of leadership marking each phase of geographic growth. New leaders are often a good thing to accelerate a company's global evolution. As the business gets ready to begin a new chapter, it needs leadership that is invested in the future state and not dragging its feet.

This is an incredibly challenging time for CEOs. Not only must they ensure that their leadership team is fit for purpose, but they must also curate company culture during the transition. Having built a successful culture in the domestic business, it is unnerving to let go of that certainty and evolve. In a reactionary way, inexperienced CEOs often double down on the company's origin story and on all of the comfortable and familiar tropes of those smaller and more intimate times. Just when a new vision is called for, they look back to the past for a sense of security. This is one reason why many companies like to deify their founders and their values, seeking comfort by connecting success in the past to future endeavors. This is a fascinating practice. Surely, what is needed is an accountable leader who appreciates the uniqueness of tomorrow's challenges. Can you imagine a navy captain comforting or inspiring their crew with stories of the previous captains of the ship? I am sure they are all proud of the ship's history, but the crew has new missions now and those other captains aren't on board.

Most growing international companies need to work through a phase of reactive and partial adaptation to their new and emerging global reality. It can be messy and, along the way, it fuels an assortment of misalignments in leadership, strategy, capabilities, and structure, some of which are visible on the surface while others are buried deep. However, these misalignments will not stay hidden forever. They are seeds of dysfunction and, if we are lucky, objective, and insightful, we may be able to dig them up before they grow and bear fruit.

Strategic Intent

As we have discussed, a global company seeks to grow by increasing its worldwide market penetration. Its global business strategy describes where and how the company wants to succeed at this. The strategy clarifies and directs both intent and action. Conceptually, this is straightforward, but practically it can be an enormous stretch. To explain this, we will start with some fundamentals and take a look at how global strategy is subject to the defining characteristics that shape a company.

The first of these fundamentals is the company's *business model*, which is the way that it creates value. This is not complicated. A manufacturer creates value when it designs, produces, and then sells something more valuable than the parts or raw materials that it used. A company with a service business creates value by charging fees for knowledge, entertainment, transportation, banking, hospitality, medical services, etc. The business model also identifies the company's suppliers and its customers as these are defining players. It also clarifies the company's value proposition, which is jargon for what the company offers. All of this informs the financial model of the company—that is, its balance sheet and income statement.

Having defined what business the company is in, the next defining feature, which is typically distinctive in that it is unique to the company, is its *operating model*. For some reason, this is often confused with the business model, but it is quite different. The operating model defines how the company is run. In short, it describes the main processes that the company follows to create and deliver value. So, if the business model captures *what* the company does, then the operating model describes *how* it does it.

As you can imagine, the operating model can be very broad and includes equipment, assets, and technology, the organizational structure of the company, who is accountable for what, where the company physically exists, its capabilities, culture, and even who, how, and when it makes decisions.

So, now with this context, we can see that a global strategy needs to do much more than define where and how the company will deliver value. That would be enough to describe an intention, but it is not enough to activate that intention, to make it a reality. To do that, we need to appreciate a powerful truth: *Global strategy must be executable by the company's operating model*. It sounds obvious. However, knowing this does not mean we can avoid its consequence. Indeed, this is where many problems start.

To begin with, the operating model of a global company is often too far-ranging and too complex for any one person to see it all. Different parts may be visible to different stakeholders, but nobody can see the whole thing. Also, not all parts of the operating model are conscious and deliberate. Typically, the core of the model is well-defined but how things work, such as how separate geographies or functions interact, or how local market differences drive unique adaptations, are frequently blind spots. It follows that the different ways that separate parts of a company will respond to a new global strategy, as it is deployed to be activated, may not be visible to top management. The complexity drives a loss of control, and, over time, these blind spots can manifest as tension or dysfunction that dilutes the strategy and its activation.

As with any complex system, just like software with bugs and bad code, the way a company operates can have unforeseen outcomes. Every company's operating model is a work in progress. There will always be unrealized potential and also barriers to performance, opportunities to uncover, and repairs and renovations to make. A successful global company will obsess about this because, if it is neglected, the operating model can go so far off the rails that it is no longer fit for use. However, if it is nurtured to adapt and evolve, then it can continue to meet its purpose, which is to bring strategy to life.

It is also important to remember that the operating model defines the accountabilities and reward systems of the company. The challenge for global strategy becomes a lot steeper when we compare the differences between what people are accountable for and what they are rewarded for. Invariably, reward systems focus most company employees on small areas of local scope. This throws global strategy into limbo for, as we all know (and both economists and psychologists tell us), what you measure and what you reward is what you get.

Takeaways

To begin, we have started to become acquainted with the motivations, objectives, and formation of global companies. Even in this short review, it is clear that geographic expansion comes with many unintended complications as outlined below:

1. There is a strange paradox in the need for market uniformity as well as diversity. As we shall see, this is a two-headed monster that can set company stakeholders against each other. While the board of directors and CEO may want the best of both worlds, they have built an organization in which some people push for consistency and compliance while others insist that their uniqueness must be recognized. Hear from Stefan, a global new business director: 'There are colleagues saying this is a healthy tension. They use these words. It is an excuse. Lazy. Like the iceberg they do not see.'

2. We also discussed the common motivations of global companies and how their formation histories will bias their thinking and behavior. It seems that every multinational has its demons. The

advantage goes to those with more objective awareness who take remedial action.

3. We briefly touched on the tension between company stakeholders who prefer autonomous control to interdependence. This topic will come roaring back again and again as we explore this dysfunction, which is so ubiquitous as to be among the top waste-creating practices in most global companies.

4. We described how the complexity of global operations inevitably dilutes control. When no one can have a full view of their company's ways of working, how can we be sure that we are operating as needed to bring global strategy to life?

In the next chapter, we will dig deeper into the dynamics of global strategy, spending time with the different stakeholders and exploring their motivations.

2. Global Strategies

Most discussion of global business strategy is predicated on an automatic and tacit assumption that all of the company, meaning all of the stakeholders within it, want that strategy to succeed and to be effective. This premise sounds realistic and believable. Unfortunately, I have some bad news. You see, there is an undeniable density of behavior that contradicts this. Indeed, stakeholders' support is anything but consistent. After all, their expectations of global strategy vary dramatically, and their commitment and accountability to its deployment, and to its results, are typically weak and uncertain. It is more accurate to say that some, although not all, company stakeholders may be open to a new global strategy, but only if it is a good fit with their business and their personal needs.

Management consultants invest a lot of time discovering and diffusing stakeholders' objections to strategy. Their recommendation can live or die, not just on the word of the chief executive officer (CEO), but on the engagement of all of the key stakeholders. Yet, they know that people often hold their cards very close and don't say what they think in a public forum. Indeed, their external perspective allows consultants to see company stakeholders for what they are: Gatekeepers, advocates, persuadable critics, or intractable barriers. Consultants are under no illusion that the strategy they propose will succeed on its own merits. Success is always more dependent on the people involved and the trust they share than on the quality of the strategy itself.

This is an important point. A strategy can be fantastic but that is not going to make it happen. Indeed, the number of global strategies that are adopted and executed as designed is painfully low. Meanwhile, the business strategy consulting market worldwide, sometimes called "boardroom consulting" or "strategic advisory," is thriving. It is growing over 10% annually and may exceed US$100 billion by 2026. It seems that we are very focused on a strategy as a deliverable. Of course, this is the easier part where we have control. Converting this statement of intent into priorities, actions, and results is where most global strategies crumble.

We are going to detail the reasons for this, but first we need to clearly define what global strategy is, and what it isn't, while appreciating how the answers to these questions will change depending on where you sit in a company. That is the focus of this chapter. First, we will review how global strategy is developed, by whom, and for what purpose. After that, we will shift gears to focus on its deployment and how it might be executed.

Local, Regional, and Global

Within a multinational company, country leaders develop their growth strategies. Within the scope of their marketplace, they decide where and how they are going to win. They assess their opportunities and advantages, and they figure out how to both minimize risk and beat their competition. Of course, the local strategy must be executable by the company's local operating model. Fortunately, most country-level organizations can adapt when they need to. This is not so hard when they are relatively small and have a simple and accountable hierarchy. Indeed, it is easier for local leaders to modify how their business is run and to build bespoke processes to improve its performance. Also, local businesses are easier to focus on, which means that everyone in the hierarchy is more likely to understand their role and what they need to achieve to meet the goals identified in their strategy.

At the regional level, companies create a regional business strategy, which in many ways is a summary and an aggregation of the separate local strategies of the countries within its purview. This is a country portfolio strategy, in which the role of each country is defined along with its objectives. The regional strategy serves to identify priorities and can offer local country leaders very tangible benefits to fuel their growth, including more focus, resources, capabilities, and expertise. Common barriers to growth can be tackled more effectively this way, just as investment in common opportunities can achieve results faster and also more efficiently.

The interdependence of regional and local strategy is clear. Plus, it helps that—in most cases, local country leaders report directly to regional leaders. So, there is certainly no confusion over accountability or rewards. These direct reporting relationships ensure that everyone is in agreement.

As a side note, some organizations create strategies that focus on a "cluster" of adjacent countries, with several clusters making up a region. The idea is that the countries in each cluster have many similarities and so this additional level of administration offers some efficiencies. This structure is often preferred by regional leaders in large companies who want to limit their number of direct reports. However, the extra layer can create an unhelpful bureaucracy because, at the regional level, we are now comparing clusters rather than individual markets. This increases the risk of missing important commonalities between countries that are not in the same cluster. After all, geographic proximity does not always mean the same market opportunities or challenges. More often than not, this approach seems to impede the ability of the region to focus on where it will have more impact. The caution here is to be aware that market clusters may be setting organizational structure before strategy, which would be, of course, back to front.

A Balancing Act

It is rare to build a regional strategy before developing the country-level strategies that it will encapsulate. Typically, we define regional objectives and goals through an iterative process that starts at the country level. We build up and look for common and compelling opportunities or risks. At the same time, corporate headquarters provides input and targets to be incorporated into the regional strategy, and their implications are then distributed throughout the portfolio of countries.

This highlights an important and unique balancing act that regional leaders need to play with their headquarters or global leadership. On the one hand, they are champions for the local markets in their regional portfolio. To this end, they will advocate for local needs and also work to protect their countries from anything that might compromise their focus on regional and local objectives. On the other hand, they are required to serve the global whole. This means that they must also support corporate or global objectives and accept their role in the broader global portfolio.

This intermediary role is made all the more difficult because it hardly ever happens that all of the global, regional, and local strategies are perfectly coherent. It would be a lot easier if these strategies were nested together like Matryoshka dolls, one inside the other, but that is not the real world. Consider that all of these strategies are developed separately, at different times, and by separate teams. So, it is best to assume that there is always a need to integrate, negotiate, and reconcile these separate geographic strategies. It can be a hard role working in the middle.

Gatekeepers

It is not unusual for a region to abandon its balancing act and cut back its interdependence with global and local strategies. We only need to watch how the different region heads in a company behave to see this play out. Typically, and this is so predictable, the leader of a more dominant region will seek to limit their accountability to the rest of the global portfolio. A classic example of this is when developed regions, such as North America or Western Europe, push to reinvest profits in their own business, rather than release them to promote the potential of emerging markets. In their defense, the dominant region heads are not directly rewarded for anyone else's operation. So, while from one perspective, their actions can seem self-serving and even opposed to a net gain in global business performance, they are simply playing by the rules of the company's accountability and reward system. They are doing exactly what they have been asked to do.

This scenario highlights another aspect of the role of regional leadership, which is highly consequential. *Regional leaders are de facto gatekeepers to the flow of global strategy* down through the organization to its local execution. In this role, regional leaders typically operate between the extremes. They neither throw the gates wide open and fully mobilize their region to deliver global strategy, nor do they hold the gates completely shut. Despite the expectation of full deployment, each regional leader filters the global strategy based on what they consider is best for their region's performance. For example, a common disconnect might be their desire for short-term wins rather than to support a strategy that offers slower returns, in which case the longer-term strategy will not be a priority for them.

Regional leaders feel that they have some license to massage the global strategy in this way. Indeed, it should not be surprising if they resent and resist an imposed directive that curtails such freedom. After all, from their perspective, they are the only stakeholders in the company with a clear view of the whole picture from global strategy to local execution. They may reasonably believe that they are the only leaders with relevant expertise in both strategy and execution for their region.

This kind of dissembling behavior is common and it is also easy to spot it. All you need to do is to ask local stakeholders who would be the executors of the global strategy if their objectives and targets were in line. Curiously, even though their secession from some or all of the global strategy is easy to detect, regional leaders are often brazen and unconcerned about any reprisal. Could it be that global leaders are not monitoring their strategy's activation? Are they too poorly connected or too far removed from local execution to know? As we will discuss later, this is a blind spot. It is hard to believe, and yet you can see how it would reinforce the theatricality of global strategy.

Figure 2.1 shows how different degrees of regional adoption can affect the overall coherence of global strategy. This simple illustration reveals the potency or impotence of the strategy. In the left-hand diagram, all regional strategies are nested within the global strategy (with their respective countries' strategies nested within them). However, in the right-hand diagram, each region makes its own choice and so can be in the strategy, outside of it, or participating to varying degrees.

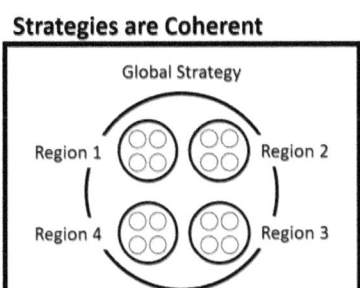 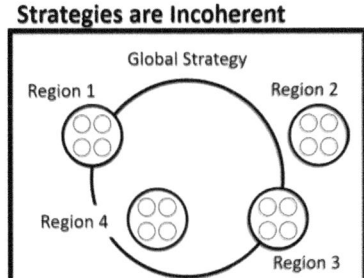

Figure 2.1. Illustration of Global and Regional Strategy Coherence

There is a breed of companies in which the challenge of regional alignment to global strategy is even harder to achieve. In these organizations, the operating model gives regional leaders greater authority than their global counterparts. It can be something simple like budgetary control that creates this scenario and allows separate regions to operate as quasi-autonomous businesses. It is interesting what happens in this situation. You might expect powerful regional leaders to use their authority to influence global strategy. However, they tend to simply reject it in favor of their own plans, presenting a fervent bias against collaboration, and even an aggressive resistance to interdependence. From my research, it seems that they interpret all things global as an undesirable and perhaps unacceptable risk to their autonomy and control. A stronger and more independent region will fight even harder to protect or increase that independence.

It doesn't seem to matter whether global leadership has notional authority or not: The challenge for global strategy is that it must offer each region sufficient value for regional leaders to be willing to give up a little autonomy. That is a very high bar.

Leadership and Operations

What is strategy? What does the word mean? Why are there so many different interpretations of something that is so universal and so important? How many unique templates have you seen or had to work with? Have you noticed that, even inside a single company, different stakeholders think about strategy in different ways? Each leader, with a history of strategy at other companies, brings an assortment of models and disparate ideas. Why does this happen? Why have we not converged on one best approach? Surely, there is only risk in all of this confusion. It really makes no sense for us to fumble around with the ways we define and develop something so essential.

Can we blame the academics, business writers, and consultants for creating a hundred buzzwords and articles stuffed with jargon? They certainly don't help us to find a single accessible definition when so many of them are marketing their own unique and novel concepts. So, what is your *strategic intent*? Your *guiding policy*? Do you know *where to play* and *how to win*? How did you draft your *business model canvas*? Does your company have *strategic coherence*? Do you have a *winning aspiration*? A *guiding ambition*? What is your *right to win*? Is a *strategic plan* really an oxymoron? Have you named your *purple cow* yet?

I am poking a little fun to make a serious point. There really are hundreds of pithily crafted concepts to help us make better and more informed decisions. There are heaps of models, tools, and clever analyses to help focus our thinking. There is also canny marketing, softly inferring that we may be behind the times or missing the mark if we don't sign up for the latest insight.

It does seem that we are going out of our way to make something that is extremely important into something that is unnecessarily complicated. Whatever the causality, there is no doubt that our understanding of strategy suffers from a frustrating degree of confusion and inconsistency.

Qualified Decisions

Every organization is made up of some people who are responsible to choose what the company is going to do and others who are responsible to get the work done in order to achieve that. For discussion, let's call these two groups "Leadership" and "Operations." This is deliberately elementary to make the point that company performance requires both of these groups. Leadership can describe decisions but they are only ideas and imaginings without Operations. Conversely, Operations can do work but without Leadership they lose perspective and will not adapt. Such endeavors are, to quote Sun Tzu, 'the noise before defeat.'

Let's focus on the connection and the communication between these two groups. To begin with, it is obvious that it is not effective for Leadership to act like a despot and to issue commands as if the group had absolute power. After all, any great idea from Leadership will only happen if Operations understands it and can get it done. To that point, a new directive that is not accepted by Operations will underperform or fail. So, to ensure that new ideas are viable, they need to be qualified. The decision rests with Leadership but the business results from the decision depend on Operations. Clearly, collaboration between the two groups will promote better decisions, and vice versa. If we describe strategy very simply as making choices and then acting on them, then a good strategy needs both groups involved.

Does this sound strange or novel? I am not proposing a radical redistribution of authority. Yet, we have been conditioned to equate strategy with decision-making and to think of it firmly and exclusively as the remit of Leadership. After all, it is to Leadership that so many strategy gurus and consultants target their products and services. Meanwhile, Operations is more likely to be presented as an obstacle to compliance rather than as a collaborative partner.

Two things happen when we follow this philosophy. First, we ignore objective truth. Leadership's expertise is not knowing how to get things done or even knowing if things can be done. Only Operations experts can qualify if new ideas will work as they have been imagined and, importantly, have the insight and perspective to predict results. The second consequence is more insidious and more consequential as we are creating conditions where strategy is owned only by a small minority. Now, in addition to the real risks to the strategy associated with feasibility and coherence, we can find ourselves struggling to engage our own organization.

Do We Need a Strategy?

If strategy is so poorly defined and variable, then it stands to reason that many companies think they are doing just fine without it or with their version of whatever strategy may be. The understanding that they have of their capabilities, their advantages, and how best to grow profitably, seems sufficient. So, what would a strategy need to articulate to make a difference?

Let's revisit our model and explore how strategy might exist either as a function of Leadership or as a function of Operations.

When there is a bias towards Leadership, we focus our conversation on choices and, when taken too far, we risk making decisions that may never happen. As Stephen Bungay wrote in *The Art of Action (2011)*, 'We have a strategy, we have long-term objectives, we all have budgets … meanwhile our people are asking, "So, what is it exactly that you're asking me to do?"'.

With a bias towards Operations, we focus our conversation on what the organization does, and the risk of over-development here is a company that becomes blindly stuck in the status quo with a rigid identity and a limited modus operandi. Imagine a company that for decades has sold just one product, such that Operational capabilities have become a rigid habit. The inertia this creates can stymie any new behavior. In fact, Operations may be too entrenched to adapt. New direction from Leadership must be assertive and specific in its expectations or no change will occur.

In spite of these risks, more companies seem to live at the extremes, with a bias towards either Leadership or Operations. We typically find the companies that don't invest in strategy falling prey to one of these biases, and their risks run the gamut from weaker results to the loss of market relevance.

In the coming chapters, we will explore why fewer global companies exist at the center and why they struggle to build a strong bridge between what their leaders say they want to achieve and what their organization is willing and able to achieve.

Control Enthusiasm

A core question, hotly debated, among strategists, is how much control to exert in order to achieve important objectives. For this discussion, let's describe the two opposing sides in the debate as Controllers and Guides.

The Controllers' approach favors managing to objectives and rigorous tracking of performance against defined goals. They focus on compliance and enforced alignment. No surprise: This is the preferred choice of Leadership, particularly global leaders who dream of an organized, uniform, and consistent world. As with most control enthusiasm, this desire for dominion comes from a place of fear. Controllers are uneasy and concerned about whether Operations will deliver what they dictate without oversight. This also infers a lack of trust and questions the competence of Operations. The Controller camp wants to create a directive quasi-legal document and then prosecute it.

You may be familiar with some of many examples of this control from the world of brand marketing, where the visual properties of a brand—its colors and shapes—are defined in detail and locked. Deviations can be punished and any changes, such as for modernization, are strictly controlled by a small team of owners. A common consequence of this is that, while the strategy is tightly controlled, those stakeholders who have no say feel little or no ownership. The strategy belongs to someone else.

Meanwhile, the Guiding camp prefers a strategy to offer more freedom. Operations like this approach because they feel respected, their ownership is not compromised and their authority in executional expertise is appreciated. This is like saying, 'We have agreed that we need to be in San Francisco next week. You know best how to take us there.' Unfortunately, by stating an intention at such a high level and then allowing for parochial solutions, this approach encourages reactive behavior and creates a bias towards existing capabilities and the status quo.

Of course, this debate is simply a surrogate for the same trick question of whether strategy should exist either as a function of Leadership or as a function of Operations. The answer, which feels like a lot of hard work, is that it is much more likely to succeed when it is a function of both. The result we are looking for is some kind of freedom in a frame, and building this requires inclusion, which means that, in spite of all the noise to the contrary, Leadership can't hold the reins too tight. After all, if you own the strategy, then nobody else does.

Developing Global Strategy

In all companies, Leadership requires a document that describes the global business strategy. Typically, this will identify the company's vision, a time-bound target goal, the primary opportunities for growth, the capabilities it already has or that it needs to pursue, and perhaps a compelling argument for success. This is the highest-level summary that still makes sense and it is designed to convey a sense of mastery and control through its focus and simplicity. This short summary document is best intended for the CEO, the company board, or investors, but it is not a document that is useful to activate and animate the ambition that it describes. For that, we need an operational document that is designed to be easily interpreted and translated into plans for execution. This is a critical requirement because there is a world of difference between communicating an intention and making it happen.

A global strategy must be more than a communication document for Leadership. It needs content that is appropriate and effective to engage each stakeholder. We need something to present to top management, which is a summary of key choices and their projected outcomes, and something else for the company's operational leaders, which enables them to build plans detailing how the strategy might be pursued.

Separation of Powers

Staying with the simplicity of describing a company in terms of Leadership and Operations, we can see that a new strategy needs both groups as an audience. Follow the logic, we see that there are, therefore, two sets of approvers of global strategy. Does your company's Leadership acknowledge this? Is Operational approval a formal step?

More often than not, Leadership assumes that, when they approve their version, what they have seen is what will be executed. Indeed, the research indicates that many in Leadership rarely consider global strategy with the complex realities of its execution in mind. This happens a lot and it is a dangerous blind spot because Leadership is at risk of approving a global strategy that will never be fully realized.

This throws gasoline on a fire that is already burning. It fuels the potential for dysfunction created by the differences between these two separate sets of approvers: the company's leaders, who approve the strategy's intention, and its operational leaders, who reside in the regions and countries, and are de facto, if informally, approvers of its execution.

Figure 2.2 reprises the earlier Figure 2.1 to show the possibility of dysfunctional differences between the two sets of approvers. Strategic Leaders only see their diagram.

Figure 2.2. Illustration of the Separate Approvals of a Global Strategy

If we accept this principle—that a company's leaders are not the only approvers of strategy—then we can play a better game. It might be useful to think of operational leaders and their teams as a kind of employee union with collective bargaining power to promote their interests. This helps to make it clearer that negotiation for mutual benefit is a necessity.

Accountability

As we have discussed, it is a lot easier to have a strategy approved by top management than it is to have it adopted, planned out, and executed by your company's operational management. It is entirely possible to have one without the other. It is also possible for there to be no negative consequences when this happens. After all, while approval of a strategy is a finite task that is very measurable, the strategy's execution can take years and involve a very large number of stakeholders. As a critical consequence, accountability for the results is, at best, postponed. At worst, there is no accountability at all.

So, remembering that what you measure is what you get, and considering that many global teams face an uphill battle to develop a strategy that will secure operational approval, should we be surprised that many global strategists will focus on managing up in their headquarters rather than on delivering results in the markets?

It may not sound very admirable but, in many companies, delivering a strategy document is the outcome that their operating model promotes and celebrates. Whether the right actions follow is an entirely separate consideration.

Value

Despite varying degrees of detachment from how their strategy might be executed, companies pursue global strategy because it offers the potential to unlock incredible value. So, what is its purpose? Here are just a few questions we might ask as we try to answer this.

- Is global strategy a tool for senior leadership to aggregate and summarize the complexities of the business?
- Is it a vital instrument to cut through the complexity of global operations and direct the company's focus?
- Is it a key to unlocking opportunity in regions and countries that could not do it alone?
- Is it a plan to marshal the company's unique set of capabilities and mobilize them wherever they are needed for competitive advantage?
- Is it a forum that responds to regional and local needs to accelerate growth?
- Is it a unique view with a longer-term perspective that enables the company to plan several moves ahead?
- Is it a way to share intelligence and market experiences, so that the whole company can learn quickly from successes and failures?

Of course, a strategy can be one or several of these things. Yet, if it is to be anything beyond a summary of existing strategies or intentions, it is clear that the scope and therefore the value of the global strategy depends on the interconnectedness, the interdependence, and the engagement of its stakeholders throughout the company and around the world.

Ideally, a company's leaders would have a clear understanding of the degrees to which their organization possessed these attributes. Yet, they typically assume that there is more connection and more good faith collaboration than there is. It is surprisingly hard for them to know without a direct investigation. Instead, they remain at the mercy of their blind spot. They buy into a fallacy that their approval of choices and intentions is all that is required. As a consequence, they are unlikely to acknowledge the informal, yet powerful, gatekeeping that takes place in regions and markets.

Architects

The architects of global strategy are most often a team of leaders, whose role is defined as *global* and that is based at the corporate headquarters. Curiously, worldwide or regional experience is not often a prerequisite to be on this team. More global leaders are likely to come from the headquarters' country than from other markets. They often take a global assignment as a temporary role, knowing that they will move back to their home market once their short tenure is complete. In fact, in many companies, there is no such thing as a global career path. Bizarrely, this frequent turnover among global leaders means that local and regional stakeholders often have more experience dealing with global strategy than some members of the global team. So, it is not surprising when these stakeholders voice their frustration at having to work with a new batch of global inductees who have limited country and regional market knowledge. Imagine how challenging it is to have such a team review your current business or tell you where you now need to focus. How tempting it must be to decline the video call or to book them a taxi back to the airport.

All of this means that global leaders not only face the huge challenge of figuring out how to be effective in an unfamiliar and difficult role, but they also find themselves developing a global strategy without a strong worldwide network of connections and trusted relationships. It is a small wonder then that local and regional leaders complain that global strategy is too often built in a silo. It is also ironic, and perhaps lacking a certain self-awareness, that these same local and regional leaders are rarely the first to initiate collaboration. Unless they need something.

Strategy Deployment

The purpose of strategy is to get the right things done.

Let us imagine that company leadership has agreed to a new global strategy. What comes next? How is the strategy operationalized to transform its ambitions and decisions into action and results? How does this strategy become the choices and the core set of priorities that the regional strategy and then the local strategy are built upon?

Deployment is a critical phase for any strategy because global teams must pass the strategy baton to others. Imagine that relay race. Whoever is receiving the baton needs to be running in sync and at the same pace for the best exchange. Indeed, the baton only makes it across the finish line if, at each transition, everyone knows it is coming and what to do with it, and then passes it along to a willing teammate. In a race like this, success is defined by interdependence.

Commitment

Starting from the top, the first steps in deployment sit with the region heads. They have the task of applying the global strategy to their business and distributing it across their organization. As we have discussed, region heads are the first, and most influential, de facto gatekeepers of global strategy.

How deployment happens here depends primarily on whether the region head feels they are interdependent with the global whole. If the connection is strong and the relationship has mutuality, then they can be confident of the relevance and value that the strategy offers to their region.

It is not unusual for region heads to operate autonomously. However, this simply means that they own the decision rights for participation in the strategy. It is not a reflection of their commitment but rather of their authority. Instead, we should pay attention to independent attitudes and behaviors. After all, owning regional decisions is not the same as acting like a separate entity, pursuing its own objectives. That said, the larger the regional business, the less likely we are to see a willingness to adapt, collaborate, and commit to a global strategy.

As senior leaders of the company, region heads typically apply considerable latitude and personal choice to the degree to which they deploy global strategy. They can be slow to change course and shift priorities, weighing the risks and benefits from their perspective, and balancing common tensions, such as the distraction from achieving important results or existing targets. Also, region heads don't expect to be held accountable for the success of a global strategy, particularly if the company updates it every few years. They may be aware of the need to demonstrate commitment for political purposes, but that is different.

Occasionally, global strategy is developed as an aggregate of regional strategies. In this case, deployment is unnecessary. We might argue that the global strategy is too.

Ownership

A top-down deployment often assumes that engagement with the strategy is automatic. It isn't. How many times have you heard local and regional stakeholders refer to "the global strategy" as an external thing, a secondary thing, and certainly not something that they are excited about? To be at stake for the success of the strategy, the stakeholders need to own it.

Truly, branding the strategy as "global" doesn't help. We can be part of a larger whole but the piece that is specific to us is the piece that we own. So, the faster the global strategy is translated into smaller, regional, and local strategies, the better. However, the more common practice is to give the global strategy a branded identity that persists. For those in global leadership, this offers some reassurance that the strategy is a real and living thing. For those who might do the work, this says that the strategy belongs to someone else. Also, the high-level global perspective is typically weak, and sometimes impotent when it comes to connecting with relevant issues and opportunities on the front lines.

Integration

The key step to building ownership and engagement with global strategy is to translate or integrate it into regional strategies and so into local operational strategies. Is the global strategy additive or is it a change of course? Remember that each region already has a strategy and the often tight-knit team of country leaders and their managers understand it, own it, and are focused on it. So, the last thing we want is to create competing or confusing directions.

In part, this is why region heads take such latitude. There is no one else with the perspective and knowledge to lead this integration. They will take the puzzle pieces and decide whether they fit together; the pieces that don't will be discarded.

Is this a bad thing? If global strategy compliance is your passion, then it is. However, the regions will push back that some parts of the global strategy simply don't fit their priorities or their operating model. There can be culpability on both sides. Global stakeholders must answer why they developed a strategy without investing in the necessary operational insight. Regional stakeholders must be transparent and not allow a misleading perception of compliance to take root.

Visibility

How do we keep track of whether a global strategy is indeed cascading through an organization? At a later date, we can set and follow specific measures associated with the new strategy. However, as a first step, we want to know how we are setting ourselves up for success.

I have seen large multinational companies send presentations and travel the world giving strategy road shows. Unfortunately, this is what we do when we create a global strategy in a silo or behind closed doors. If we need a road show, then that tells us that our company's operational leaders have not had a seat at the table. That strategy is almost doomed before it starts. It is a classic example of global strategy theater because the road show presentation is a political performance only.

Ideally, we want to create a roll-out plan and the focus is not to present the strategy but to integrate its objectives into regional and local priorities. A measure of progress, then, is when a new global strategy triggers the review and possibly the revision of regional and local strategy.

The best measure of an effective global strategy deployment is how quickly it disappears as it is infused and absorbed into operational plans.

Takeaways

In this chapter, we have discussed some of the most important and consequential ways that different company stakeholders engage with global strategy. We have also seen that our systems and the ways that we typically operate can raise the bar for success.

A Fiction of Unity

Here is a summary of the key points from this discussion:

1. A global strategy must do more than describe where and how the company will deliver value. That is a statement of intention, but it is still not clear whether the company can act on it. To do that, the global strategy must be executable by the company's operating model (how the company is run).

2. Regional strategy can offer local country leaders very tangible benefits to fuel their growth, including more focus, resources, capabilities, and expertise to combat shared barriers to growth and to pursue common opportunities across their geographic portfolio.

3. It hardly ever happens that all of the global, regional, and local strategies in a company are perfectly coherent. These strategies are developed separately, at different times, and by separate teams. So, there is always a need for integration and reconciliation of geographic strategy with regional leaders working in the middle.

4. Regional leaders are critical gatekeepers who control the deployment of global strategy through the organization.

5. The purpose of strategy is to get the right things done, which means that global strategy needs to serve two masters: The company's senior leadership and also its operational leadership. Serving just one of these leaves us with either a hopeful intention or a company biased by today's capabilities.

6. There are two sets of approvers of global strategy: The company's senior leaders, who approve the strategy's intention, and its operational leaders, who reside in the regions and countries and are de facto, if informal, approvers of its execution.

7.   A successful deployment of a global strategy has that strategy integrated into regional and local strategies and operational plans that those stakeholders own and understand.

We have taken a brief tour through global companies and strategy to set the scene for the next chapter. We have been chasing the idea that a global company can be more than the simple sum of its parts, but we have already seen complexity, confusion, and many reasons why we might fail. Our next step is to name and define the forces that oppose our vision.

A Fiction of Unity

Forces of Fragmentation

The world acts spontaneously to minimize potentials or to maximize disorder.

Rudolf Clausius on the Law of Entropy (paraphrased)

In the following chapters, we will discuss the separate but often combining forces that pressure global companies to fragment, to misalign, and, so inevitably, to dilute their results and their potential. This chapter may feel like a deep dive into negativity. Indeed, the challenges and the behaviors that we will explore are probably not the outcomes nor the characteristics you imagine for your global company. Yet, repeated observations, assessments, and feedback from global, regional, and local leaders tell us how real and common these forces are.

In general, we are all aware of tension and dysfunction within our global company. Yet, it is common for company leaders to focus just on managing the symptoms and to avoid investigating the root causes. When asked about this, global, regional, and local leaders confess to concern and discomfort, which includes a fear of personal jeopardy, if they were to publicly name the motivations that drive many of these problems. So, while some of our colleagues and counterparts are willing to take some action when performance starts to break down, they are hesitant and cautious. Of course, inaction is not a solution. Indeed, if we choose not to treat the underlying causes, then the symptoms typically worsen.

Understandably, we prefer to imagine an organization of harmony, collaboration, and shared interest. We know it is naïve but we prefer the comfort of this assumption: Our global company, our strategies, and the decisions and actions that span this multinational business, are all rooted in the presumption of a committed, connected, capable, and collaborative organization. In this soothing scenario, all of the leaders of our company are not only willing to serve the global gestalt but also capable of doing this—and in a system that supports their efforts.

However, as we will explore in a moment, this assumption is neither realistic nor reliable. The coherence of our global company, the deliberate and hard-fought unity of purpose that is necessary to fuel and achieve our global ambition, is under siege at all times. As a consequence, without intervention, our global organization will, to varying degrees, split, splinter, and divide into progressively independent, autonomous, and disconnected parts. Worldwide performance, current and future growth, profitability, speed, efficiency, and competitive advantage in capabilities and talent are all predictable casualties.

The word "fragmentation" means to break into smaller or separate pieces. The forces acting to do this, to splinter our global business, originate from the people, processes, philosophies, and structures that comprise it. The fragmentation itself can be focused geographically or functionally, or both, and it can happen slowly or it can grow dramatically fast.

All global companies experience fragmentation. It is a constant headwind. I hope that, by naming these forces and detailing their origins, I will provide you with a framework to recognize them so that you can start to moderate their dysfunctions. Each of the forces discussed in this section is discrete in that it creates unique challenges and can lead to specific and damaging consequences. At the same time, the forces often coexist, even fueling each other to multiply the risk of degradation. Some are inescapable, and can only be managed and mitigated. Others are entirely preventable.

This idea of nesting and multiplying forces is important, particularly when we need to call out certain behaviors. We will see that, when leaders take actions that are contrary to the collective interest, there is nearly always a complex context, often not of their own making. I am not excusing bad actors and there are always more of those than we would like. Yet, it is enlightening to hear global and regional leaders, particularly senior executives, describe dysfunction as inevitable given the conflicting pressures that they are navigating.

As you read these coming chapters, you will find that I have chosen to use frank and fearless language. In business, and some cultures, we are often intolerant of such parrhesia. However, these fragmenting forces persist, in part, because we continue to dodge the clarity that comes from objectivity and candor—so, no sugar-coating. There is no point in dancing around these issues. The risks are real and, in this space, there is a long history of complacency and inaction. Consider that, in my research, over 90% of global, regional, and local leaders agree, or agree strongly, that there is dysfunction in their organization that reduces the effectiveness of global strategy. Almost everyone can see it. Let's stop hiding.

So, what can we do about it? Well, as a first step, we are going to shine a bright interrogator's spotlight in the face of these forces.

My intent is that you will never think about global collaboration and dysfunction in the same way again. You will have a new understanding that links symptoms and causes. You will also realize that global success needs vigilant and expert guardians to combat the daily pressure toward disorder, dysfunction, and separateness.

3. The Fallacy of Globalism

As a global leader in a multi-billion-dollar international company, I was spearheading a new channel growth strategy. One morning, my boss, who was the head of global business strategy, stuck his head through the door of my office and asked, 'Do you have the top ten markets aligned yet?'

It was clear that he expected the leaders of our ten most important markets to agree and commit to the new global strategy. My job was to persuade them. He believed that we, the global group, had devised the best growth strategy. It was a superior alloy of insight, thought leadership, and with all of the benefits of a global perspective. We knew the business well and this strategy would work for all of the markets. Curiously stubborn, they just needed to be convinced. Meanwhile, there were many questions we were not asking.

- Is that how global strategy should work?
- Does this approach help each market grow its business or is this about something else?

- Is a single umbrella strategy the best way to grow worldwide?
- Is such a strategy so efficient that there is a meaningful net gain?
- Does the global strategy coexist with market-level strategies?
- Does it replace them?
- If this works for the top ten markets, what about the next ten?
- What if it doesn't work for them? Too bad?
- Can markets opt in or opt out?

We will get to these questions, but the fact is that a single global business strategy, even if it features an impressive array of insights that decipher all common growth drivers and barriers, is never better for everyone.

The key to understanding this is in the motivation. A one-size-fits-all strategy is invariably developed and promoted by those whom it serves best.

Most global, regional, and local managers agree, sometimes grudgingly, that—somewhere and for someone—there are benefits to global strategy. Yet, disagreement invariably occurs when we ask whether they receive a fair return for *their* contribution. Indeed, the consistent reality, and it is always there—right in front of us—is that different stakeholders share the investments, advantages, and profits of global strategy unequally. Their frustration, therefore, and a cause for their possible disengagement is the biased and irregular distribution of value.

In this chapter, we will examine the lie of globalism. On dissection, this invention turns out to be, more often than not, a play for dominance and a deliberate disregard for meaningful differences. We will see how actions based on a belief in this concept—the idea that a single global strategy is better for everyone—will always come up short. We will also explore how this mindset, which prefers to ignore meaningful geographic differences, creates waste, fuels discontent, and undermines the credibility of global leadership.

We must understand this philosophy and why it is a fallacy because, despite its flaws and its limiting consequences, globalism is tempting in its simplicity and also, depending on where you sit, by its biases. In asymmetric multinational companies that favor certain geographies, perhaps a large home market, globalism is the least disruptive approach that protects a comfortable status quo. At the same time, building an international strategy that accommodates all meaningful market differences looks incredibly hard and very slow. For one thing, local leaders everywhere are notorious for overstating their market's uniqueness. Inclusivity seems like a fine thing but, in practice, too many cooks in the kitchen means laborious progress and delayed action. That said, globalism is still not the solution to these challenges if the intent is for more balanced multi-regional growth.

Let's start the dissection.

Selling Globalism

Imagine that you are an American global leader discussing global strategy with your French colleague Jean-Louis and he just gave you the world-famous 'but we are different' speech (which would be just as likely with the nationalities reversed). You probably saw this coming. After all, as a global leader, you hear that speech so many times you could write the script yourself. When Jean-Louis pushes back, he lists considerations that he claims are important but don't fit your strategy. Taking his focus away from these things, he says, will dilute his opportunity in France. His list could include national culture, customer preferences, trends, market structure, regulations, profitability, resources, and capabilities, to name just a few. As these local considerations are areas where he has more expertise than you, do you accept his warning? Do you trust his expertise and judgment? If he is right, a mistake could become a serious barrier to success.

On the other hand, it may also be true that Jean-Louis is simply offering a common and very human response. To him, your global strategy may seem like an imposed incursion that could feel like an annoying distraction or even outright overreach and a substitution of his leadership. He may have invested years of his life building a mastery of his business. Does your process respect and value this expertise or does it undermine his significance? Such a reaction is not unusual. As we will discuss in later chapters, in addition to the importance many of us place on our status, we share a common desire for autonomy. This will always be a challenge to international collaboration. After all, being part of a collective, of a larger whole, means being less unique, and that means having less focus on individual actualization and gain.

Let's return to Jean-Louis. When he pushes back, is your first reaction to focus on your shared relationship as a way to win him over? Are you thinking that a good next step might be to listen to his concerns and build a nice rapport over dinner and a bottle of wine? If so, ask yourself why it is so important that you secure his buy-in. What are you trying to sell him? Why? Does he need it? Why do you want him to compromise? Are you curious or frustrated? If you can't persuade him, will his reaction be an obstacle to ignore, bypass, or even overrule?

Intuitively, we know that the benefits of global business strategy are not automatic or certain for every market or stakeholder. However, we are frequently guilty of proselytizing the idea of "global" as a singular, consolidating, and positive force for meaningful scale and efficiency. Many global strategies are truly umbrellas that direct all markets beneath their span to pursue the same goal. Why do we do this? Where does it come from?

Globalism is a collection of beliefs and values. It asserts that everyone around the world will be better off if they embrace the benefits of an interconnected and interdependent approach. That doesn't sound too crazy but, in practice, it goes further and becomes the inflexible belief that a single global strategy is better for all.

Nobody would argue that one-size-fits-all is a valid approach for hats. Hat size is a single variable and if people's heads can be modeled in a normal bell-curve distribution, it is not complicated to calculate how many heads a single hat size will fit. In this case, the effectiveness and the relevance of a one-size-fits-all strategy are fine. Very few will have a hat that fits perfectly but, for many, the fit is good enough.

Who would make the same argument for business? There are indeed common variables, like market penetration, that are consistently important everywhere. However, every real-world complexity adds more variables. Globalism fails because it chooses to ignore the variables that are inconvenient, but inconvenient doesn't make them irrelevant. Its forced simplicity is a deliberate or negligent decision to overlook selective considerations without diagnosing their significance. And the outcome is predictable.

To return to our colleague, Jean-Louis. When he says, 'Look, I don't want to do these things because I don't believe that it is best for my business,' he is rejecting your global strategy based on local fit. This is perfectly understandable. A single strategy is, by definition, not optimal for every market. So, what do we do now? How do we resolve this tension? Is this a negotiation? Are there going to be winners and losers? As a global leader, how do you define success with Jean-Louis? Again, are you there to help him to grow his business? Or do you simply need him to comply?

No Rising Tide

The inherent flaw in globalism is the naïve position that *global* business strategy is better for everyone.

It is a seductive idea but it fails every time, even when forced. The ideology of globalism under-delivers its supposed value because the actions that we would take under that doctrine ignore meaningful diversity and therefore demand too much compromise from its executors. In particular, above and beyond the question of fit with local business, globalism demands a bigger sacrifice. It requires local leaders to give up some of their autonomy and self-determination. This flies in the face of human nature and the very consequential reality that most companies are not designed to reward this behavior. Just the opposite. Indeed, the notion that a senior leader will voluntarily choose to give up even a modest slice of their power to be a good corporate citizen is a pipe dream. Few regional or country managers will accept such a demotion unless they receive something very compelling in return.

Let's examine the recent misfortunes of economic globalism as a parallel example to reveal some valuable and hard-won insight. For context, the leaders of the world's largest and most developed markets have stubbornly pushed the principles of globalism for the past 20 years. As a direct result, the acclaimed global political scientist, Ian Bremmer, described the world as entering a "geopolitical recession" in which alignment and collaboration for common benefit are deteriorating. He described globalism as a doctrine, which claimed it 'is going to be good for people inside the United States and these other advanced industrialized democracies, and [therefore] they should support that politically because they will be taken care of.' Bremmer then qualifies this by stating, 'And that's a lie.'[3] We have all seen the consequences and the backlash. As they questioned the return on their investment, and in the absence of fair mutuality, nation after nation began to deliberately reduce the connective tissue between themselves and what felt like an imposed global machine. Meanwhile, country after country responded to the inequity by advocating for some form of introspective national populism.

This economic and political upheaval underscores the point that not everyone is enjoying the fruits of global progress. Consider a key tenet

---

[3] Ian Bremmer, Center for Global Business Annual Forum at University of Maryland's Robert H. Smith School of Business, April 2019.

of economic globalism: The strategy to create efficiency by moving production to where resources and workers are cheaper. Such global arbitrage enables low-cost products but, at the same time, it can weaken manufacturing innovation and displace jobs in developed markets. So, even in this simple and common example, there are both winners and losers. Our world is simply too complex to put any faith in the idea that a rising tide will lift all boats by a similar amount.

The rebellion against globalism throughout the worldwide economy is a powerful example. It shows what happens and how we start to lose our way when we decide that everyone should adopt a single strategy even though we know it will only work hard for some. Today, there is remarkable public anger towards the governments that advocated for economic globalism. In large part, and avoiding the ugly politics, this is because they failed to be responsible for—and to show a duty of care towards—those for whom the strategy was not best designed.

Globalism may be positioned as mutuality, common cause, and shared opportunity but it is fundamentally hegemonic. It picks favorites and its benefits are exclusive. This is why it inevitably fails as a principle upon which to build a global strategy. It only truly serves a shortlist of winners. This is why it sees other markets' differences as inconvenient or even inconsequential. Globalism is not valuable worldwide. It is, ironically, not *global* at all.

Breeding Disengagement

Most global companies expand into new markets to increase both their global market penetration and to create protective diversity. Indeed, we deliberately assemble a geographic portfolio for the very reason that these separate markets—or regions or clusters—are not meant to rise and fall together. We rely on the fact that it is the uniqueness of the characteristics of each market that dictate the value it derives from any strategy. From customer trends to supply chains to government regulations, these differences are often inseparable from the market opportunity itself.

Yet, in this context, many global teams craft one-size-fits-all global business strategies that define singular and worldwide objectives and priorities. Typically, we label these as important and relevant for a period of, let's say, three to five years. This is such common practice and yet it makes so little sense. We risk investing in a strategy that at best is only partially executed, that diverts investment from where it would have more impact, and that distracts operational teams from pursuing local opportunity.

We also miss the chance to support markets for whom the strategy is a poor fit. There is some cruel irony here. Smaller markets, which are typically disadvantaged by globalism, often have fewer resources and so have more need for external support and additional focus. They can least afford to divert resources from what is most relevant to fuel their growth.

Imagine what it is like to be Jean-Louis: To be on the receiving end of a one-size-fits-all strategy that does not fit. Then imagine how you might react when you learn that this strategy describes where the company's resources will be focused for the next five years. Perhaps you are also told that you must adopt these priorities as well. From Jean-Louis' perspective, this is crazy. If he goes along with this, then he and his market may underperform. As we will learn from the research study, at this point, his most probable course of action is to ignore the global strategy, deliver his target results, and worry about forgiveness later. His formal performance objectives are unlikely to reflect the global strategy and this provides excellent cover for his actions. Jean-Louis sees no reward for the sacrifice of being a good corporate citizen. It is just the opposite.

A global business strategy is not better for everyone. Yet, we have global teams working hard to persuade every market and region to get on board, pushing hard and using political chicanery to squeeze key stakeholders for commitment. We also have local teams shaking their heads and going back to business as usual the second the global team leaves for the airport. In the end, stakeholder engagement is always going to be the deciding factor in a strategy's success. Engagement is a necessary precursor to execution. This is the inevitable flaw in the globalism doctrine and why it is clear how this will always play out.

Globalism does serious and long-lasting damage to the idea that there is value in global collaboration. So, it is not surprising, and as you will see later in the research, local market leaders see global strategy as less important and less valuable than either their regional or local strategies. To many local and regional managers, the word "global" means "corporate compromise." Small wonder, then, that for any stakeholders except for the strategy's favorites, globalism breeds disengagement.

Three Behaviors to Watch For

Why do so many strategic leaders push for compliance with a one-size-fits-all global strategy when most operational leaders believe it is a mistake? Why are the strategy's executors not being heard? After all, at some point, the strategy will need to be operationalized. Why are we pretending that there is no risk?

This is a dangerous disconnection. It creates many symptoms of dysfunction and, fortunately, they are very easy to spot. We can't miss the loud and repetitive warnings that we are heading into danger. The challenge, and the reason that globalism is such a powerful and fragmenting force, is that we still find it very difficult to change course.

Here are three common signs that a belief in globalism is fragmenting the performance of a global company:

1. Oversimplification

Global strategy, a set of decisions for the business to thrive and grow, is going to be complicated if it is truly global. Each of the regions, clusters, and markets within the scope of the strategy will present varying degrees of difference. We can't ignore this because winning in these geographies, and competing successfully with serious locally focused competition, often depends on our ability to deliver against very specific needs.

Globalism tries to brush these differences under the rug. Ignoring the complexity of the real world, its devotees often capture the essence of global strategy in a short presentation or a one-page high-level summary. In reality, for operational stakeholders, these all-too-common summary documents are meaningless. It is an inexcusable own goal to suggest that our business's worldwide complexities and opportunities can be represented by something simple. Simplicity is certainly reassuring but it is an illusion. It is an attempt to show control and mastery by summarizing, averaging, and omitting. Oversimplification, fueled by a belief in globalism, is likely to carry our so-called global strategy across the line into impotence and irrelevance.

Ask different regional and local peers if they can see themselves in a simplified global strategy. Is it clear to them how the strategy helps them to succeed? Do they know what to do? How many of them want this?

Different parts of a global strategy have different meanings for different stakeholders. An area of focus for some markets will never be equally relevant and valuable everywhere. However, an oversimplified global strategy obscures this—so much so that we may be left wondering whether the authors know the extent of the strategy's relevance. At the same time, without seeing the specificity of their particular business landscape reflected in the strategy, local stakeholders are more than likely to conclude that the strategy is not meant for them.

Of the trappings of globalism, perhaps the easiest to spot and the most glaring is a strategy that works too hard to show its mastery of a complex world by presenting that world as a simple construct. You may have seen examples with all opportunities rendered down into a small handful of *growth pillars*. This sense of control may calm our fears, but it is not always grounded in reality. There is no rising tide to lift all boats and this strategy is likely to truly serve only a subset of its stakeholders. This is made abundantly clear by the tension created when some of those who would be executing the global strategy show concern that it is disconnected from their business realities. Meanwhile, watch its advocates oppose this disagreement and avoid calls to acknowledge the messy complexity of the real world.

Here is an uncomfortable yet powerful diagnostic question: Is the global strategy designed for presenting or for doing?

2. Enforcement

Globalism may be a fallacy, but it is very seductive to its authors. It powers a tribal tension whereby global strategists are convinced that they are promoting what is best. They may believe so strongly in the superiority of their perspective that they resist the legitimacy of any dissension. They may even feel frustrated that regional or local stakeholders who don't share their vision are being inappropriately rebellious.

A global strategy built this way will not be widely embraced. However, if authority rests with the global team to enforce the strategy, then they may attempt it all the same. If so, we see global leaders promoting or even dictating their strategy, but there is a classic tell, a signal that shows that they know that this approach is flawed. In the final analysis, they do not stand accountable for their strategy's results. They know that their regional and local colleagues, who are of course the executors of any strategy, may endure the initial enforcement, but—sooner or later— they can, and probably will, disengage.

It is fascinating that we can be aware of what is going on and still do this. In the end, if compliance with global strategy is coerced, then the strategy is revealed to be a political exercise only. It is revealed as theatrical with nobody committed to, and accountable for, its performance.

Strategic governance, forced compliance, and oversight are all clear signs of top-down globalism and its guarantee of collaborative failure. Without voluntary engagement, every global strategy is in trouble.

3. Ad Hominem

Globalism does not tolerate naysayers very well. It is not a doctrine that likes to endure objective scrutiny and be debated. As we saw in the example with Jean-Louis, it is hard to argue with the expertise of a stakeholder who is telling you that the strategy does not fit his market.

So, in a telling symptom, some global leaders will respond to this criticism with ad hominem attacks. They will claim that those who dispute the value of the global strategy are simply opposing a challenge to their autonomy, their authority, or their ego.

To some degree, this is probably true. Autonomy is an important motivator and senior leaders will always have ego. After all, most days they are the boss. Also, put yourself in Jean-Louis' shoes. Every day, he is the man in the arena fighting hard and giving all that he can to win within his territory. How would you respond to a new direction that does not reflect your expertise? You may not have all of the answers but how would you react if you didn't have an opportunity to be heard and to have influence?

However, while the ego response to global collaboration is very real, here it is a red herring. Look past the ad hominem attacks. Can we objectively and rationally promote the value of the global strategy? Can we debate its merits and its flaws? If not, then you know that you are dealing with a one-size-fits-all doctrine.

When we realize that we, or others, are not curious about the cause of dissension, then we need to ask why. Globalism takes a hard inflexible stance. It does not promote mutuality. The sooner we are aware of this then, the sooner we can hit the brakes.

Takeaways

Globalism is a pervasive and tenacious force of fragmentation. While belief in this doctrine is disconnected from much of marketplace reality, it is very seductive for global strategists and also for top-level leadership.

At its core, globalism is not about service: It is authoritative. It does not listen and it is pushy. Globalism says, 'I know better' and 'Get with the program.' It even apportions blame if the results don't materialize.

A global structure offers top management greater visibility and control of their organization. However, there is a trap if we take the desire for control too far. This is happening when we reject meaningful complexity because it interferes with the streamlined view of things that we would prefer. We inevitably fail when we insist that markets compromise just to align with a more manageable and directed approach.

Here is a summary of the important takeaways from this discussion:

1. Globalism is the belief that a single one-size-fits-all global strategy is the right answer and that all the participants will benefit in a similar way.

2. Globalism fails because a) it ignores meaningful diversity, and b) the actions that we take under that doctrine demand too much compromise when the strategy is a poor fit. These strategies are

hegemonic. They are designed to serve only a shortlist of favorite geographies and they see other markets' differences as inconvenient or inconsequential.

3. It is common practice for many global teams to develop one-size-fits-all global business strategies that define worldwide priorities for up to three to five years. This approach demands a grand compromise in which local and regional participants are required to set aside or deprioritize their marketplace differences. Such a settlement risks serious and long-lasting damage to the idea that there is value in global collaboration.

4. Globalism is seductive in that the simplicity of a single strategy feels like mastery. Its proponents are frustrated by stakeholders who don't share their vision and who reject any dissension that might undermine their sense of control. However, these stakeholders are the inevitable executors of the strategy, and they can't be ignored or compelled without harming their engagement and their results.

In the next chapter, we will expand on the tensions between global, regional, and local stakeholders. Unfortunately, globalism is not the only force that creates silos and pulls separate stakeholders apart to place them on opposing sides. As we shall see, fragmenting forces often combine and they can do real harm to trust between leaders, and so, predictably, to global business performance.

4. The Unspoken Power of Tribalism

On 29 May 1985, English and Italian soccer fans of Liverpool and Juventus football clubs had gathered in Heysel Stadium in Brussels for the European Cup Final. As they waited for the match to begin, the crowds became rowdy and then increasingly hostile. One hour before kick-off, Liverpool supporters suddenly broke through a fence and charged at the Italians. In the ensuing tragedy, as most fans tried to escape, a wall collapsed and 39 people were killed, while another 600 were injured.

I chose this example of tribal animus deliberately for its excess. Yet, why choose an event so appalling and so dramatic? Why describe actions so primitive that you might reasonably question their connection to professional business behavior? Well, it is exactly this extreme behavior, behavior that appears to set rational and civilized judgment aside, that makes this story so valuable for our discussion.

It is human nature to be tribal. We may not like this, but it is undeniable. Indeed, tribal attitudes and behaviors are a shared reality of our social evolution. However, when we see or hear stories like this, we are lightning fast to deny our tribal attitudes and behaviors. We tell ourselves that we are more rational in our choices, more evolved, and certainly not that primitive. We are not emotional and unrestrained animals!

The takeaway here is not the example of Liverpool versus Juventus. The lesson is in our response to the story. How quickly do we label those soccer fans as *others*? How strong and immediate is our conviction that they are not us and we are not like them? Do we judge them to be less than us? Do we give them a derogatory name to create further separation, like "hooligans," thugs," or "a mob"? Perhaps, we identify that they are part of a different socio-economic or demographic group. Just look at the surprising lengths we go to in order to say who belongs in our tribe and who does not. While judging others for their tribal behavior, we don't even notice how tribal our own reaction is.

So, we are barely into a conversation on tribalism and already we have seen how easy it is to prefer to belong to certain groups and to reject others. Let's be consciously competent about this. We confront a shared blind spot when we recognize and admit to just how quickly, and almost unconsciously, we can discriminate against other groups.

Tribalism is a very human trait. It is found everywhere and every day. It is so ubiquitous that, while we may not be aware of our tribal attitudes and behaviors, they are normal. Our tribal thoughts and actions often feel perfectly acceptable, defensible, and dismissible. Yet, the label of tribalism is so disdainful. We would rather not name it, and, if you or I were called "tribal," we would be insulted. Certainly, in a business context, we like to maintain that our professionalism trumps any such primitive impulse. As a result, this is not a behavior in ourselves, or in our group, that we prefer to acknowledge and so it is not something we choose to grapple with. Ironically and hypocritically, we won't hesitate to acknowledge tribal discrimination from other groups.

So, this is a hard topic. If we are to understand tribalism and to manage its influence, then we are going to need to look it in the eye. We will also need to look at ourselves in the mirror. The alternative is to choose to keep the blindfold on and to accept the direct consequence, which is that our global company will never be more than the sum of its separate parts. Instead, it will behave as an association of groups that may collaborate for a time, or perhaps compete, so long as each group can maintain its separateness and as much independence and autonomy as it can.

In this chapter, we will discuss how tribal antagonism is pervasive, and how it undermines the performance of global business in obvious and insidious ways.

We will begin by digging up the root causes. We will learn why our tribal instincts were important for our social evolution and survival. And so, by understanding our behavior a little more, perhaps we can chastise ourselves a little less. It also means that we must accept that, as humans, we are hard-wired to prefer our tribe. It is who we are. We don't need to apologize for it. We need to accept it.

Fair warning, tribalism can be a distressing and depressing topic. We don't like this human quality in others and even less in ourselves. However, it is always there, a stubborn weed in the garden. So, it is important that we need to learn to stop denying our tribalism or treating it like a dirty and embarrassing secret. Tribalism will oppose or damage trust between groups. However, there will be a lot more damage and dysfunction if we pretend that it is not in the room.

As we dig deeper, we will learn how most companies have reward systems that promote tribalism. This is particularly true between separate geographic organizations. Typically, when we ask these groups to collaborate with others, we still only reward them for their own tribe's achievements.

The odds are against us. Social evolution is against us. However, we are not defenseless. It is possible to learn to accept our tribalism and to call it out in others. Tribalism's impact is best diffused by leaders who are vulnerable, inclusive, and curious. Unfortunately, these proficiencies are rare and progress is often fragile. So, in most cases, this is a force of dysfunction that will not go away. We need to anticipate it, prepare for it, and never pretend that we don't also bring it to the table.

Humans Are Tribal

As humans, we all need to belong to groups and we discriminate in favor of these groups. We like our group more and other groups less. We form bonds of trust, affinity, and loyalty within our group and tend to see those outside, or those who identify with other groups, as different, as competitors, or even as threats.

In business, we are quick to acknowledge feelings of identity, belonging, and even of antagonism when it comes to competing externally with other companies. We even celebrate these emotions. Indeed, we encourage and reward a competitive tribal mindset with money and prestige. For so many, this is the mindset that is needed to win.

Tribal behavior is instinctive and normal. It makes perfect sense to measure our success benchmarked against the performance of our rivals. However, let's not fool ourselves that it only applies externally, between competing companies. Tribalism is everywhere—it is certainly present internally and it is particularly consequential in a global organization.

Every global company is inevitably made up of separate factions. Tribal identifiers of geography and function are the most obvious and real. We even promote tribal separateness. I knew a region head who led "Team Europe." He cultivated his own team culture and was openly proud that he protected his organization from what he considered to be external interference. Meanwhile, his annual meetings celebrated the region's successes and cemented team members' bonds with one another. His people were loyal or they were encouraged to leave. Does this story sound familiar? Isn't it interesting how easily we conflate building a strong team with building an independent team? It seems that the stronger our tribe becomes, the more self-reliant we want to be. I will add that this region head was fired by a new chief executive officer (CEO) who refused to put up with his need for separateness. However, his replacement was one of his lieutenants who had advanced in that same tribal milieu. Today that culture of separateness is less visible but still very much alive.

In a global company, tribalism erodes collaboration. It opposes common objectives and undermines collective strategy. There is no sweeping this under the rug. Internal tribalism, particularly geographic tribalism, is a bad thing. It is damaging because, even at low levels, tribal antagonism shapes and drives cognitive distortions. By poisoning trust and fueling biases that muddy our thinking about critical issues, tribalism warps our reason. When we view the world through the lens of *what is most favorable to my tribe*, then we compromise our ability to have a balanced and objective understanding of current and future opportunities. By definition, we are at a disadvantage to any competitor with an impartial fact-based strategy.

At the same time, let's not make the mistake of attaching shame to tribalism. That will make it so much harder to have accepting and productive conversations that open the door to progress. We are built to be tribal. Yes, it is a force of fragmentation but let's expect it and treat it as something normal, especially from our leaders.

We Are Not Wired to be Global

Human brains are not adapted to working in large populations. We are social creatures but our abilities to trust and to collaborate have physiological limitations.

The *Dunbar Number* describes the maximum number of stable interpersonal relationships that people can handle. This idea was proposed in the 1990s by British anthropologist Robin Dunbar. He posited that, for humans, the number of social relationships that we can manage averages around 150. Above this number, we need laws and norms to keep us together because groups larger than 150 people will fragment and separate. Studies of Stone Age society reveal that a village size of 150 people was the average above which they split into separate groups. It is also interesting to note that the size of military units in professional armies, from the ancient Romans to today, also reflects this phenomenon.

Business relationships form just one subset of our total. Family, friends, neighbors, and even that old acquaintance from high school, all compete for a place in our maximum social capacity. Not everyone is equal of course. Dunbar noted that we devote approximately two-thirds of our time to just 15 people. So, what about everyone else? Well, those whom we don't choose to connect with, or for whom there is simply no room left in our limited brains, are labeled as *others*. This is important to understand because we are more likely to stereotype such people and less likely to think of them as individuals.

Dunbar observed that the cohesion of tribal groups is maintained through physical and social interaction. Today, with our ability to communicate instantly and worldwide, we can form connections with almost anyone. However, the strength of these connections is limited by the frequency, duration, and intensity of each interaction. So, in the end, with an upper limit on the number of strong connections that we can form, we are more likely to invest in the connections that are easy to reinforce. This is why proximity matters. A global company organized with strong worldwide connections can create tribal groups that span geographies. Even so, the connections are almost always stronger between people who are physically close because their connections are easier to reinforce.

As Allen Buchanan, Professor of philosophy at the University of Arizona and author of *Our Moral Fate: Evolution and the Escape from Tribalism (2020)*, puts it, 'Groupishness is in our genes. We will always tend to divide the world into Us and Them and tend to think We are superior.' Statements like this suggest that tribal animus is instinctive and inevitable. However, Buchanan points out that 'Our moral nature is not exclusively tribalistic but also includes the capacity for inclusion.' So how do we come out on the right side of this? What can we do to promote more inclusion?

The key is to understand that, while we all have strong and sometimes unconscious biases toward tribal thinking and behavior, different environments can stimulate our potential either for tribalism or for inclusion. If we can be sufficiently objective to diagnose how we encourage tribal thinking and then change those structures or processes, it becomes possible to make lasting progress in being more inclusive. It helps to think of tribalism and inclusion as opposing and competing forces. Feeding one starves the other.

Tribal Leaders

Admitting that you have a problem is always the first step. However, when it comes to tribalism, we struggle. While we might accept that there may be tribal biases and preferences inside our company, between departments, teams, offices, regions, or markets, it is much more difficult to admit, acknowledge, and point out the rivalry, the animosity, and the opposition. Perhaps we avoid this confrontation because we don't know what to do about it. It is clear is that we don't like to address our internal antagonism. Even when it is staring us in the face, it seems that we would rather not call it out.

In particular, we avoid calling out our senior leaders. This behavior may be normal, but it feels like a terrible indictment. Surely, we say, a good leader would not be in that important position if they yielded to such basic instincts. They would not place such self-serving and primitive ideas ahead of opportunities to collaborate. Anyway, look at their team's business results. The leader is a strong performer. Making excuses like this is a mistake. Leaders are human too and, in reality, they are more tribal than anyone else. After all, they represent the identity of their group and they have a duty of care only to that group. Many leaders bring experience and expertise, and they have earned their authority. Our leaders set the tone and reinforce the sub-culture of their groups. Let's be objective: Leaders are tribal chieftains.

Do we shy away from this reality because to hold other leaders accountable for tribal antagonism is to admit that it exists within ourselves? Of course, this is self-defeating because any denial ignores an obvious and important insight: It is the leadership of each company that has the most power to fuel or diminish tribal behavior. However, we make this almost impossible. Consider that we almost always measure and reward a leader's performance for actions that they control within their tribe. Indeed, we focus both functional and geographic leaders on their separate and unique tribal objectives. This makes sense of course, given their expertise and their specializations, but, with scale, this inevitably fuels a desire to develop or maintain tribal independence. This separateness, they argue, is necessary to protect their power to control their ability to perform, which they now claim is critical to delivering their required results. And the more the company depends on these results, the stronger the tribe's negotiating authority.

In a small company, the CEO may be successful in forging strong connections. However, in companies above a few hundred employees, this becomes increasingly difficult and before long the CEO will find themself in the role of the high chief who leads and depends on other chieftains. In a global company, the regional presidents are the most powerful of all tribal leaders.

Let's put ourselves in their shoes. Imagine that you are the head of North America and charged to deliver specific regional objectives. What is the value to you of anything you might do to support another region? Is it a distraction? Do you want to help other leaders who may also be rivals for a promotion one day? If you need resources or support to deliver your goals, then mutual collaboration and interdependence may be your mantra. If not, how magnanimous are you prepared to be? You enjoy your position and want to control your ability to deliver your goals, which means directing the focus of everyone in your region. Why would you put this at risk?

A time-honored illustration of this bias towards tribal independence can often be seen in large regional business teams within a global company. For example, in many Western multinational companies, it is common for the US business to have disproportionate scale and resources, and for its leaders to want to go their own way. It doesn't matter if the business is mature and so less profitable and projecting little growth. Rather than support and fuel other regions or markets, these US teams often prefer to invest in their domestic capabilities, pursue independent innovation, and reinvest profits to fuel their own agenda. Protected by the power of their scale, large regional businesses often ignore their company's geographic portfolio strategy even if it impedes global growth and harms the protective power of market diversity. It is fascinating to see this tribal power on display. It is often so brazen and unapologetic. Of course, this dicey autonomy creates significant tension and so it is always predicated on the continued ability to deliver strong results. If results fail, then grab some popcorn and settle in to watch a dramatic rebalancing of tribal power.

We Have More in Common

In July 2004, Barack Obama delivered the keynote speech at the Democratic National Convention in Boston, Massachusetts. His most famous lines were a call for unity. He said:

> ... there is not a liberal America and a conservative America—there is the United States of America. There is not a Black America and a White America and Latino America and Asian America—there's the United States of America.

Obama was praised for his incredible oratory but the claim of national unity, while sounding so commendable, has proved to be fantasy. Indeed, 20 years on, the polarization and fragmentation of America is greater than ever.

In business, having recognized the separateness and the divisive behaviors of tribal groups within their company, global or regional leaders often make a similar appeal. Faced with disconnected regions or markets, they cite company values, common threats, and a shared mission. They highlight similarities between opportunities, competition, channels, customers, consumers, etc. They claim, 'We are more alike than we are different.'

If you have ever been a recipient of this message, if you have been asked to set aside your tribal identity for the greater good, then you know that the tactic fails. It can sound laudable, but it is not effective and it does not stick. Human connections and the sense of belonging that they create need feeding. The frequency, duration, and intensity of our interactions with others create and strengthen the bonds between us and, because we can only manage a finite number of relationships, only the strongest bonds survive. We don't build lasting connections with conceptual ideas, but we do with the people right in front of us whom we see often and with whom we spend time doing important things.

A request to set aside differences can have the opposite result. It is a huge error to assume that tribal differences are not important to those in the tribe. To say this out loud can show indifference, even disrespect, to what a person holds as some valuable defining characteristics of their identity. This can fuel even more tribal thinking. Indeed, a common response to this appeal is for tribal members to double down on their differences. They may even create new differences to reinforce their separate tribal identity.

A rational appeal is not going to overcome the baked-in tribalism that comes with being human. Remember the violent soccer fans in Heysel Stadium? They had much in common, such as demographics, socio-economic status, and a deep love of their sport, even a common desire to watch the game that they eventually disrupted. Yet, all of the similarities that the fans of each team shared failed to bring them together and instead strengthened their identities as separate rival groups. Similar tribes are easily rivals and a rival tribe competes for the same objectives and resources or superiority. Rivals are similar in many ways and yet they are absolutely "other" and a threat. In a global company, we can have many rivals. That we share so much in common is why we compete.

It is a fool's errand to try to dismantle tribal identity. Remember, we will create separate tribes from almost identical people as soon as there are enough of them to make it work. Tribalism occurs not because of differences but because we have evolved to associate with relatively small groups. The differences can be useful identifiers, but they are not causal. This is important. Trying to remove or to ignore differences reveals a fundamental misunderstanding of tribal behavior. Tribal differences are just the symptoms of our need to manage the size of our social groups.

Each tribe needs its distinctive characteristics to describe and maintain its identity. To give these up is like asking a country to abandon its flag or asking a sports team to lose their uniform or their association with the town or city where they play. It is not going to happen. These distinctive attributes of the tribe are necessary to create an all-important sense of belonging. It is the differences that tell us we belong here and not there. So, a request to set aside these differences, to effectively merge tribes, would weaken our sense of belonging, and this goes against, according to Abraham Maslow, some of our most fundamental emotional and social needs.

To make matters worse, this petition, to recognize common needs and so come together, can also be interpreted as a veiled attempt to convince regional or local market stakeholders of globalism. The argument infers that everyone will reap similar rewards because we are all so similar. This is untrue. While there may be similarities between regions or countries, it is their differences that determine what value a common strategy offers to each.

Last but certainly not least, the appeal to focus on what we all have in common rarely comes with an associated reward. Most companies' financial incentives are aligned with tribal results. It is much easier to measure specific individual contributions all within their limited scope of influence and that of the teams they lead. At the same time, many people become very uncomfortable, and often demotivated, when their performance is linked to results outside of their control. So, colleagues struggle with incoherence, a kind of cognitive dissonance, from leaders who ask for one thing but reward another.

Since tribalism is going to win out in the end, we are better off positioning this request as an *and* —that is to say, recognizing and respecting all of the differences *and* recognizing all of the similarities. The idea that we don't have to give up our tribal identities to be a part of a larger whole is inoffensive and reasonable. It is extremely hard to reject the idea that we are different in some ways and similar in others. It is less tidy and certainly more complex, but it is also real. Indeed, it is surprising how collaborative separate tribes can become when they don't have to focus on defending themselves and justifying their differences.

Three Behaviors to Watch For

In business, tribalism is a constant force that erodes and fragments broader connectivity and collaboration. It is always there and we are all a part of the problem. That said, it doesn't pay to be overzealous in trying to root it out. We must allow for normal behavior. Several times a day, we may aggregate or label a group in discussion. Not every *Us vs. Them* conversation is a bad thing. Again, this is normal behavior. Accept it.

The performance gaps that result from tribal animosity are common, and are typical symptoms of poor trust and half-hearted collaboration: strategy failures, clumsy coordination, missed opportunities, unsolved problems, finger-pointing, etc. Somewhere, in all of that mess, one or more tribes is probably feeling disrespected. Yet, must all tribal differences be indulged? Surely, some of the differences are overstated. If so, we need to learn where the line is. Where is the point at which we go beyond investing in a stronger team to rejecting outside influence purely on the basis that it comes from outside?

Let's imagine that there is good and bad tribalism. Think of it like this: Good tribalism is inclusive, and invests in more and stronger connections within the tribe; bad tribalism is exclusive and seeks isolation, preferring fewer and weaker connections beyond the tribe. So, for example, a tighter-knit team is the result of good tribalism, but this often comes with an exclusive loyalty, which isolates that team, and this we want to avoid.

Behaviors that exclude are not hard to spot. For example, pay attention when there is no clear or transparent explanation for a disagreement or disconnection. A local market leader who rejects regional strategy claiming a poor fit and then presents a fair rationale is not being negatively tribal. A local leader who commits to a strategy but takes no action to support it may be.

Also, watch your behavior. We are all going to struggle with this. If you are a global leader, then watch that you are not suffering from the dangerous global-knows-better syndrome. This is a classic tribal attitude that says global thinking is superior to that of the regions and their local markets. Why this mindset is so common is a puzzle when we consider that, more than anyone, global leaders need to encourage connectivity between geographic tribes. Disrespecting those tribes and their expertise will achieve the opposite.

Here are three of the most common examples of negative tribal behavior in global business.

1. Fake Commitment

More often than not, negative tribalism is hidden and unspoken. It does not react well when you shine a light on it. It is also emotional and it does not stand up to a rational objective review. This is why, in business, negative tribal behavior is often passive-aggressive or duplicitous. After all, it is easier for a tribal leader to offer that fake commitment than to engage in reasonable debate to justify the separateness or independence that they desire.

Therefore, an easy test is to check that everyone is putting their words into action.

Some years ago, I worked with Fred Hassan, the CEO of several global pharmaceutical companies. He would meet with local managers during his business trips. Among other things, he would ask them about their role in the global strategies that their regional and local leaders had agreed to. Their replies spoke volumes. It was such a simple and powerful act of leadership and governance.

Of course, not every missed collaboration or failure to cascade strategy is deliberate. However, if the diagnosis of a snafu suggests that not all parties are prioritizing as expected, then it is worth checking whether something else is going on. We all recognize the normal signs of shared dedication to a mutual undertaking. So, if engagement, proactivity, and enthusiasm, and of course execution, don't fit your expectations, then these may be warning signs of a faux commitment.

2. Justification Research

Market research that acknowledges local or regional differences can satisfy tribal bias and allow for inclusion. However, it can also be used to justify exclusion.

Many times, as a global leader, I have seen a local or regional team present the findings of a research study to justify their uniqueness to opt out of a shared initiative. The argument is that their consumers or customers have different needs or preferences and therefore their market or region needs to go its own way. It is always important to listen to this. Never forget that not all boats rise together. This work may be legitimate. However, when the study comes as a surprise, when it is a response to a call to collaborate, when you can feel the tribal tension, you should hear the alarm bells ringing.

Research to justify independence that is performed under the radar is a common tribal trick. Often the work done is rushed, imperfect, and blatantly biased, but it makes a point. Indeed, the quality of the work is not that important. The findings, whatever they are, don't need to be a statistically accurate insight: This is a political message that says, 'We don't want to do this and, if you force us to, it will fail.'

Global teams can be just as guilty of this behavior. They are not above using multi-market studies as a cudgel to push those markets into compliance. So, be careful when global or regional teams present research that ignores or minimizes market differences. Only if the individual markets agree with the findings will all be well.

3. Tribal Chieftains

What are the expectations for interdependent collaboration within your global leadership team? Is your company a loose assembly of regional businesses or are you aspiring to operate as a collective global whole?

If the latter is your company's declared intent, then does your global leadership team deliver the goods? Are they a collaborative and interdependent group that is committed to pursuing shared successes? Do they work together to mutual benefit as connected parts of that whole? Or, at the other end of the spectrum, is your global leadership team an uneasy gathering of tribal chieftains? Are they uncooperative rivals who pretend to play nice but value prestige and status and will go to great lengths to maintain their separateness?

A global leadership team of tribal chieftains often pretends that there is harmony because it is politically risky not to. For appearances, the chieftains will make a faux commitment, and then they will hope that time and circumstances will allow them to quietly renege. Here is a true story from the world of consumer-packaged goods. You will see how each tribal chieftain knowingly allows an expectation of interdependent collaboration that turns out to be false.

A global team was leading a project to harmonize separate regional brands into a single global brand. The heads of each region demanded that consumers in all regions must prefer the new global brand in six different ways over what they currently had. This was a deliberately high bar that could sink the project. However, if it could be achieved, then the new global brand would be truly superior and fuel sales growth everywhere. The project succeeded and the results were shared in a global leadership team meeting. There, in a startling reversal, the region heads angrily rejected the findings. Within minutes, their cordial facade fell away and senior executives, typically calm under pressure, started shouting and arguing. This was anything but a calm and reasoned discussion. At issue was their loss of autonomy, and this was worth a lot more to them than stronger sales and a more preferred brand.

Your global leadership team will set the tone for collaboration, connectedness, and mutuality. Which of them will 'walk the talk'? If you can, examine circumstances where everyone agrees that collaboration is important and where they need each other to achieve something valuable. Real or faux commitment is easy to spot. Indeed, a lesson from the story just told is that it is not a good idea to continue working when the commitment is not real.

Consider that regional presidents, in particular, have incredible authority to fuel or diminish tribal animus and behavior. This is because they are the most powerful tribal leaders in a global organization. Yet, at the same time, each regional president must, by definition, represent the interests of their tribe. That is their purpose and it is what they are rewarded for. All of this places them in what can be a challenging situation. Do they see their interests best served by connection and collaboration or by isolation?

Takeaways

In the quest for global advantage, the hardest and most protracted battles we ever fight are internal. In every organization, teams form bonds of trust and loyalty and, to varying degrees, they tend to see others outside their team as threats, rivals, and competitors.

While we may not want to admit it, in any global organization, tribalism is a real and omnipresent problem. We are part of that problem. We like to pretend that we are above it, but senior global leaders are no more immune than junior local managers. The most vulnerable players are regional presidents, who are the most powerful tribal leaders in a global company.

Forces of Fragmentation

Tribalism is a constant force eroding and fragmenting our connectivity and collaboration. Tribal antagonism shapes and drives cognitive distortions that muddy our thinking: It warps our reason. However, we are not powerless. There are many opportunities to diffuse tribal tension and to promote inclusion in its place.

Here is a summary of the key points from this discussion:

1. We all need to belong to groups and we discriminate in favor of those groups. We like our group more and other groups less. We form bonds of trust, affinity, and loyalty within our group and tend to see those outside, or those who identify with other groups, as different, as competitors, or even as threats.

2. Human brains are not adapted to working in large populations. We are social creatures, but our abilities to trust and to collaborate have physiological limitations. We all have strong and sometimes unconscious biases towards tribal thinking and behavior. However, it is possible to make lasting progress in being more inclusive. It helps to think of tribalism and inclusion as opposing and competing forces. Feeding one starves the other.

3. Admitting we have a problem is always the first step. Yet, we struggle to admit to tribal behavior. In particular, we avoid calling out leaders. However, the reality is that we actively encourage leaders to be tribal. After all, it is typical to measure and reward a leader's performance for actions that they control within their tribe.

4. Global or regional leaders often appeal for unity, claiming, 'We have more in common than we have differences.' This tactic is not effective. Tribalism will not go away because we ask it to. Also, while there may be similarities between groups, it is their differences that determine their unique potential and the value that a common strategy offers to each. Tribes need their separate

identities and this fuels our sense of belonging. If anyone tries to dilute our tribal identity, then our knee-jerk response is to double down. A better appeal would be to acknowledge both differences and commonalities.

In the next chapter, we build on the themes of forcing alignment and blind spots as even the most valuable strategy is tested by the company's global matrix organization.

5. The Incoherent Matrix

Imagine the global matrix, your company's worldwide and interconnected operating structure, as an electronic circuit. This distinctive combination of wires and components enables simple and complex operations to be performed. There are transistor-like switches, which are gatekeepers to the flows of energy, decisions, and resources. Resistors too, which do just what you might expect. And diodes, which allow energy and information to flow in one direction only. Some components collect and release potential, smoothing the flow of processes or providing focused bursts of power and performance. There are sensors, too, that detect important changes in external conditions. This electronic circuit has many different components. It is often large, diverse, and complicated.

The more we study the global matrix, the more we appreciate how critically important it is to understand this complex circuitry. The effective operation of your company depends on it. Indeed, just like an electric circuit, the structure and performance of your matrix define and direct if, how, where, and by whom, work is done.

A Fiction of Unity

The analogy of a complex circuit, with wiring designed a certain way and with diverse components that can fail, is very useful to highlight not only the structural constraints but also the fragility of the system. Also, while we may have a general sense of how the circuitry works, such as what is supposed to happen where, this is not enough. Most of us don't understand exactly how the different components interact. We see symptoms of performance, or dysfunction, but their causes are often lost in the complexity. This means that there is a good chance that we are going to struggle to diagnose and then remedy any performance problems.

In larger organizations, we might extend this analogy into a system of several connected circuits, which becomes even more unwieldy. As scale and complexity grow, we need to recognize that nobody may be able to fully grasp and appreciate all of the intricacies of the whole system. Inevitably, this will affect performance. It is especially worrying for global initiatives, which, by definition, seek to engage the entire system.

In this chapter, we investigate the global matrix of an organization to review its opportunities, the barriers it creates, and the most important dynamics at play. The matrix is where all of the global leadership, management, debates, collaboration, strategy, and decision-making play out. When it is working correctly, the matrix opens the way to energize collaboration and focus performance across the entire organization. When it fails, performance degrades as our company machine doesn't behave as we expect it to. Instead, we find unexpected silos, barriers, and dropped connections. Decisions become impotent and company focus becomes fractured. For global strategy, the matrix contains the vital thread that leads through the maze to link strategy development to the local commitment to execute. Even minor dysfunction can snip that thread.

No two companies follow the same blueprint when they create a global organization. Often how they get there is unique. Indeed, their structures reflect their individual journeys to build international scale.

This means that each global matrix is going to be different. Later on, we will learn to diagnose these differences. In this chapter, we will highlight the most common features and their implications.

Some form of a sophisticated matrix is essential for running a large and complex global organization. We are going to focus on its two core dimensions—geography and function—but these are not always the whole story. Some companies also try to integrate discrete structures into their matrix, adding layers that focus on customers, channels, products, or even processes. The complexity can become mind-boggling and the risk of inertia or performance drag or internal waste grows along with it.

The matrix is an important answer to global complexity and it is a high-risk problem all at the same time. We will start by reviewing why and how we create a matrix organization. We will then take a critical look at the challenges unleashed. As we will learn, the coherence between what a company says it wants to do and what its matrix allows it to do is vital, and there is always a gap. It is so important to understand what is happening here—in part, because this is a chronic blind spot. Many leaders assume that their matrix is a self-correcting system that will automatically adapt to match the decisions that they make. In reality, parts of the matrix are almost guaranteed to be incoherent with global directives. This coherence can be repaired and improved. Yet, before we can reclaim our effectiveness, we first need to understand the dysfunction.

A Matrix is Born

As companies develop international operations, they create groups to control and manage their business strategy. The make-up of these teams is driven by geography and their structure follows a simple linear hierarchy. The role of head of international business is created and the person in this role directs several country leaders. In turn, each of these commands a team of function leaders (operations, finance, marketing, sales, human resources, etc.). Finally, these function leaders direct their teams to deliver the local business strategy.

In this structure, the international head reports to the company chief executive officer. This is important to ensure that there is a high level of accountability to top global management. Direct access also ensures that top management pays attention to international operations. Typically, if the ratio of international to domestic sales is low, the head of the international business will have a lot of autonomy and authority.

In this phase of growth, decision-making and accountability are well-understood by all of the players. Everyone can place themself in the hierarchy and by physical location. So, they all know who and what they need to get the job done.

This international organization, with a structure based on geography, works well when the business spans just a few countries. As the number of countries and complexity increases, there are advantages for top management to focus the attention of some business functions by adding a new global structure. So, at this point, we introduce a second company-wide hierarchy in which functional departments are responsible for their activities around the world.

This new function-focused structure increases accountability and central control. It reduces headcount by shrinking duplication and it also improves worldwide access to expertise. This is good. A global functional hierarchy directly addresses some of the challenges that would impair the profitable growth of this developing company.

Typically, companies look for these benefits by first globalizing back-office functions, such as finance, information technology, human resources, and supply chain. Typically, this evolution yields substantial value without much drama.

So, now we have two management structures that coexist and overlap. While each structure is built separately, and has different priorities and focus, the intent is for them to be interdependent. Fused, they form a matrix that connects the geographic hierarchy with the global functional hierarchy. This hybrid system is intended to connect the complex global business, combining separate hierarchies in an interactive and reciprocal relationship. In practice, this approach is double-edged: It is partially successful but it is also seriously flawed.

Conjoined Structures

To understand how the two management structures integrate, it is important to remember that each was originally designed to unlock separate opportunities and solve separate challenges. While we were able to globalize back-office functions with mutual benefits for both hierarchies, the integration becomes vastly more challenging when we consider sharing the ownership of strategy, prioritization, resources, and decision-making.

Table 5.1. The Intent of Geographic and Functional Organizations

Intent	Geographic Hierarchy	Functional Hierarchy
Control	Improved visibility to direct the business	Improved visibility to direct the department
Strategy	To deliver sales and profit	To deliver capabilities
Efficiency	To exploit similarities between countries	To reduce geographic duplication and headcount
Perspective	Competitors, customers and consumers	Functional experts
Resources	To focus local resources	To allocate global/regional resources
Decisions	Decentralized decisions	Centralized decisions
Results	Discrete and short-term	Strategic and longer-term

Table 5.1 above details some of the strategic intentions of each structure. There are similarities but there are also meaningful and contrasting differences.

With this information, we can ask a better question, which is where do these structures reinforce and support each other, and where do they compete or create roadblocks?

The two management hierarchies are separate systems and each is designed for its own purposes. Importantly, they are not designed or redesigned to work together. Rather, they are fused, imperfectly combined, and connected with participants rewarded for actions under either geography or function. In fact, by retaining the separate tribal reward systems of the geographic and global functional hierarchies, we all but ensure that mutuality is a rare thing. As a result, it is not unusual to experience conflicting objectives, misaligned strategies, and different priorities, together with what seem to be irreconcilable preferences, processes, cultures, and behaviors. The two systems, forced together, are too often in disagreement and they resent their dependencies, easily find themselves at odds.

To deliver the synergies top management is looking for, the two overlapping organizations need to complement each other in their collaborations. However, if the objectives and results that they are seeking are not the same, then we can expect more tension and confusion than headway. How do we make decisions in this combined organization? How do we collaborate when the two organizations define success differently? How do we hold each other accountable when we report into different hierarchies? How many matrix bosses need to sign off on important decisions? What have I done to deserve two bosses who have different goals?

This global matrix is not a new idea. We have had decades to practice and refine it. Yet, although many companies continue to experiment with modified structures and different approaches to sharing or mandating authority, the fundamental and often conflicting biases created by fusing two separate organizational structures have not changed.

Matrix versus Strategy

The organizational matrix of a global company will inevitably present some degree of incoherence and dysfunction in response to global leadership and direction. What may have been the clearest, focused, and well-communicated input is translated by this complex machine into a partially diluted output with often unexpected and surprising alterations. Yet, with our understanding of the inherent conflicts in an assembled matrix, this should not surprise us. Remember, large parts of a global matrix organization belong to regional and country management hierarchies. When we built them, we structured these organizations to deliver specific tribal objectives. So, when we introduce global strategy or any directive outside their designed scope, we are asking these parts of the organization to do something they were not built for. This is a structural problem of our own making.

We expect regions and countries to engage with global strategy. However, we also expect them to remain consistent and deliver their primary function. For example, we need local teams to focus on their specific opportunities to drive short-term growth. Being pulled in two directions, local support for global strategy will not be the priority. If local and global objectives are too different, the global strategy may not be a priority at all.

Strategy leaders often struggle to appreciate this reality. They hold a common misperception that company operations are subservient to strategy. It is a seductive idea that seems logical and appropriate. However, this often proves to be simplistic and naïve. The complexity and dysfunction of the matrix show us that any top-down decision takes a convoluted and risky journey before it is translated into execution.

It follows then that a matrix organization will never be fully coherent with global strategy, and all that hand-wringing about how difficult it is to build global alignment exposes how little this is understood. Imagine how differently we would approach collaboration if we set our expectations in the right place.

This is an important operating principle to understand and therefore to manage. A degree of incoherence between strategy and operations is a predictable tension that needs our awareness and proactive interest at the highest levels. The structure of our organization, and the characteristics and quirks of its global matrix, are going to fuel some actions and restrict others. We need to expect this and to be able to diagnose it.

Organizational Inertia

Per the aphorism, "Organization follows strategy." If so, it makes sense that a global matrix will be structured for the strategy it is designed to deliver. However, in the real world, we are not in the habit of checking this. Instead, we take for granted that our strategy and our organization are coherent. We also assume that, if they are not, then the organization will adapt as necessary. Indeed, we are often guilty of giving new strategies the green light without questioning whether our organization is set up to successfully deliver.

When we do recognize the need to adapt our organization, we prefer to tweak and modify what currently exists. We create new roles and new teams, and we introduce new ways of collaborating. You may have seen new global and regional sub-teams created to bring focus. Common favorites are a speed team to prioritize a global product launch or a global project team to roll out and accelerate the adoption of a new process. However, these are temporary bolt-on attachments to the existing structure and, overall, the matrix stays the same. So, while we agree to these temporary or incremental solutions, we rarely explore whether a larger change to the organization is necessary.

Why do most leadership teams not review the fitness of their matrix structure when approving a new global strategy? Where does this inertia come from? It is hard to accept that we don't know that the global matrix is operating under tension. If we agree that organization follows strategy, then surely we must conclude that we need a new organization when we adopt a new strategy. Yet, many ignore the risk completely. Very few companies design strategy and organization in the same conversation.

I have a theory that strategists have a bias toward focusing outward. We tend to view strategy-building as a practice to lend influence and predictability to all of those external variables that are beyond our direct control. If this theory holds, then it is ironic that in our search for control we overlook the opportunity to adapt our organization and to optimize the mission-critical factors that we wholly dictate.

Three Behaviors to Watch For

When the matrix misfires, global strategy pays the price. Sometimes the misfire is immediate and obvious, such as a power struggle or misalignment. On occasions when the tension is ignored or buried, the impact is revealed later and often too late to recover the lost opportunity.

1. Decision Flow

This topic is covered in detail in Chapter 7. However, it is worth a mention here because the matrix makes up the communication network through which decisions flow. The matrix is the arena in which global strategy decisions are proposed, debated, agreed, deployed, pursued, or ignored.

Let's go back to the analogy of electric circuitry and imagine that each management structure is a separate circuit. In each circuit, the energy to do work flows in a direction that follows the structural wiring and, in the two management hierarchies, decisions flow easily with the simplicity of command and control. So, what happens to the flow of energy when we combine the two circuits? To begin with, we find that decisions move more slowly. Compliance and commitment are less automatic. There is more confusion, delays, and debate. There is more disagreement and often much more energy expended to avoid the appearance of disagreement. We see a lot more risk-averse behavior and we gain a healthy appreciation for the true levels of trust between leaders. A signal to watch for is the practice of pre-aligning leadership ahead of a decision, specifically to avoid open disagreement and maintain a fake facade of harmony.

Poor decision flow is an easy symptom to spot. It is a common feature, particularly in companies that try to manage the matrix by seeking overly broad consensus in decision-making. With too many cooks in the kitchen, the service is going to be slow.

Decisions made in a global matrix require deliberate curiosity and the highest levels of engagement. Disagreement and lively debate are very good and very necessary. Decision flow may have stopped, but this is a sign of a functioning matrix. More dangerous are decisions that you thought were agreed to but then resurface later for re-litigation. Worse still are decisions that you thought were agreed to and then you hear nothing. A global matrix with operating practices or a low-trust culture that allow this to happen is misfiring dangerously.

2. The Fog of War

If decision flow is at risk in the matrix, then the work we have decided to do is also in jeopardy. However, a diagnosis of decision flow may not raise flags and, still, the work may not get done. The reason is simple: The global matrix is easy to hide in and its complexity offers plausible deniability when expectations are not met. Too many stakeholders and a flabby bureaucracy create a "fog of war" in which actions and intentions can be obscured.

In the last chapter, we talked about "faux commitment." This is not just a symptom of tribalism but also a common and duplicitous behavior that is enabled by the matrix. It is fueled by self-interest, politics, culture, or an unhealthy enthusiasm for control. Is it an ugly idea to suggest that colleagues are deliberately misleading us? Would it be more comfortable to view the world through the lens of positive intent? If so, then let's think of the global matrix as a fragmenting force that puts people in challenging situations. Pulled in conflicting directions, we feel pressured to make choices but unable to make everyone happy. That said, it is harder to maintain a belief in positive intent when, rather than being transparent, stakeholders use the matrix to hide their actions.

Uncertainty and limited visibility are the hallmarks of a global matrix. The remedy is to improve precision and trust. We need effective mechanisms for accountability and performance measurement to know if the agreed work is getting done or if the matrix is misfiring. The Russian proverb *doveryai no proveryai* means *trust but verify* and that is very good advice here.

3. Time-Based Separation

Geographic and functional management hierarchies pursue business results in different time frames. Local organizations are more likely to focus on short-term, perhaps quarterly or annual, results. Global teams may be focused on the impact of a three to five-year strategy. This can be a major cause of fragmentation and it is one that the matrix magnifies. It is also a well-known tension that we seem to know is there but then do nothing about.

Partnership and collaboration require that the stakeholders involved not only need each other but that they are working to the same end. There needs to be some overlap in their objectives for a win-win to be found. Two groups that don't share the same objectives have little basis for meaningful partnership. If they are somehow forced to work together, then—to produce results—one or both will need to compromise their initial objectives, which neither wants to do. This is a variation of the prisoner's dilemma, in which cooperation is irrational and self-interest has a better pay-off. Yet, many of us are guilty of hoping that this disconnection will spontaneously resolve itself. The most naïve believe that our expressed company values or cultural solidarity will see us through. It can be a hard pill to swallow, but the matrix eats culture for breakfast.

Imagine a multinational company with centralized product innovation. The global team directs a product pipeline to deliver their growth strategy, which will be launch-ready in three years. Meanwhile, local markets are begging for new products to compete now. While a few large and dominant markets get their wish, most of these requests are denied. Both global and local teams want growth, but they define the time frame differently and, in this case, the global team holds all the cards. Ironically, the global group says that its role is to help the markets win. The markets find no humor in this.

The dynamics of this example are more common than you might think. I have seen both global and local teams invest in separate product pipelines as a way to resolve their disconnection. The inefficiencies were ridiculous, of course, but this was not viewed as a failure but rather as a way for all the stakeholders to get what they want without giving up any autonomy. Performance was less important than maintaining control.

It is common for the time-based separation between different stakeholders in the matrix to reinforce negative perceptions. Local teams are seen as hungry, demanding, and tactical, while they see the global group as a slow and disconnected cost center. These tribal points of view are typical in a matrix structure. However, left unchecked, this disrespect creates the conditions for global and local strategies to be developed separately. When each hierarchy crafts its strategy alone, and then they inevitably collide in the matrix, it is too late to reconcile the differences. If you have seen this movie before, then you know it doesn't end happily.

In a later chapter, we will explore how to bridge the time gap. Mutuality is not out of reach. It is not impossible for different stakeholders, or even separate branches of the matrix, to become invested in each other's success.

Takeaways

Most company leaders don't think too much about the coherence of strategy and organization. While the strategy may change, they tend to assume that their organization is already designed for what is to come. At the same time, given the duality of a global matrix, a system with both overlapping and competing objectives, we see that the matrix is never fully in sync to support global strategy.

Do you smell burning?

It stands to reason that companies that do adapt, to better align their organization to deliver new strategies, have an advantage. In their book, *The Essential Advantage (2010)*, authors Paul Leinward and Cesare Mainardi capture this point well:

> … most organizations are "sticky": their identities, cultures, and relationships are by nature slow to adapt to changing conditions … but by becoming more coherent, like a boat moving toward a lighthouse at night, you align your organization toward a clear, more visible, more consistent goal. You are no longer as vulnerable to external events—or to your internal fragmentation.

It is worth streamlining and reassigning Darwin's theoretical concept here. Let us agree that the global organization that is best able to survive is the one that can adapt and best adjust to the changing environment in which it finds itself.

However, we have learned that a global matrix has powerful inertia. It is likely that, without powerful intervention, this self-competing complex organizational structure will remain unchanged. It will certainly not evolve spontaneously to best fuel our strategy. While necessary to connect our global organization, the matrix represents a constant fragmenting force that degrades the effectiveness of strategy and makes us vulnerable.

Here is a summary of the key points from this discussion:

1. A global matrix is created by fusing two or more separate management structures. Typically, this matrix connects the company's geographic hierarchy with its global functional hierarchy. While each of these has different priorities and areas of focus, the intent is for them to be interdependent. This connected global organization relies on a network of collaborative relationships. However, this coalition is only partially successful as they struggle to reconcile their different priorities.

2. Geographic and global functional management hierarchies have separate objectives and priorities. This is particularly evident when it comes to decision-making and business results. To energize these differences, stakeholders in a matrix are rewarded for actions under either geography or function. Typically, there is little overlap. In fact, by retaining the separate tribal reward systems of the geographic and global functional hierarchies, we all but ensure that mutuality is a rare thing. It becomes unexceptional to experience conflicting objectives, misaligned strategies, separate priorities, and conflicting preferences, processes, cultures, or behaviors.

3. While we expect regions and countries to engage with global strategy, we also expect them to remain consistent and deliver their primary function. For example, we need local teams to focus on their specific opportunities to drive short-term growth. Being pulled in two directions, local support for global strategy will not be the priority. If local and global objectives are too different, the global strategy may not be a priority at all.

4. We tend to take for granted that our strategy and our organization are coherent. We also assume that—if they are not—then the organization will adapt as necessary. We are often guilty of giving new strategies the green light without questioning whether our organization is set up for success.

More than survive, if our global company is to thrive, then we need to start accepting and acting on these realities. We are structured for dysfunction and we undermine our success when we leave this fragmentation unchecked.

6. The Wrong Leader

My stepfather was an Englishman who owned a large Volvo and he took it with him when he went to live in France. At almost seven feet tall, there was no way he could fit inside a little Citroen or Renault. A plausible excuse perhaps, but it meant that, while driving in France, his UK driver's seat was on the right, placing him on the outside of the driving lane, which limited his visibility around corners. He also suffered from nerve damage in his feet and, as a consequence, he couldn't feel the pedals very well. Imagine then, these factors combining along the narrow and often single-lane French country roads with their tall hedgerows. As a passenger, his sudden accelerations and convulsive braking as we shot around blind corners were terrifying.

Was he ignorant of his capabilities and the risks he was taking? Probably not. Yet, he was not objective about the danger. Our terror notwithstanding, he would always insist on driving. Being the driver, and sitting in the driver's seat, were incredibly important to him, more important than our fear for him or ourselves for that matter. The role gave him a sense of value, status, identity, and fulfillment that he was not prepared, under any circumstances, to let go.

This story is not so unusual, is it? Many people insist on being the driver. I'm sure that you know someone who always prefers to drive than be the passenger. Perhaps they are also somebody for whom the role and identity of being the driver are important. Indeed, many of us enjoy the power of the driver's seat. We relish this central role, making decisions for everyone and exerting control. Once it becomes a habit and a part of our identity, we don't want to switch places. Indeed, it is so rewarding that many of us want to be the driver regardless of our performance. Is performance something we even think about? Do we ever consider that, because *we* are driving, we might not reach our destination on time. We not going to change roles just because we don't know the way. We are the driver.

This is a great metaphor for business leaders. Particularly, as for many, it seems that what matters, more than results in fact, is that they are doing the leading. Of course, we want to get things done, solve problems, and create positive results, but only, only if we are driving.

Over the past 20 years, Gallup claims to have studied performance at hundreds of organizations around the world and measured the engagement of 27 million employees. Their findings proved a point that should have been obvious to everyone: *Business performance depends on how people are led and managed.* In particular, Gallup exposed just how much the critical measures of business success, such as profitability, customer satisfaction, productivity, quality, and employee retention, all depend on having managers with the necessary talent. Unfortunately, their research also revealed that 82% of people currently in managerial roles do not have that talent. In fact, less than one in five managers has the talent to lead people to perform.

Does this fit with your experience? Thinking back to the bosses you have had, how many were able to help you to unlock your best performance?

How many of your ex-bosses were leaders in the sense that you would have chosen to follow them? Does one in five seem about right?

Gallup's findings are powerful, but they are less surprising when you look at the reasons why we promote people into managerial roles. In most cases, promotion happens based on availability, tenure, and seniority. Of course, these have nothing to do with whether the individual has the right talent and mindset to thrive in a leadership role. Intuitively, how we choose leaders has to be one of the most consequential factors in business. Yet, the data is very clear: We don't seem to know how to get this right. We are terrible at choosing leaders. We make a bad choice more than four times out of five.

To make matters worse, leaders don't improve with time. If you have read *First, Break All the Rules* by Buckingham and Coffman[4], you may recall the insight that was echoed by tens of thousands of great managers: *People don't change that much. Don't waste your time trying to put back what was left out.* Yet, in 2019, companies spent more than $370 billion globally on leadership development training. If Buckingham and Coffman were right, then this wasn't the best investment. However, it shows that we know that we have a leadership problem. Sadly, a poor or average leader will never become a great one. Missing talent is not a weakness or a development opportunity that can be fixed with training.

Being a good leader is a lot harder than we pretend it to be. For global roles, this challenge is compounded dramatically because international leadership is a torture-test scenario. To begin with, in each tribe, our senior chieftains promote those who best mimic their own behaviors. So, leaders are selected based on tribal fit, but what they learned in order to get ahead in their tribe will not be enough in a diverse international milieu. Compared with directing a local team, leading colleagues across a global matrix presents a whole new standard of difficulty. People with

---

[4] Buckingham, M., Coffman, C. (2016). *First, Break All the Rules.* Gallup Press

the necessary talent and relevant experience are, therefore, extremely rare.

This topic is so important. While many of the forces of fragmentation that compromise our global companies' performance are inescapable, the ability to appoint effective leaders can be learned, which means that this source of dysfunction can be mitigated or even avoided.

In this chapter, we will explore how the wrong people with the wrong skills are too often in the driver's seat, where they undermine and even sabotage global collaboration. We will also tackle our shared aversion to acknowledging the reality and the incidence of this dysfunction. Indeed, you may be surprised by the pull-no-punches candor of this chapter. Yet, if we want to improve on Gallup's scorecard, then it is about time that we stopped dodging the issue.

Choosing Global Leaders

As we consider global operations, it is important to appreciate that global business acumen, as opposed to domestic business acumen, is not really recognized as a formal discipline or competency. Instead, it is commonly overlooked and treated as an extension of existing functional capabilities. If you can do one job, then you can do the other. This is a fatuous mistake that harms careers and business results. It is particularly risky for those new to a global role who often realize very quickly that they need help, mentors, and guidance. Learning to be effective in a global role is often an on-the-job drink-from-the-fire-hose undertaking. Typically, It is a highly visible and high-stakes role with the very real probability that to succeed you will need to disaffect or even frustrate some of your companies' most powerful leaders.

An experienced mentor can make an enormous difference, but there are not many of these. Unfortunately, it is more common for global roles to feature as temporary assignments rather than a long-term career path.

This means that tenured gurus who have solved some of the riddles of global effectiveness are hard to find.

The practice of moving domestic leaders into global roles belies the reality that global expertise requires a different and more complex skill set. Leaders who are used to command and control will struggle to influence their peers in a global matrix. Those who prefer to avoid conflict are also unlikely to thrive. That said, most managers, and at all levels, agree that they are better leaders as a result of their experience.

I once worked with a US-based global company where there were several vice presidents (VPs)_ of marketing. Each was responsible for a separate part of the total portfolio. They all had long tenure and every few years they would rotate positions and exchange businesses. This was a game of musical chairs where eventually, through performance, attrition, and political maneuvering, one VP would be declared the winner and successor to the US chief marketing officer.

By coincidence, the company's global strategy team was co-located with the US headquarters and so one of the tour-stops for each VP was a global marketing role. This was a two- or three-year assignment with little definition and even less accountability. Each VP would take their turn to enjoy a novel and temporary role knowing that ex-US results were not important in their career. Indeed, it wasn't long before they would focus their energy on planning their next assignment. In the US office, there was no awareness of the international contempt for these pretend global leaders.

Having the wrong leader is perhaps the most destructive force of global fragmentation because it is so widespread, so impactful, and therefore so risky. Most global leaders have neither the talent nor the mindset for the role. If we don't define any qualifying criteria, then we set ourselves up for failure and we also leave these colleagues exposed and vulnerable. In the earlier example, meaningful qualifying criteria for effective global leadership were never considered. The global role was

VP-level and this, together with physical proximity, not having played the role before and therefore inexperienced, were the only boxes necessary to check.

If only 18% of local business leaders have the talent to induce others to deliver top business success, what must this mean for global leaders? There can be no doubt that a global leadership role, which operates in the murky gray of the global matrix, requires the highest levels of influence, empathy, and engagement. Experience in the command-and-control world of local business is no help. Cultural sensitivity, patience, negotiating, trust-building, and (perhaps above all) the ability to forge meaningful connections are likely to be new skills that take years to be mastered and are extraordinarily rare—especially in one person. So, how many global leaders have the rare talent and mindset to engage their international colleagues to get things done and to deliver the best results? It may be optimistic, but we might estimate that fewer than 1 in 10 global leaders have what it takes.

Perhaps we should flip that around and agree that almost everyone is going to struggle in a global leadership role. The qualities that make a great global leader are simply too rare and we don't select for them when we put someone in that role.

Gallup's data and findings were published over 20 years ago. Sadly, there was no seismic shift and no sudden bloom of self-awareness. Promotional practices and the criteria for managerial roles have not changed. This problem is not going away. But we choose to ignore rather than confront it. Practices of measuring leader performance, such as tracking team engagement, are not widely used. Replacing leaders is very disruptive and so we waste a lot of time and performance accepting mediocrity or hoping for change that will never come.

How does this fit with your experience? If you are a regional or local leader, then I wonder if you agree with the research study, which found that only a minority of regional and local stakeholders have confidence in global leaders. The three areas we explored were global leaders' behaviors, capabilities, and how they tackle critical issues. We asked top-, senior-, and mid-level managers, and all agreed. Surprisingly, confidence was low even among top-level company leaders, which in this case were regional and country presidents. Middle managers in regions and countries claimed to have the least confidence in their company's global leadership. Most of these stakeholders did not agree that their global peers earned trust, empowered team members, or even led their teams to deliver meaningful value. The shared insight, common to both regional and local colleagues was this: *Global leaders are not at stake for my success.* There seemed to be very little trust.

Let's get into the details and look at some everyday examples of how the wrong leader can trigger dysfunction and fuel the fragmentation of global performance.

Trust and Candor

The foundation of any relationship is trust. However, trusting others and building trust are not always easy, particularly when it feels like there is personal risk. Strong connections are crucial and this is why international collaboration can be something of a worst-case scenario. The challenges of building trust in a global matrix amplify the difficulty of some foundational requirements. To begin with, we need a viable reason for collaborating that all parties can agree to. We must need each other for something important and need to work together to achieve this end. This sounds simple but, in the matrix, that sense of mutual need for common value is not so easy to find. Remember, the benefits of a global strategy are not the same for everyone. So, from the very start, a collaboration will have a different value for different stakeholders.

In a high-trust environment, we might expect each member of the team to reveal the true value to them of the collaboration and therefore the commensurate commitment that each is prepared to offer. This candid conversation, this level-setting negotiation, is an appropriate and effective way to begin. However, without a foundation of trust, stakeholders will not be forthright and transparent. Rather than take this risk, they will keep their opinions to themselves. The wrong global leader, hoping that silence means consensus, will forge ahead but alone. Ironically, the candor and transparency that are needed up-front to build a constructive partnership, are finally revealed when stakeholders feel they have been pushed too far. Unfortunately, at this point, they may reject the collaboration altogether.

The Tidy Trap

It is common for global leaders to fall into the trap of trying to be tidy. This happens when they believe that global strategy equates to a simple and focused narrative. Mistakenly, the wrong leader will assume that neat simplicity shows their command of strategy, and the growth and efficiency that they hope to unlock.

This is a top-down mindset. It is simultaneously naive and arrogant, and it fails to earn trust. Rather than build an inclusive collaboration, the wrong global leader believes that stakeholders' differences are messy and unimportant. They believe that this diversity is unnecessary complexity and they will ignore or minimize it. Of course, as we have discussed, it is the differences that determine the value of the collaboration for each party. So, any attempt to dismiss these differences signals that there is probably no good reason for collaborating.

In such cases, the wrong leader may present a global strategy to an international audience, detailing its shortlist of priorities and the required capabilities, but they will never explore the spectrum of reactions in the room.

Strategy as Product

Let's talk about a company-wide error that completely undermines trust in global strategy. Do your global leaders see the global strategy as their product? Not the results but the strategy as an approved document? Is the strategy document a deliverable that they create and then sell-in to the organization?

This happens often. After all, nobody else has 'build a global strategy' as a personal objective. So, if this does happen, then what does success look like? What does the global leader need to check the box? Where do operational alignment and commitment fit in? Indeed, what if there is not much interest in their new strategy? Must they ask their regional and local colleagues to opt in? If so, then what control do they have over their success? The wrong global leader reads this interdependency as vulnerability and finds it to be unacceptable. They see the risk of failing to secure agreement to an inclusive strategy as a threat to their success. The result is a mindset that is anything but curious. Exploration, debate, and the search for compromise are unwanted and dangerous distractions. Meanwhile, their international colleagues can sense that they are not listening and that they are not flexible. They then disengage.

How do you start to trust a leader who is not even curious about your success?

Fog of Dishonesty

Open and candid conversation is a crucial, if high, hurdle for a new team of international collaborators. With different backgrounds, cultures, styles, biases, and preferences, and of course separate business objectives, it takes work for the team to learn about each other. It takes deliberate choice and effort for team members to open up. Unfortunately, human nature makes this process even harder. How can we be honest and vulnerable when we have such a propensity to lie?

A study by University of Massachusetts psychologist Robert S. Feldman, published in the *Journal of Basic and Applied Psychology*, found that 60% of people will tell on average 3 lies during a 10-minute conversation. When the pressure is on and self-perception or self-esteem is being threatened, people will lie at much higher levels. To make matters worse, according to a study by Jennifer Argo of the University of Alberta, people are more willing to lie to coworkers than they are to strangers.

We lie or mislead to promote perceptions of ourselves that we prefer. We lie when we are uncertain and when we don't want to offend. We are nice but fake to avoid disagreement. We lie to senior leaders because we want to curate their opinion of us. We even pretend to have professional respect when we are convinced that the other guy is a complete jerk.

In a global context, this fog of dishonesty can become a real handicap. Even if they communicate with candor, international stakeholders can hold very different perceptions based on the same set of facts. Indeed, the more time you spend working with people in a global matrix, the more it becomes clear that individual perspectives are very different. Coming from a diversity of geographic and functional roles, the views from these different positions can vary greatly. Also, a person's place within each hierarchy, their proximity to execution versus the board room, creates its own perceptions and blind spots. So, taking the time to understand team members' perceptions is immensely important. Yet, it is almost impossible to make progress doing this if we can't sort fact from fiction. These are serious barriers to trust and collaboration.

An effective medicine to treat issues of trust and candor is a powerful double dose of curiosity and vulnerability. The wrong leader is focused on their success. By contrast, servant leadership serves as a solid basis to build trust among international stakeholders. This requires behavior that is almost the opposite of trying to force them to get on board with a pre-defined strategy. The wrong leader is in a rush and doesn't ask many questions. Trust builds slowly with each step an incremental and authentic experience. With confidence in global leadership so low, the opportunity here is to model the right behavior and take the first vulnerable steps.

Negotiating Strategy

Global strategy often struggles to find the right balance between focusing the organization and representing the diversity of its opportunities. There is a sweet spot out there that reflects important local priorities, while also concentrating resources and attention on the company's most critical path forward. On either side of this delicate point of balance is a no-man's-land of either disengagement or fragmentation and waste. And, of course, that sweet spot is a hard-to-reach territory achieved only through curiosity, courage, persistence, and the expertise of an experienced navigator. It is not a place that one team can reach alone and we charge global leaders with getting us there.

Inevitably, in the quest to find this strategic balance, a global leader will find themself negotiating with their international colleagues. To succeed, they need to do more than identify mutually beneficial outcomes: They need to design and promote an inclusive focusing recipe that feeds all possible stakeholder value and engagement. This is an incredible challenge. Indeed, their international colleagues are likely to be skeptical and indifferent, if not openly hostile.

Effective global leadership requires the highest levels of skill and training. Not the least of these skills is understanding the right way to negotiate.

Adversarial Negotiations

Developing a strategy should involve healthy disagreement and debate among the stakeholders. However, the wrong global leader, who perhaps is more comfortable in a command-and-control structure, creates confrontation when they attempt to force acceptance or compliance with their preferences and decisions. That is not to say that global strategy negotiations are easy. Far from it. Some stakeholders refuse to consider the bigger picture; others prize their autonomy above everything and demand to go their own way. Sometimes the task is just to build enough trust so that colleagues will even entertain a win-win outcome. The mountain is very steep, and the terrain is new and different for many global leaders. If one of them is not ready for it and not willing to adapt, and if they can't bring both assertiveness and empathy to the discussion, then their audience quickly becomes unsympathetic and unreceptive.

When negotiations feel competitive, the wrong leader fights their corner. However, smart leaders see these situations as opportunities to build stronger relationships and to problem-solve. How can we reach a mutually beneficial outcome without compromising what is important to each?

A win-lose result, such as dismissing a local priority that does not fit the global list, is short-sighted. Typically, when international stakeholders return home, they will continue to prioritize as they see fit.

Collaborative Negotiations

Working together to build a global strategy based on common ground sounds positive, but it risks letting the pendulum swing too far. Collaborating in this way works well when two sides are negotiating, but it's not possible when we have multiple stakeholders with different needs and whose relative importance is not equivalent. Global strategy is not democratic, and it also brings objectives and perspectives that are not always common to local business. Sometimes, the Venn diagrams don't overlap. This means that responding to the demands of each stakeholder and looking for a middle ground can be a recipe for disaster. Consensus like this does not ensure an appropriate course. Rather, it is a timid stance that gives away authority in a quest to appear inclusive, fair, and harmonious.

In a room of international stakeholders, global leaders are outnumbered and can feel the pressure. It is very tempting to appease all these representatives with a message of collaboration and to allow that cooperation to be optional if they see sufficient value. This is a terrible concession that probably dooms any chance of a focused global strategy.

Consultative Negotiations

This approach offers the greatest chance of finding that elusive sweet spot. Its trademark is curiosity as the task for the global leader is to understand how each stakeholder perceives their opportunities or challenges. In this way, a global leader hopes to shape how each stakeholder understands the value of the global strategy, including what they will gain and what they might lose otherwise. This takes a lot of work and, while some local leaders complain of having to teach others their business, that friction doesn't last. If the global leader can become an informed voice representing local issues, then they will be accepted and appreciated worldwide. The wrong global leaders fear to reveal their limited local expertise and so avoid asking questions.

It is important in these negotiations to understand the difference between fixed and flexible needs. Local and regional leaders often present all their needs as fixed and non-negotiable, but this is not the case. The power of this consultative approach comes from the starting assumption that individual stakeholders may not be fully aware of what constitutes the ideal strategy for them. This mindset allows the global leader to guide and control the negotiation as the stakeholders clarify their underlying needs. An early discovery phase is typically well-received. The value of this step not only comes from asking the five whys and digging up the root cause of each stakeholder's critical needs but also the act of inquiry itself.

Pushing and Pulling

It is well-accepted that a critical capability of global leadership is the talent to influence others. With international teams made up of peers, and leaders from regions or key countries, a global leader needs to motivate and drive outcomes with a group that may have the same or greater seniority. These colleagues have different bosses, different objectives, and different reward structures. They enjoy being in the driver's seat of their own business and they may not recognize authority from outside their management hierarchy. So, influencing this group is not easy. Indeed, it requires masterclass influencing skills.

A candidate for global leadership without talent and experience in this area is going to fail and fail badly. The tools they used in other roles to motivate others with factual arguments or compelling visions may do more harm than good. As we have discussed already, leaders used to direct-reporting relationships have learned habits that can sabotage them in a global matrix.

Influencing is persuading people to think and act differently in ways that are to their benefit. There is no trickery or force. In fact, fundamental to success or failure is the underlying reality that the power to influence is given by the influenced. They volunteer. They must choose to opt in and accept the influencer's proposal or line of reasoning.

In his book, The New Influencing Toolkit[5], management consultant Tim Baker gives us a handy 2×2 to deconstruct how we influence. He identifies separate styles in which we either push or pull in either a logical or an emotional manner. For example, in a logical and pulling approach, we might promote the benefits of a proposal while highlighting the flaws in the status quo, effectively inviting our audience to make the right decision based on a reasoned argument. In an

---

[5] Baker, T. (2015) *The New Influencing Toolkit*. Palgrave Macmillan.

emotional and pushing approach, we might create a compelling and inspiring vision to motivate and provoke our audience.

This simple breakdown of influencing style is useful because, in a team of equals where no one has a basis for authority, stakeholders from different management hierarchies find it hard to successfully push and pressure one another into an agreement. Even if this works on the day, a pushing influence fades over time, particularly when stakeholders are separated by thousands of miles. Yet, this practice is not uncommon. Global leaders visit, there is a meeting, they assert facts and figures, they push their conclusion, and then they leave. The next day, the local or regional players shake their heads, pretend it never happened, and go back to business as usual.

Influence by pulling is more effective in the global matrix because we need stakeholders to choose to participate out of self-interest. Indeed, successful influencing requires the global leader to offer something of value. This is achieved through curiosity and a thorough investigation to figure out what this value might be. The telltale symptom of a wrong leader is their impatience with discovery and their urgency to converge to a decision. Yet, their international colleagues want to feel that they are invested in their success and their ability to influence them depends on this. There is no faking it. Influencing for a genuine win-win is easy to see and feel, and so is its opposite.

Leadership Teams

It is common practice for a global matrix to be directed by a leadership team. Typically, this is a group of senior managers who represent key functions and geographies, and who connect to make decisions and coordinate work in different parts of the world. Just as individual leaders can either unlock engagement or drain performance, a global leadership team carries its risks. Indeed, it is a crucible that will concentrate and magnify either the right or the wrong behaviors.

First, it is important to understand that the so-called leadership team is probably not a team at all. Rather, the team members are representatives of geographies or functions that are linked only by their senior positions in the company hierarchy, and not necessarily through shared wants or needs. Also, it is evident that the authority and the autonomy that are their habits and preferences make them less willing to subordinate their desires in a team setting. It may be more accurate to describe this group as a council of tribal chieftains, possibly rival tribal chieftains.

The wrong global leadership team can cause tremendous dysfunction and damage to an organization. Unfortunately, by their nature, these teams are usually insulated from critical feedback and it shows. We wrap our leaders in a thick protective blanket that insulates them from candid feedback and accountability. The more senior the leader, the thicker the blanket, until they live in a pandering and disconnected world.

Earlier in this chapter, we discussed how we learned from the research that confidence in global leadership teams is low. In addition, we found that over half of middle managers, whether they have global, regional, or local responsibilities, agree that their global leadership team does not communicate effectively. Almost two-thirds of regional and local managers are not aware of this team's recent decisions. However, the real bad news is that global leaders don't know this and don't seem to be interested. None of the global leaders who participated in the research have ever asked these questions.

This is dangerous. These global leadership teams are not global, they are not leading, and they are not teams. Let's look at some of the most serious traps they fall into.

To Command or Serve?

Is the role of your global leadership team to serve or to be served?

A commanding leadership team is easy to spot as membership conveys a coveted status. Even joining the meeting has prestige. 'I'm sorry Julie. I can't right now. I have been asked to present at the GLT (Global Leadership Team).' Look at me. I am going places!

The desire to be served leads to more focus on the experience of the meeting itself than on outcomes and impact. The meeting becomes a prestigious event. A classic indicator of this is when more work goes into preparation before the meeting than there is the communication of desired actions afterward. Information flows in but little flows out. There is a meeting, but the team is not leading.

This is also the type of environment where the highest-paid person's opinion (HiPPO) is alive and well. Indeed, when the power of position overcomes the power of ideas, one of the first victims is self-awareness. Indeed, managers learn to convince themselves that the HiPPO's idea is superior. Dissent and debate, which are so vital for informed decision-making, disappear.

A leadership team that seeks to serve is rare and offers a very different experience. The role of this team is to consult, remove barriers, and guide decisions if necessary. These meetings are precursors to the work—they are not the focus.

To Tell or to Delegate?

A leader with a bias towards telling has assumed that their organization is not capable. If the necessary capabilities were there, then they might delegate. Good leaders adapt their style to fit the appropriate situation. However, when it comes to decision-making, many leadership teams act as if they are the only ones who can do it. Worse, they create a forum that they control where all decisions must be made. This slows the business. Important action must wait for next month's global leadership team meeting. Hopefully, the agenda is not too full already.

Is this self-indulgence? After all, decision-making can be a lot of fun. It is certainly validating. Deciders feel important and powerful. There is probably a little endorphin rush to it as well. According to Tony Robbins, *significance*, which is our desire to feel important, recognized, and to be acknowledged for what we've contributed, is a core human need. However, I am not sure that this is about making a valuable contribution, but it is linked to ego and status. After all, most drivers will not give up the driver's seat, regardless of their performance.

Of course, the right leader will push decisions down in the organization to engage and develop talent.

Another reason to avoid delegating decisions is fear. This happens when leaders conflate decision-making and control. This can be the top reason not to delegate because, when we are accountable, we fear losing control of performance. Global leadership requires more interdependence than most people are used to. This can create a sense of vulnerability and personal risk, which can fuel this self-protecting and decision-hogging behavior.

In the global matrix, delegating decisions is always the smarter play. There is something incredibly deflating about a small group thousands of miles away making decisions about your business for you. And, since they are thousands of miles away, if you don't like their decision, do you need to listen?

Feigning Harmony

When the global matrix is misfiring, some leadership teams work very hard to keep up the appearance of partnership and collaboration. They understand what their managers want to achieve and they present an image of a healthy alliance with them. Yet, beneath the surface, trust is straining and politics are intruding. All of the team are aware of the tension, but they plaster over it and avoid conflict—at least in the meetings.

Matrix failure can have many causes. Indeed, the global matrix is primed for conflict by design. So, it is much more effective to openly accept this than to pretend otherwise. There will only be trust when leaders are candid and transparent about their priorities, reservations, and differences. Avoiding reality wastes everyone's time.

Leadership team theater is consequential conflict avoidance. It is very common and not just in companies that prize harmony and consensus. Where there is a personal risk and no upside for leaders to address tough topics and lead candid debates, we should not expect it. If the difficult conversations don't happen, then the crippling consequence is that hard decisions are not made, or they appear to be made but they don't stick.

Have you ever seen leaders who, seeking a certain outcome, try to position the meeting minutes as binding proof of everyone's commitment? This tells you things are going off the rails. Think about it. Rather than having a debate, they are circulating a memo hoping it will pressure others into compliance. This is a parody of leadership.

As a side note, it is important to recognize that different national cultures approach conflict very differently. Sensitive management of these preferences may require pre-meetings and some good old-fashioned *nemawashi* (a Japanese term for quietly laying the foundations). However, avoiding conflict is always an abdication of leadership.

Three Behaviors to Watch For

It is not hard to spot the wrong global leader. The most obvious signals of their performance can be seen by looking at the international stakeholders that they are supposed to be leading. We gauge a leader by their followers. How engaged and committed are they? Is everyone on board or are people pretending and playing politics? Is there alignment or theatrics? How open and transparent are the conversations? Does the team debate with candor or is every disagreement "taken offline" and hidden from view?

In addition to the many indicators already covered in this chapter, here are three examples of red flags that are unique to the global role.

1. Career Risk

A global leader often has access to senior- and top-level executives across the span of their company's worldwide operations. Career-wise, this exposure is valuable. At the same time, it can be risky because global collaboration is so often a cause of tension among a company's senior leadership. It is not unusual for a global leader to find themself caught in a difficult situation and facing hard decisions as these tensions rise. This is another reason why it is so important to choose global leaders with the necessary talent. I have seen career mobility and growth cut short when a global leader pushed too hard. I have also seen consequences when they held back to avoid conflict. It is a hard job and showing up without the tools to succeed can be personally risky.

When global leaders realize that they are out of their depth, they can resort to a common set of behaviors that are easy to spot. The right global leader will ask for help. The wrong leader will focus on managing up to ensure goodwill and support within their hierarchy. They may also try to protect themself by making ad hominem, and sometimes tribalistic, criticisms of their more challenging counterparts.

Another form of career risk comes from the difference in measuring performance in global and domestic roles. For a domestic leader, results are tangible, particularly for commercial roles. However, a global position can feel quite unquantifiable. When you are used to concrete deliverables, your efforts to lower barriers or to create focus can seem intangible. With no direct control and maybe no feedback, a global leader can find it hard to gauge their success. Often, they are hard-pressed to enumerate the value of their contribution.

In addition, it is not unusual for a new global leader to feel abandoned when they leave the connected community of a domestic team to start an international role. Their boss, who used to be an advocate, is now focused on other people. Many leaders complain that a global assignment, which was sold to them as a skill-building career accelerator, actually froze their progression.

To make a difference, to make their company stronger, global leaders must be change agents. However, delivering change, particularly in a global matrix, is not easy. As a species, we don't like it. Those senior leaders who prefer their autonomy, and those who benefit from the status quo, will reject the change if they can and resent it if it is imposed. It is not unusual for change agents to become unpopular and to create adversaries and critics, and frequently they don't receive the protection to emerge unscathed. Faced with all this risk and very little upside, we should not be surprised if our global leaders focus instead on self-protection to ride this out. They quickly realize that it is not hard to escape accountability in this role and many play out their tenure delivering the bare minimum to avoid creating any tension.

2. Bluster

I have known several top and senior leaders who would shout and scream about what they were going to say to their international counterparts, but only when these people were not present. They would tell their direct reports to write authoritative memos and to push for their agenda. However, when the meeting or call finally happened, these leaders would roll over and capitulate. Their bravado was a vain attempt to hide the fact that they could not handle conflict. Meanwhile, their direct reports, who thought they would be protected, were exposed to retribution and felt betrayed.

There are some obvious capabilities that global leaders need. Among these is a thick skin and the ability to disagree and debate with their peers and more senior colleagues. After all, it is only by unpicking the cause of conflict together that we understand how we might move forward.

Bluster suggests that the necessary, if challenging, conversations between stakeholders are probably not going to happen. It is the action of a leader who wants to be seen as powerful but outside of their immediate reporting structure is not respected.

3. Avoiding Tension

Global leadership is the pursuit of complex problem solving in which separate parts of the problem have different owners and no single person can see the whole thing in its entirety. Even when there are common objectives, how these will be tackled and achieved by different stakeholders can be obscured in the intricacies of the global matrix. All of this requires new interdependent relationships and new distributions of authority. This rewiring of power is always going to feel unusual, which in turn means that misunderstandings, disagreements, and tension are inevitable among the problem solvers.

A positive way to view global collaboration is as a puzzle that needs many stakeholders to solve. Whenever there is tension, it means that we have revealed another part of the puzzle to unlock. So, tension is a good thing. It is a clue that we need to take action to make more progress.

The wrong global leader sees tension as bad and wants to avoid it. Some see tension as a failure, thinking that it reveals poor leadership. Others don't feel comfortable taking it on. However, this means that the puzzle will never be solved.

The right leader helps others to feel comfortable disagreeing and debating. The wrong leader avoids it and, as a result, we can't find the right solutions.

Here is an example. I worked with a global company based in America's Midwest, which had a culture that prioritized conflict avoidance and the appearance of harmony. So, how an individual performed and whether they were well-liked was at least as important as their results. This was an organization of delightful people but they did not know how to handle the typical tensions that are a normal feature of the global matrix. Candid conversations, healthy debates, and disagreements were deliberately avoided. As a consequence, regional leaders did not challenge global strategy or try to improve it, but instead made fake commitments, knowing that they would not be held to account if they went their own way. Global leadership was nothing but theater.

Takeaways

In the quest for global advantage, the hardest and most protracted battles we ever fight are internal. In every organization, teams form bonds of trust and loyalty and, to varying degrees, they tend to see others outside the team as threats and competitors. Our global leaders need to bind these teams together, respecting their different needs while focusing their energies. This is a demanding role that requires a mastery of expertise. However, as we are so poor at selecting leaders, most people in these roles find that they are out of their depth or do not know how to be effective.

Here is a summary of the key points from this discussion:

1. Even with enormous quantities of data to guide us, we remain incredibly bad at selecting and promoting leaders with the necessary talent to engage their teams and inspire performance. Only one in five leaders has what it takes. In global roles, which require a more specialized and hardcore skill set, the situation is even worse. Most global leaders are not a good fit for the role. As a consequence, only a minority of regional and local stakeholders have confidence in global leadership.

2. Many global leaders struggle to build trust with their international colleagues. Often, they are focused on their success in delivering a strategy document rather than the results of the strategy. Instead of building an inclusive collaboration, the wrong global leader believes that stakeholders' differences are unimportant. Regional and local colleagues are unable to trust a leader who is not curious about their success.

3. Global strategy often struggles to find the right balance between focusing the organization and representing the diversity of its opportunities. Yet, there is a sweet spot that reflects important local priorities, while also concentrating resources and attention on the company's most critical path forward. Consultative negotiations offer the greatest chance of finding this balance. Its trademark is curiosity because the task for the global leader is to understand how each stakeholder perceives their opportunities or challenges. In this way, a global leader hopes to shape how each stakeholder understands the value of the global strategy, including what they will gain and what they might otherwise lose.

4. Influencing is persuading people to think and act differently in ways that are to their benefit. Fundamental to this is the underlying reality that the power to influence is given by the influenced. They must choose to opt in and accept the influencer's proposal or line of reasoning. Influence by pulling is effective in the global matrix. Indeed, successful influencing requires the global leader to offer stakeholders something of value.

5. Often what we call a global leadership team is not a team at all. Indeed, it is unlikely that its constituents share in common goals and incentives, which is a defining characteristic for teamwork. Some may even compete with one another. Instead, all these leaders have in common is their seniority in a company's

geographic or functional hierarchies. In some cases, it may be more accurate to describe this group as a council of rival tribal chieftains.

6.   When a global leadership team has a desire to be served this leads to more focus on the experience of the meeting itself than on its outcomes and impact. The meeting becomes a prestigious event and more work goes into preparation than there is communication afterward. Many global leadership teams want to make all key decisions. This disengages their organization and slows the business.

Global leadership has so much riding on it and yet our report card is miserable. Among all of the fragmenting forces, this is the most pervasive and most destructive. Yet, it is also an area of capability that most companies choose not to address. Later, we will cover several easy practices and tools that can greatly improve our trajectory for the better. We can not only get out of our own way and stop doing so much business with ourselves but al so bring clarity and purpose to this role. There is so much value to unlock.

In the next chapter, we will focus on the factors that impede effective decision flow. This is more than a symptom of the global matrix and of our leadership: It is a force unto itself. We will learn how even small inconsistencies in our philosophies, capabilities, and processes for making, distributing, and effecting good decisions can cause dysfunctional, even invisible, blockage.

7. Decision Cholesterol

Decision Cholesterol is a useful concept because it helps us to visualize the challenge of decision flow in a way that highlights how high the stakes can be. We can imagine that, in a healthy organization, energizing decisions should flow freely from its heart to the tips of its toes. We also understand that the organization is complex with different components and processes, and that, just like us, its functionality is fragile. It is not hard to believe that decision flow can be restricted or even dangerously obstructed. Also, like cholesterol, these clogs and blockages are not so easily detected without a specific diagnosis or until unwanted and possibly dangerous symptoms manifest. Fortunately, we know that, with the right information and perhaps some new choices, we should be able to lower our risk. And we need to. Decision cholesterol is a killer and the health of the entire company is on the line.

High levels of decision cholesterol become a dangerous force for global fragmentation. The causes are structural, philosophical, and individual. At first glance, decision cholesterol seems to be a symptom resulting from all the other forces. In fact, it is all that and more.

For decision-making to be effective in a global organization, we need a new guiding philosophy. As we will discuss in this chapter, today's practices are surprisingly inept.

Adapted Decisions

In the previous chapter, we discussed how, as leaders, we love to be the driver. We embrace that status and make it part of our identity. And with that comes authority, significance, choice, self-determination, and even self-actualization. As a leader, we have an amazing responsibility as people look to us for direction and advice. We set their objectives and rate their performance. We are the arbiters of what is important, and we choose where to focus and how best to win at what we do.

At the same time, each leader has a boss, and our boss has objectives. Typically, we negotiate and agree on how best we can support these objectives. We figure out what success looks like and we commit to achieving appropriate goals. Our boss has a boss also. We probably never see their objectives. Rather, we assume that our boss has done the work to cascade the appropriate direction and focus to us.

Let's define an objective as something that we want to do or achieve based on a choice. Broadly speaking, at the highest levels of the company, leaders' objectives are more conceptual and, as we move closer to the front lines, objectives become more specific and increasingly measurable. So, we can see that, at every step as we descend through the hierarchy, there is a certain amount of translation and adaptation. In effect, senior leaders' objectives become increasingly deconstructed as we follow this process down through the company. As work progresses, our boss may check in with us to ensure that we are keeping on track. Our understanding of the objectives may have shifted as we have learned more about achieving them. We may also need to adapt based on new experience, and we may have a more accurate appreciation of our capabilities and their effectiveness. Of course, we do the same thing with our direct reports. Throughout the company we ask, 'What can I do best to support the objectives of my boss?'

Is this real? Does it sound too neat and tidy to belong in the real world? Well, if you ask senior leaders to describe how their decisions transmit through their company, many will explain a process that is similar to this. Every year, senior leaders communicate new objectives and expect that every manager below them in their hierarchy will align with their priorities. However, and this is less true in small companies, they rarely inspect the alignment process and typically take it for granted. Very few senior leaders examine the coherence of performance objectives beyond their direct reports. Indeed, most senior leaders stop after making and communicating a decision. When asked, they clarify that their task is to set direction and now that work is done. Later, they may check in with their team, but compliance is expected.

It does seem reasonable that, once a decision is made, alignment and action will follow throughout the organization, but there are limits to this. To begin with, this model process works best in a linear hierarchy where there are no conflicting priorities. Think back to the overlapping circuitry of the global matrix and you can appreciate what a confusing and convoluted journey of reinterpretation each objective can undergo. Intent, outcome, priority will all change, and the changes may not be consistent in similar branches of the matrix.

The model process also works better when there are fewer points of authority in the chain. This is because, even with the best will in the world, there is going to be some adaptation each time the decision is translated through the lens of each subsequent leader. Like a transmission chain experiment, the initial intent and objective will experience cumulative modification. Every small adaptation will compound and, therefore, the longer the chain, the greater the risk of degrading the intent of the original decision.

The linear process and the mindset that we use for making decisions, and defining and cascading appropriate performance objectives in a small domestic company, are not suited for a multinational organization. Yet, until we learn a new trick, we will continue to dilute our leaders' decision-making. This reduces our company's focus and coherence, which is how fragmentation starts.

Matrix Obstruction

In an ideal world, good decisions, made quickly, flow swiftly through an organization, result in committed execution, generate more value at greater speed, and build competitive advantage. If we needed proof of this, when Bain & Company studied 706 organizations, they ranked them according to decision-making effectiveness and found that the top 20% delivered stronger earnings, greater return on invested capital, and higher revenue growth.

When the Decider is Not My Boss

As we have discussed, between the act of decision-making and the act of execution, in a global company, our important decisions must journey through the global matrix. Unlike a small and linear management hierarchy, the matrix is complex and wired with inherent conflict and tension. As a decision travels through the matrix, it will pass through diverse points of authority and each time there is a risk. Yet, this goes beyond the typical adaptation that comes with reinterpreting objectives because the various leaders in the matrix may have no reporting relationship with either the originator of the decision or their management hierarchy. Without a formal need for compliance, each leader in the matrix will assess and understand the decision through their individual lens, which will inform their interpretation of the relevance and value of the decision. So, in the matrix, every decision or objective is evaluated, interpreted, and translated, and the original intent may be diluted, deformed, diverted, or even denied.

Global strategic decisions are managed across the three layers of global, regional, and local leaders. How do we ensure that, once critical decisions are made, they are not changed, delayed, or obstructed as they work their way through the matrix and between these geographical hierarchies, toward execution?

In addition, we need to appreciate that a decision will flow down several paths in the matrix. For example, a global decision will encounter each geographic region and also each functional management hierarchy separately. So, a single decision will be reinterpreted in several different ways at different points of authority. How do we avoid the confusion that this generates?

We can start by accepting the surprisingly short-range effect of decision authority. For example, it would be realistic and practical to recognize that decisions made by global or corporate leaders may be supported by global subordinates, but they are more frequently revisited, revised, or refused by regional or local leaders. If this doesn't happen through transparent and candid negotiation, then it will happen through a quiet filtration based on regional and local priorities and preferences. Even when the issuing authority is so strong that everyone complies, this only lasts while there is scrutiny. What may have been a specific directive initially is often treated as a suggestion when it is imposed on parties elsewhere in the matrix.

To return to the earlier example from the world of brand marketing, it is common practice for chief marketing officers or global brand directors to mandate very specific branding requirements. This can be something very simple, such as the shape and color of a logo, and— on paper—they have the formal authority to define how their brand is experienced everywhere in the world. However, by the time regional marketing, local marketing, and their communications agencies have finished with the strategy, you would think those requirements were optional. Indeed, without draconian governance, the creative energies of these marketing and advertising stakeholders will not be denied. Indeed, they view the strategy as an initial prototype or a proposition to be improved. The idea of adopting a strategy as is and adding no value is never considered.

Most deciders seem to be unaware that in the matrix their decision will be reconsidered, and possibly rejected or adapted multiple times, and that its execution as intended is therefore always uncertain. Many hold to a mistaken belief in the strength of their decision power. As a consequence, it is normal practice to allow only a finite and often short period of time to focus on making and communicating a new decision. This is never enough time to understand how the decision might travel.

In the matrix, organizational complexity creates a net of ambiguity that allows leaders to camouflage their actions. As we have discussed, the choices made in global strategy do not offer equivalent value to everyone. In particular, complex decisions, too many decisions, and imprecise definitions of success all reduce the likelihood that a new decision will travel. For neutral parties and dissenters, the fog of the matrix offers plausible deniability if they choose to prioritize elsewhere.

While we described the compound adaptation of objectives as a risk, the act of translating global or corporate decisions into local plans is entirely appropriate. It is absolutely necessary for local leaders to translate global strategy to achieve results in their local context. The risk occurs when the adaptations are not understood by the deciders. However, when the process is shared, then there can be a lot of benefits. Indeed, the insights that prompt the modifications of new objectives are valuable. Often these changes bring the original objective more in line with the company's capabilities and operational strengths. This is critical information that is hard to find any other way.

No matter how informed you think you are, making decisions when you are too far from the action carries serious risk. In the matrix, which is too large and complex for anyone alone to encompass, there is a better process for managing effective global decisions that embrace an operational feedback loop. When we engage more of our organization in developing decisions, we can improve how relevant and actionable our strategies and choices are.

Bad Decisions

We have been discussing how hard it can be to align and focus a global organization on a new decision. So far, we have concentrated on structural issues because the global matrix can play havoc with decision flow. For this purpose, we have assumed that all decisions have equal merit but what about bad decisions?

In a McKinsey survey[6] of over 2,000 executives, only 28% agree that the quality of their company's strategic decisions is generally good. At the same time, most agree that their company makes bad decisions about as frequently as good ones. Meanwhile, a second study reveals that executives spend nearly half of their time making these decisions and they are frustrated knowing that this is not working.

Digging deeper, senior executives point to a shortlist of frequent failings that undermine strategic decision-making. High on this list is leaders' cognitive bias, which is the systematic tendency to deviate from rational calculations. This is hard to manage even with self-awareness and is often left unchecked. The list also captures some universal, if embarrassing, home goals, such as bad forecasting, failing to anticipate competitors' responses, and mismanaging budgets.

Let that data sink in because this is shockingly poor performance and it should change the game. Three in ten decisions are generally good, the same number are bad, and the rest are neither good nor bad. Put simply, the number of good decisions made by senior executives is too small for us to think that the key to countering decision cholesterol is to improve

---

[6] The McKinsey Quarterly 2008. McKinsey & Company, Strategy & Corporate Finance.

alignment and compliance. It is starting to make sense why some international stakeholders dissemble and simulate agreement. Can you fault the behavior of regional and local leaders who question the merits of global decisions when most of those decisions are not good?

Imagine that, in your company, stakeholders are aware of a history of only 28% of good decisions. Every collaboration is an investment of trust and personal capital. Nobody likes to be burned twice but many will have been. Every bad decision that is made by global leaders and then executed locally for poor results increases the likelihood that next time decisions will not flow so smoothly. When a significant proportion of all these decisions are bad, as McKinsey suggests, then it is safe to assume that every new decision will be met with caution and apprehension. Calls to collaborate may be met with inertia and neutrality at best.

The McKinsey study explored several components of decision-making practice, such as fact-gathering developing of insights, good judgment, and process. Of these, they learned that the quality of the decision-making process itself was by far the most important factor in delivering strong performance and return on investment. This is a powerful insight although it may be hard for senior leaders to hear. Executives' expert assessments, critical thinking, and experienced opinions are not the primary drivers of good decisions. This is not how it happens. Instead, it is the process. It is how we make decisions that makes the difference to our results.

McKinsey also learned that an important driver of process quality, and therefore decision quality, was the prioritization of skill and experience above rank and company status in discussion and debate. In fact, including perspectives that contradict the opinions and biases of senior leaders turned out to be a necessary practice for better results.

While it is easy to knock the highest-paid person's opinion (HiPPO) in a book, the real world is very different. Senior leaders like to make decisions and many will insist on it, refusing to even consider the inclusive process that this study suggested. They don't want to be contradicted. If you recall the story from the last chapter, most leaders like to be the driver regardless of the outcome. To this point, for many senior leaders, it is a source of pride that they can make decisions under pressure and on only partial information. They love it. Many are equally proud of their instincts and crow about listening to their gut. Crucially, for them, decision-making is an important expression of their authority, prowess, and expertise. It is a part of their identity and it is how many understand their role.

I remember working with a US-based company whose leaders would take the corporate jet to Florida for a two-day strategy meeting. This leadership team could not have been more exclusive and the event itself was closed to contrary opinion by design. Perhaps it should not be a surprise that their performance at that time mirrors McKinsey's conclusions. The company lost valuable market share as category innovation eroded what competitive advantage it once had. All this despite the fact that many managers close to the front lines had been flagging this risk for some time.

So, just like the Gallup research, which taught us that business performance depends on how people are led and managed, over 80% of leaders don't have the talent to do this effectively. We now have more shocking data. Company executives lay bare that over 70% of their strategic decisions are not good. So, where does this leave us? Waiting for a seismic shift?

Disagreements

We don't need management consultants to teach us that a healthy field of diverse opinions is important for good decision-making. Also, it is not a huge mental leap to appreciate that involving the stakeholders who will execute the decision can make an enormous difference to both feasibility and commitment. That we don't do these things every time is a mystery. However, what is clear is that these best practices can only function through healthy disagreement and debate among diverse and sometimes contentious groups. Yet, more often than not, we avoid even low-grade conflict like it is the plague.

Evolutionarily speaking, work today is such a low-risk situation that the drama of a fight or flight response seems so out of place. Yet we lash out, we go silent, and we even pretend to agree, all because a sense of opposition floods our brains with chemicals that make it hard to be objective about the issue at hand. Instead, we are triggered by fear and so we focus on defense. While it is some comfort to know that, in this behavior, we are all the same and that it is not our fault, this all-too-common atavistic response is such an impediment to collaborative progress.

Behind Closed Doors

We know disagreement delivers better outcomes. That is why it is a deliberate feature of our democratic and judicial systems. In these contexts, we easily recognize that the collision of ideas and the resolution of differences are necessary for progress. Built on centuries of iterative improvements, each of these systems has well-defined rules and conventions to manage the conflict, and they share defining characteristics that promote a healthy debate, which includes the relative equality of the contestants and processes that gives each a fair and full hearing.

However, in business, in many cultures, senior leaders shy from authentic debate, believing that they need to project a calm and confident demeanor at all times. Indeed, it is often considered a serious misstep to disagree and to argue a different point of view unless it is behind closed doors. So, we subscribe to the myth that the best leaders have perfect poise, they project harmony, and they are in control. And, on the one hand, this makes sense. After all, if leaders are not calm, then their followers become nervous. Yet, on the other, if we limit how we disagree or contend with each other, we are ignoring the best tool that we have to make better decisions.

Many senior executives have learned the practice of minimizing the audience to any disagreement. However, this can be taken too far. For, while it makes sense to limit the disruptive impact of a dispute that may get out of control, or to protect an individual's reputation and allow for more personal and difficult conversations in private, there is a priceless capability called *productive disagreement* and we need more of this. Are we building these muscles? Are we modeling good disagreement behavior? When we say, 'Let's take that offline,' which is a euphemism for 'Stop disagreeing in public,' we may be overlooking a vital teaching moment.

Tension Reveals the Cracks

If we don't know how to have a productive disagreement, then we will try to avoid it. This is really common behavior and we see it or feel it almost every day. Yet, avoiding friction has consequences. At a personal level, we suffer when we don't stand up for ourselves. At a company level, tension reveals cracks in our company's coherence and internal compatibilities. And when tension stays unresolved, the cracks can widen, which means that connections dry up, collaboration slows down, and commitment fades.

If we have the awesome responsibility of steering a company, or just a part of it, and if we have a duty of care to our organization, then we need to identify and then find answers to all of the different tensions in our purview. Pretending that the cracks are not there is just like plastering over a fracturing foundation—it is a crazy and immoral deceit. Sure, we may not like doing the work and we may not be very good at it, but the cracks are there, they are real, and the sooner we act the better it is for everyone.

A more useful way to understand disagreement is to think of it as signposts or waypoints on the path to better decision-making. Per Marcus Aurelius, 'What stands in the way becomes the way.' So, if we think that a disagreement is an obstruction to a decision or a block to decision flow, then we are looking at it backwards. Disagreement is the only path to good and shared decisions. The more disagreements that we solve, the more our decisions are well-informed, well-reasoned, and better accepted. Productive disagreement is vital for effective decision-making. It is fuel for performance. So, the right answer is actually to seek out tension rather than to avoid it.

Of course, when we remember just how few of executives' decisions are good decisions, according to their own self-assessment, we should expect a lot of tension. We should want it. If decisions are bad, then this reaction is our company's defense mechanism. This is not an affront to leaders' authority to be ignored or steamrolled. It is feedback from engaged and expert stakeholders. It is gold.

If, like many people, we fear to dispute differences, then this sounds like a perverse reversal. Indeed, many believe it will be hard to build this capability, but, with support and a few solid wins, confidence quickly shifts. To succeed, we need to develop a curiosity or a radar sense that detects and then propels us toward each source of tension.

Genuine, Thoughtful and Caring

Learning to disagree well is a game-changing skill that can put our differences to work, unlocking the power of organizational diversity. There is no better way to challenge our biases. What is more, the ability to productively disagree is the definitive sign of a high-trust relationship. The opposite is also true: Leaders who do not share trust will not disagree and debate with one another to build a productive outcome.

We don't trust people if we suspect that they may be inauthentic, or if we don't respect their reasoning or competence, or if we sense that they don't care about us. As a global leader and decision-maker, you cannot allow any of your international counterparts to feel this way about you. However, as we will see in detail later, most regional and local leaders do feel this way. The bar should be low. Essentially, all that is being asked is to be genuine, thoughtful, and caring.

Yet, global leaders are not well-trusted. To be fair, this can be influenced by a company's operating model and attitudes to strategy. Global leaders engage across a matrix with stakeholders who prioritize different objectives. They are not in a role where it is easy to make everyone happy. Yet, that is not the point. The key to better global decisions that are less likely to get stuck or be diluted is to build enough trust for us to disagree productively and then to do so as much as necessary.

Three Behaviors to Watch For

There are many contributors to decision cholesterol. While each of the fragmenting forces we have discussed in prior chapters can impair global performance in its own way, they all have an impact on decision-making and its flow. Globalism promotes top-down silo-built decisions, while tribalism and the matrix foster promote separateness and ways to hide obstruction. Meanwhile, having the wrong global leaders or exclusive VIP leadership teams can be a powerful trigger of high decision cholesterol with all of its risks to a company's health. Indeed, this is such a prevalent symptom that measuring decision effectiveness is a first-line diagnostic tool to identify global fragmentation and dysfunction.

Here are three common risks to our ability to make and then operationalize good decisions:

1. Culture and Conflict

Both national culture and company culture can skew our willingness and ability to disagree openly, which means that it is a lot more difficult to build trust and make well-informed decisions together. In a global matrix, these different attitudes and behaviors toward disagreement inevitably collide. Indeed, it follows that, for global leaders, cultural knowledge (and the sensitivity that comes with it) is a must-have skill to lead and guide decision-making and flow. Yet, it is hard to build this capability without direct experience. By all means, read, seek mentors and advice, learn languages. However, most global leaders, certainly those with limited time in the role, are going to need to improvise.

Feeing ignorant of different cultures is a tough spot to find yourself in and it is easy to feel out of your depth and ineffective. Yet, the good news is that the feeling of team engagement seems to transcend culture. So, watch out if there is too much silence and no sense of converging toward agreement and action. Do not push ahead. There may be a blockage or there may not. It may be as simple as a misunderstanding or there may be a real disagreement. Curiosity, patience, and a servant-leader mindset will serve you well. Take your time and remember that disagreement reveals a gateway that everyone needs to pass through. Don't leave any stakeholders behind.

While you may wish it otherwise, some disagreements will not surface in public. If you are ever unsure how stakeholder culture will have an impact on your ability to reach an agreement, learn the art of *nemawashi*. This is a Japanese word for a gardening technique and it translates into English as "going around the roots." In business, this means laying the groundwork and removing obstacles in an informal, and perhaps more private, way before a decision meeting. It is a powerful approach to ensure that you truly understand your stakeholders. The investment you make in one-on-one exploration sends a positive message that helps to build trust. What you learn can help avoid any nasty surprises later on.

2. Power Balance

An unequal balance of power among stakeholders can be a red flag to signal that decision cholesterol is high. Stakeholders are always more authentic in an equal group when their sense of status and significance is upheld.

Local and regional leaders may be the big boss in their day-to-day. Imagine how unsettling it is for them to find themselves in a context where they are suddenly less powerful and with less authority and respect. If you have ever attended a regional meeting of country general managers, you will have seen the uncertainty and the discomfort behind their bravado and the jockeying for position that goes on.

It is not cheap flattery to recognize the significance of others. It is important to acknowledge both their value and status if they are to feel secure enough to relax their need for autonomy and to lessen their itch for independence. Conversely, when stakeholders feel unappreciated or pushed, they can go to great lengths to reassert their sense of status.

When we are feeling powerful, we are relaxed and happy to look for a win-win solution. When we feel others exerting power over us, and this is not our norm, we tend towards disengagement or aggression. Disagreement and decisions are always easier and better among more equal groups.

3. Regional Authority

Do you work in an organization that is structured such that each geographic region has a leaning toward independent authority? If so, your expectations of global strategic decision-making may need an overhaul. In this structure, global leaders may make decisions, but decision flow is owned by regional executives and their leadership teams. The company may consider itself global, based on its footprint, but, in truth, it is a hybrid entity. These organizations tend to be exceptionally tribal and miss out on the advantages of globalization.

Previously, I described a company in which regional sovereignty was a legacy of its geographic growth, and each region maintained a separate product development group and had its own innovation pipeline. Regional managers would tell you that they needed to meet their specific market trends. Yet, this was a smokescreen. Competition from other companies, which innovated centrally, was stealing market share.

Regional executives are perhaps the most important figures in global decision-making. Their authentic engagement and their commitment to global decisions are vital. If they disagree, you need to know. After all, they control their region's participation.

Takeaways

Effective decision-making drives greater profitability and growth. Yet, as we have learned, despite their massive investment of time, less than 30% of senior executives rate their company decisions as good. This reveals a broken approach and a huge opportunity to improve. Indeed, it is clear that, today, the way that we tend to make decisions is critically flawed. The central cause is the belief that seniority grants permission and capability for effective decision-making, decisions that are well-informed and will also be received with enthusiasm and commitment throughout a company. This is symptomatic of a grave underappreciation of the limitations of command-and-control authority, particularly in a global matrix organization.

Here is a summary of the important takeaways from this discussion:

1. Senior leaders expect compliance with the decisions that they make but, at every point of authority in their company hierarchy, their initial intent is progressively reinterpreted, diluted, and modified. The changes are cumulative and so even small

adaptations compound. The longer the chain, the greater the degradation.

2. A global decision will encounter each geographic region and also each functional management hierarchy separately. So, a single decision can be reinterpreted in several different ways at different points of authority, which leads to a diversity of compliance.

3. In the matrix, complexity creates a fog of ambiguity. Complex decisions, too many decisions, and imprecise definitions of success can all feed this risk of uncertainty. As global decisions do not offer equivalent value to everyone, it is normal to find neutral parties and dissenters. For these stakeholders, fog in the matrix can give them plausible deniability if they choose to prioritize elsewhere.

4. In a McKinsey survey of over 2,000 executives, only 28% agree that the quality of their company's strategic decisions is generally good. At the same time, most agree that their company makes bad decisions about as frequently as good ones. Meanwhile, a second study reveals that executives spend nearly half their time making these decisions and they are frustrated knowing that this is not working. McKinsey also learned that an important driver of decision quality was the prioritization of skill and experience above rank and company status in discussion and debate. In fact, including perspectives that contradict the opinions and biases of senior leaders turned out to be a necessary practice for better results.

5. Productive disagreement is a hard yet important skill to learn. For if we don't know how to, then we will avoid it. And many do. Yet, avoiding friction has consequences. At a company level, tension reveals cracks in our company's coherence and internal compatibilities. And when tension stays unresolved, the cracks

can widen, which means connections dry up, collaboration slows down, and commitment fades. If we have the awesome responsibility to steer the company, or just a part of it, and if we have a duty of care to our organization, then we need to identify and then find answers to all of the different tensions in our purview. Pretending that the cracks are not there is just like plastering over a fracturing foundation.

6. If we think that a disagreement is an obstruction to a decision or a block to decision flow, then we are looking at it backwards. The more disagreements that we solve, the more our decisions are well-informed, well-reasoned, and better accepted. Productive disagreement is vital for effective decisions and therefore a fuel for performance. So, the right answer is actually to seek out tension rather than to avoid it.

Our report card for global decision effectiveness is far below expectations. This shows us that not only are the decisions themselves often flawed and uninformed, but also that the processes of development and deployment risk creating misalignment, distrust, and dysfunction. This is very serious. To repeat the analogy: decision cholesterol is a killer and the health of the entire company is on the line.

As we pile each force of fragmentation, one on top of the last, we create a powerful and depressing inertia. Stick with it. I promise that there are whole sections to come of diagnostic tools and proven practices to help us to climb out from under this. Yet, we have one more chapter to go in this section and, in many ways, it is the hardest.

8. Global Strategy Theater

Not so long ago, I watched a senior executive present a five-year global growth strategy and it was mostly fiction. You see, he realized that his objective during his short tenure as a global leader was not to lead or to activate this strategy, or to fuel its results, but simply to author a strategy document and to present it the chief executive officer (CEO) and the company board. He probably had a formal objective to define the global business strategy and that is exactly what he did.

The presentation was tidy and reasonable. It simplified opportunities and threats into a shortlist of focus areas and described important enabling capabilities for each of these. Action against future trends was defined and aggregated financials were mapped on attractive waterfall charts. Structurally, the presentation was familiar and plausible.

However, not one regional or local stakeholder had seen this strategy document before that day. Each geographic region had already defined its separate growth strategy and, while some elements from these were included in the global deck, the objectives and targets were not the

145

same. Yet, nobody objected during the presentation. Regional presidents, who were present, did not draw attention to the dysfunction and so, by their silence, it was clear that they assumed no accountability for the global strategy.

The CEO, who believed that this was a collaborative effort, approved the strategy and was none the wiser. Afterward, the global strategy document was condensed into a smaller roadshow version, which the global team presented to confused audiences over the next six months. At this point, the executive moved on to another role.

After that, the global strategy quickly disappeared. Having never existed as a unifying and mobilizing endeavor, it had no sponsors or supporters. It had no roots in the organization. Regional and local leaders carried on as before and never gave it a second thought. With the author gone, even the global team moved on after a couple of months.

There was no outrage. There was no accountability. But there was complicity. Indeed, the highly paid executive leaders of this multi-billion-dollar global company were all players in a theatrical performance.

In this chapter, we contend with the ugliest secret. It is ugly because on its face this behavior is duplicitous, and it is ethically and morally unfit. It is also a topic that nobody talks about. So, it's a secret that the skeleton is hidden in the cupboard, but, trust me, the skeleton is there. In well over a hundred interviews with global company stakeholders, the interviewees assigned this behavior to people whom they knew. They confirmed that, in matters of strategy and collaboration, too many company leaders are knowingly participating in a performance, a theatrical exercise. They put on a show with the semblance of strategy leadership and international partnership, but it is really just a parody of what could have been and, crucially, there is no accountability to implementation and results.

There is no doubt that global strategy leadership is extremely challenging. In the preceding chapters, we have explored a portfolio of almost inescapable dysfunction. So, should we be that surprised when leaders give up and let the boulder roll back down the mountain? Indeed, most global leaders agree that they are not set up for success, and most of their regional and local counterparts would prefer to choose their priorities themselves. When we are losing this fight and the forces of fragmentation run amok, global strategy leadership feels laborious and futile. Many report feeling stuck, trapped even, and also anxious about the risk of very public failure that will damage their personal advancement.

We can empathize with this sense of frustration. Without the expertise to diagnose and remedy the dysfunction, it can feel hopeless. Many global leaders describe feeling cornered with no way out of a no-win situation. Yet, rather than say, 'This is not working,' far too many choose to save face by pretending that it is.

Some executives present unreal strategies without admitting to themselves that it is just an act of what-if storytelling. Somehow, they make themselves comfortable playing a role in which global strategy is restricted to a presentation of recommended choices. The hard tasks of exploring fit, relevance, and value with operational leaders are avoided and left to others if they happen at all. This is still theater, although the defense is self-delusion rather than deliberate artifice.

Why does this happen? How do people get away with it? These are the questions that we will try to answer in this chapter.

Global Strategy Theater

Global strategy theater is an organizational poison. Most of us are either complicit, uninformed, or in denial and, in all cases, the subterfuge remains untreated. Understandably, we don't want to accept how real and commonplace this is because such mendacity is outrageous and shameful. If true, it would undermine how we prefer to understand our colleagues' integrity and commitment to our shared vision. It is so tempting to avoid or suppress the idea of this behavior. Without a doubt, if we confront this, then we are going to feel very uncomfortable.

We have already discussed how regional and local stakeholders can make fake commitments, quietly opposing or simply ignoring global strategy. Well, let's not hold global leaders to a different standard. Global strategy theater simply puts the shoe on the other foot. With a similar motive, which is the desire for autonomy and separateness, coupled with the determination to bypass the difficulties of building an inclusive strategy, these global leaders create home-baked presentations that are divorced from business operations and with no supported promise of results.

How does this happen? Well, for many, a little deception is a lot easier than negotiating and much better than compromise. For all senior leaders in a global matrix, the feeling of impotence, which comes from roadblocks that they are powerless to pass, is often intolerable, and so they find ways to change the game. Ask your tenured global and regional leaders. They can probably hold court for days telling stories of the games and the creative subterfuge that they have seen.

The entire strategy doesn't need to be theatrical. A global strategy is very likely to be grounded in real opportunities and real challenges. Of course, this makes it harder to spot the fictional plugs, those priorities or capabilities that are simply written in without any operational validation.

For example, many a global strategy will overstate the worldwide relevance of its ambition and direction. This should make us question the appropriateness of certain choices and, in particular, the operational commitment to those choices. However, there are many leaders to whom this seems quite innocuous. In these companies, inexact aggregation is the hallmark of a global summary. It is assumed to be the appropriate trade-off for focus and prioritization. Yet, this is a huge and shiny invitation for play-acting and parody. The oversimplification of global strategy throws the doors wide open for every supposed stakeholder to avoid accountability. Without enough specificity, it multiplies the challenge to hold others to account. This is not a global strategy—it is a broad discussion of possible intent.

A powerful driver of the problem is the flexible relationship that many global leaders have with accountability. Not only does the success of global strategy depend on many factors and individuals beyond the global leader's control, but also the time frame to realize that the strategy is probably a few years away. It is very typical for global leaders to move on before the strategy that they developed is realized. So, how can a global leader demonstrate their value? What can they deliver during their tenure? This is an inevitable outcome whereby we have a role with short-term tenure leading a medium- or long-term strategy. It becomes impossible to hold the global leader accountable for the strategy's results and so we default to requiring only the appearance of a tangible strategy document.

This might still be fine if we could tell fact from fiction. However, this would require that all regional and local stakeholders were fully engaged, sending a strong signal of approval or disapproval. Yet, most of them are not and they don't want to be. Global strategy like this is a distraction but it goes away. So, regional and local leaders can maintain their autonomy and separateness if they just quietly wait it out. They are not held accountable to the global strategy either.

Editing a Complex World

In the research, only 45% of senior regional leaders claimed to have read and applied global strategy to their business. The number for senior local leaders has a high variance but for countries that self-identify as a top ten market, it averages at 26%. Behind these low numbers are several factors, including all of the other fragmentation forces that we have discussed. Yet, in addition, we need to consider the utility of the global strategy documents themselves. Could it be, as in the shameful example that started this chapter, that too many global leaders focus on strategy production and put less attention on its activation and impact? Are we mistaking the approval of global strategy for the finish line when, in fact, that is just when the work starts?

Among regional leaders, there is a common perception that global leaders mislead others to make their case for a common cause. They are seen to have a bias to present the world as simple with convenient themes and aggregated opportunities that spin objective facts into a more compelling and focused narrative. For example, global leaders often downplay or ignore inconvenient differences, such as local competition or trends, when they contradict, complicate, or simply confuse the story that they would prefer to tell.

This approach might make sense for audiences like investors, shareholders, and maybe the company board, but how can it be practical or actionable for actually running a global business? Of course, it can't, and this highlights the important difference between a practical strategy for instruction and action, and a storytelling presentation of possible intent that may go nowhere. Global strategy theater is a lot easier to get away with if company leaders only focus on simple and tidy narratives. If we want a practical and actionable strategy that will engage its executors, then we need an inclusive strategy development plan, which will probably blow up any tidy summary by injecting the messy complexity of the real world.

When you think about it, the idea of representing global strategy in a single short presentation is always going to be an aggregation and an over-simplification. However, we respect a simplified summary. Indeed, it is not unusual practice to squeeze the entire strategy on to one page. If we can have just a few growth pillars to rally around, then we feel much more in command of our opportunities. If a single SWOT analysis can describe our entire global enterprise, we feel a greater sense of control. Somehow, we have all agreed that simplification is the same as mastery. We seem to be saying that our grasp of all of the complexity, and all of the details and insights necessary to fuel competitive advantage in different markets around the world, is so strong that we can omit it from the strategy. Or, it is not relevant.

Global oversimplification follows a common recipe and when we break it down the flaws are self-evident. First, when faced with a complex and confusing reality, we choose not to understand all of its subtleties. The task is certainly daunting but that is no excuse to avoid it. Yet, we frequently decide that these details and finer points are trivial, unreal, or irrational. This is the key point of failure when we decide that our subjective lack of understanding is appropriate because all of the minutiae are muddled and inconsequential. Against a world full of evidence, we tell ourselves that complex systems can't thrive and rationalize any consideration that is untidy. We then create an idealized version of what reality ought to be, and claim that the simplicity and orderliness of our vision are proof positive of our mastery.

And here we have the heart of it. In effect, by setting legibility and orderliness as the measures of good strategy, we are confessing to creating a strategy to impress rather than to achieve.

The Audience Pretends

Global leaders are not the only thespians at large. Indeed, even when global leaders develop and present strategy, albeit imperfectly but with integrity and good intentions, their audience, made up of regional and local leaders, is notorious for expressing commitment that does not materialize.

There are many reasons why regional and local leaders choose to fake commitment to global strategy. The fragmenting forces that we have discussed—globalism, tribalism, conflict in the matrix, or bad global leadership—typically send the message that global strategy is not in their best interest. There is too much compromise for not enough return. This assessment may be valid. How would you feel about adopting a strategy when you had little or no role in its development and it was presented to you as a fait accompli? How frustrating must this be when your most urgent challenges are not recognized? How insulted would you feel when your expertise is disregarded? From the standpoint of the recipients, the arrogance of such a strategy is maddening. However, and as we have discussed, all of this, including how the leaders are rewarded for regional or local achievements only, helps to fuel their preference for autonomy. It is a self-reinforcing dynamic, which results in these leaders feeling justified to give every indication of engagement but have no intention of actually following through.

When the global strategy is developed clumsily, particularly when regional and local stakeholders don't feel ownership, then it becomes something that is being done *to* them rather than *by* them. And, since there is little or no accountability, then it is easy and low-risk for them to opt out. It is, without doubt, unprincipled and slippery behavior. Yet, it should not be a surprise when stakeholders do this and keep the decision to themselves, particularly if they feel trapped and there is no forum for healthy debate and disagreement.

For regions and countries that have enough resources to go their own way, this pretense happens more often than you might think. Although, if they are large enough, they may not work too hard at hiding their dissension. However, and this is curious, more senior global executives are less likely to say that they see this behavior. In the research, when asked if regional leaders are misleading in their commitment to global strategy, 56% of mid-level global leaders agreed that they see this sometimes, often, or always. However, only 21% of senior global leaders agreed with this. Interviewees offered two hypotheses. The first is that senior global leaders are more removed from operational activities and so regional commitment is simply less visible to them, and so they are easier to mislead. The second is that these executives prefer to maintain the appearance of harmony at senior levels, which means that they may be aware of the risk to in-market results but choose to pretend that everything is fine.

So, here we have some global and regional leaders knowingly acting out a performance. On the one hand, they are adversarial but, on the other, they may both be complicit in this game. Both groups may be aware that the other is faking it, but that is acceptable because they are too. We have achieved a version of the prisoner's dilemma whereby both parties act as if they are cooperating while in truth, they are both defecting.

The only losers are those who think that global strategy is important and valuable to the business.

Three Behaviors to Watch For

Global strategy theater is a common response to the challenges and improbability of finding the right balance in inclusive strategy development. It makes a mockery of global strategy and not least because we are betrayed by our own.
Once we start to ask whether what we are seeing is performance art or a real endeavor, then we find it is quite easy to identify the behavior. For example, siloed and independent creation of a global strategy often gives it away. Even when the strategy is a clumsy mix of real and staged content, we can often spot the difference.

Here are three less obvious clues to look out for.

1. Strategy Reconciliation

A predictable consequence of global strategy theater is that, in a few short years, the decisions laid out in that strategy will become increasingly unrepresentative of actual performance. So, a telltale sign is the curious practice in which global leaders are asked to *refresh* the prior strategy. What is happening here, of course, is that local business priorities and results are starting to become awkwardly incoherent with the global strategy. *Refresh* really means *realign* or *reboot*.

It is unacceptable, even embarrassing, to have objectives and goals that are approved by the company's leadership and that are not reflected in the choices and the performance of the business. So, this is a great opportunity to harmonize global priorities with local business needs. It is a chance to compare and contrast, to anticipate new challenges and opportunities, and, importantly, to bridge the gaps.

In an ideal world, the impetus to refresh a strategy would be triggered by an external change and might come from regional leaders who need the company's focus and associated resources to achieve new goals. If the decision to refresh strategy comes from global leaders instead, such as from executive leadership, then this is likely to be more political. It also hints at the impotence of global strategy to direct company action.

This may be a great opportunity to refresh how strategy is developed. However, the first question to ask is why company leaders allowed global, regional, and local strategies to exist at the same time, even though they were incoherent. Have circumstances changed or will this be repeated?

If you are asked to refresh your global strategy, then tread carefully, particularly if you are dealing with the same actors who were involved in the last one. Spend time defining success because your task may not require strategy leadership at all but may simply be to paper over the differences. Conversely, if the need for change is market-driven, you may have a real, exciting, and valuable opportunity on your hands.

2. Thought Leadership

In many companies, the idea persists that global teams will bring *thought leadership* to strategy development. Global teams certainly offer a unique and valuable perspective. Yet, it can be harmful to aggrandize their contribution in this way. To suggest that global leaders will devise new strategies though their superior insights and reasoning is, more often than not, an embarrassing home goal. To begin with, most regional and local leaders do not agree that global teams are capable of this, and many find the idea to be arrogant and insulting. Indeed, the majority of country leaders judge that their global colleagues are not very knowledgeable about their business. To make matters worse, thought leadership is understood to be non-collaborative. It means *created in a silo by people who think they know better*. This is a very bad idea. Do we want the executors of a global strategy to feel inspired or disrespected? What is the intent behind this approach? It is largely ineffective to promote global thought leadership to regional and local stakeholders. So, we have to wonder whether there is another purpose. Why would global leaders want to promote the idea that the global team's reasoning, done in a silo, is still superior?

There is only one reason why that would that be necessary, and it is a red flag for failed cooperation and obstructive tension. It indicates that one group wants to overrule the other and this is a recipe for dysfunction. After all, a strategy built on global thought leadership is unlikely to receive much advocacy and follow-through from outside of the global group. Therefore, this also suggests that the global group is much more focused on authoring a strategy and not concerning themselves with its impact.

Building a strategy based on global thought leadership is just writing a screenplay ready for more theater.

3. Global Strategy Roadshow

What does it say when your global team schedules a multi-region or multi-market tour to present the new global strategy?

Well, first, let's remember that regional leaders are de facto gatekeepers to the flow of global strategy down through the organization to its local execution. Ideally, then, the best approach would be for regional leaders to own the new strategy and show their teams their commitment to it. Their understanding of the region makes them the perfect leader to adapt the new strategy to their markets. To the operational audience, they have relevance and respect that global leaders can never match. Also, never forget that the region has a strategy already and local leaders don't care all that much about global strategy, whereas they pay close attention to regional strategy. So, the endorsement of regional leaders is not a step that can be skipped.

To answer the question, we need to understand the purpose of the roadshow. If global leaders are invited and they facilitate or consult only, while regional leaders sit in the driving seat, then all is well. However, If there is any indication that the roadshow is an independent initiative led by the global team alone, then the alarm bell should ring as this looks like an attempt to compensate for missing collaboration and a strategy that was probably created in a silo. Perhaps the global team believes that, by presenting their strategy outside of the global headquarters, it becomes more real. Perhaps they believe that a roadshow will make it appear to their senior executives that the strategy has traction and regional engagement. This is more theater. Yet, if both regional and global stakeholders are complicit in the performance, then this may work.

In all probability, a global strategy roadshow is an unprincipled stunt carried out for personal advancement and it can cause damage even beyond the failure of the bogus strategy. In particular, global functional teams—for example, global product development—might swallow the performance and believe that the global strategy presentation represented the company's new direction. Only later, after they have shifted focus and invested erroneously, will they realize that the strategy is not real, and that regional and local business leaders are ignoring it.

Takeaways

Global strategy theater is an unprincipled abuse of trust. It is an unpleasant practice that places personal advancement ahead of company performance and makes a joke of global decision-making. When the work to develop a common strategy is difficult and potentially fractious, and when nobody is held to account for a global strategy's performance, it is all too easy for the participants to fake it. Global executives pretend to lead and achieve their objective of delivering a strategy, while regional executives pretend to agree and then leave, ignoring that presentation and preserving their autonomy and control.

The tacit joint complicity among senior executives is often a demoralizing surprise, particularly for newly minted global and regional leaders who have not yet learned this cynical game. Tread carefully. You don't want to be the one person who is not play-acting.

Here is a summary of the key points from this discussion:

1. In matters of strategy and collaboration, too many company leaders are knowingly participating in a performance, a theatrical exercise. They put on a show with the semblance of strategy leadership and international partnership, but it is really just a parody of what could have been, and, crucially, there is no accountability to implementation and results.

2. All senior stakeholders, global, regional and local, have a desire for autonomy and control. When regional leaders indulge this impulse, they quietly resist or even ignore global strategy. When global leaders surrender to this need for independence, or in

some cases, for sovereignty, the result is a global strategy that ignores its executors' realities and is therefore, inevitably, a work of fiction.

3. A powerful driver of the problem is the flexible relationship that many global leaders have with accountability. Not only does the success of global strategy depend on many factors and individuals beyond the global leader's control, but also the time frame to realize the strategy is probably a few years away. It is typical for global leaders to change assignments before the strategy that they developed is realized. So, it is unlikely that they will be held accountable for the performance of the strategies that they lead.

4. Global leaders have a bias to present the world as simple with convenient themes and aggregated opportunities that spin objective facts into a more compelling and focused narrative. For example, global leaders often downplay or ignore inconvenient differences, such as local competition or trends, when they contradict, complicate or simply confuse the story that they would prefer to tell. This oversimplification follows a common recipe. First, when faced with a complex reality, we choose not to understand all of its subtleties. We decide that these details and finer points are trivial, unreal, or irrational. This is the key point of failure when we decide that our subjective lack of understanding is appropriate because all of the minutiae are muddled and inconsequential. Against a world full of evidence, we tell ourselves that complex systems can't thrive and we rationalize any consideration that is untidy. We then create an idealized version of what reality ought to be, and claim that the simplicity and orderliness of our vision are proof positive of our mastery. By setting legibility and orderliness as the measures of good strategy, we are confessing to creating a strategy to impress rather than to achieve.

5. Global leaders are not the only thespians. Indeed, even when global leaders develop and present strategy, albeit imperfectly, but with integrity and good intentions, their audience, made up of regional and local leaders, is notorious for expressing commitment that does not materialize. Typically, both groups may be aware that the other is faking it, but that is acceptable because they are too. We have achieved a version of the prisoner's dilemma whereby both parties act as if they are cooperating while, in truth, they are both defecting. The only losers are those who think that global strategy is valuable to the business.

    Global strategy theater is an unsettling practice and not least because it reflects poorly on the integrity of the senior executives in global and regional roles who participate.

When interviewed, executives who would discuss this felt justified and claimed extenuating circumstances of structural pressure, conflicting objectives, and misaligned incentives. Regional leaders cited the unreasonableness of global leaders and vice versa. Both groups also questioned the other's competence. None regretted saving face by acting and playing out a role that was not real.

* * *

After a dark voyage through these forces of fragmentation, a surprising but common reaction from many interviewees is validation. This articulation of what is often not dealt with is a confirmation of their struggles. It triggers a genuine delight to learn that others share their frustrations and they are not alone in this fight.

Chief among their aggravations is the institutional practice of avoiding, and then failing to name and address, the causes that are behind the symptoms that so many experience. Many global and regional leaders express that the status quo is unfit for purpose. Yet they are unable to overcome this inertia and they feel powerless to lead meaningful change.

In this section, we have seen that the systems and processes, the structures, the philosophies, the leaders, and the decision-making in global companies can all conspire, often together, to subvert a company's cohesion and business potential. With the bar set so high and no true accountability for participation or performance, global strategies often fail before they start, or they fragment quickly, disappearing into the global matrix. Worse still, knowing that there is no alignment or commitment to the strategy presented, some global and regional senior executives put on a theatrical performance in which they pretend to be partners in a shared endeavor but are really independent players, each planning to go their own way.

The interwoven complexity of all of these fragmenting forces should tell any global leader that they have much to achieve if they want to make a difference. This is no task for the faint-hearted and there is often personal risk. However, for those who accept the mission, there is a surprising degree of power in naming the enemy. Combined, all of these negative forces can seem unstoppable. Yet, each component can be identified, assessed, and then mitigated, modified, and sometimes even neutralized.

Later, we will work through a suite of diagnostic tools that offer new and effective ways to label and evaluate these challenges. After that, you will find a whole section of guiding principles and road-tested advice to empower you on your journey.

Before this, and now that we have labeled the difficult terrain and the headwinds to expect as we traverse it, let's hear from company leaders. Let's bring these forces of fragmentation to life and hear how they affect our colleagues in their different roles. Let's listen to their experiences as they witness the dysfunction.

Suffering the Symptoms

**Being in a minority,
even a minority of one,
did not make you mad.
There was truth and there was untruth,
and if you clung to the truth even against the whole world,
you were not mad.**

George Orwell, *Nineteen Eighty-Four*

9. A Global Report

How do we experience these fragmenting forces?

In the chapters that follow, you will find the summary of a research study, featuring the findings from surveys and interviews with 142 global, regional, and local business leaders. This research is valuable because it brings to life the incidence and the consequences of dysfunctional behavior in global leadership and strategy management. The attitudes and behaviors that the participants report are surprisingly congruous, and they compound to reveal a hot mess of wasted opportunity. Yet, it seems that any way they turn there is no escape. For, even though they feel trapped, many leaders can't see a way past the status quo.

While some of the observations that follow might be predictable, it can still be jarring to see in print some conclusions that we may intuit but don't say out loud. Feedback on the study's conclusions has been consistent and along the lines of 'This is shocking and yet entirely plausible!'

As you will see, the participants use direct and often emotive language. They are frustrated by the inertia of a broken system in which they feel impotent. Some observations are critical and blunt. Yet, we need to hear them. If we condone these fragmenting behaviors and continue to look away, then we will learn nothing and nothing will change.

Overall, our report card for global effectiveness is not satisfactory. Multinational companies permit a smorgasbord of global dysfunction. This chapter is a treatise on the consequences of that choice.

Here is a short description of the methodology. After this, we will mine the insights in a series of thematic summaries.

Approaching this work, I was already alert to an onslaught of symptoms that telegraphed some serious underlying problems with global effectiveness. Of course, I was not the only one paying attention. Many stakeholders in global organizations were aware of these. Yet, the problems never seemed to go away. So, a question that I wanted to answer in the study was: Why do global companies that suffer from serious dysfunction choose to allow the malady to go untreated?

This leads to more questions as we try to explain our understanding of the problems and our limited motivation to do something about them. Is the dysfunction somehow less visible to senior leaders? Is the challenge so entrenched and systemic to a global organization that we are complicit? Are there benefits to global incoherence that divide company leadership? Are there winners in this game?

In 2019, to help frame some of the questions and to inform the methodology, I kicked off a pilot study of 22 global, regional, and local managers. During these interviews, we learned very quickly that perspectives from different places in the global matrix were quite distinct and the contrasts were powerfully revealing. In particular, there seemed to be real differences in opinion between senior leaders and local executors when it came to global strategy.

The full research study featured a formal survey, followed by an interview and then an open discussion with 142 respondents sourced from over 50 different multinational companies based in the Americas, Europe, Asia, and Australia.

To explore their different perspectives, I asked the participants to identify themselves within the simple 3×3 array shown below in Figure 9.1. Their responses were aggregated into these nine separate groups. Each respondent defined their scope of responsibility as Global, Regional, or Local. The labels Top, Senior, and Middle were used to describe management seniority, which helps us to normalize the differences in job titles that we find in different countries.

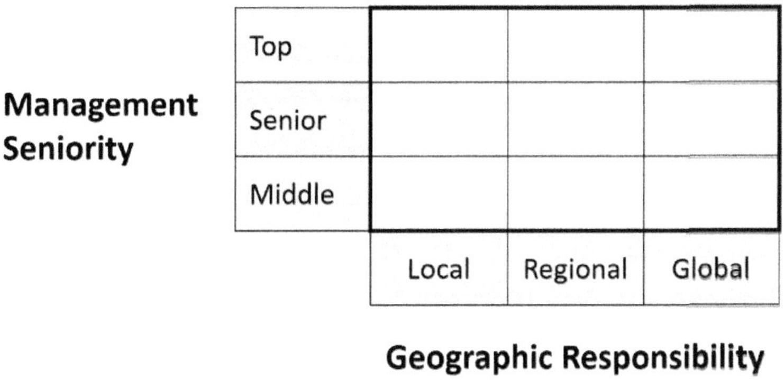

Management Seniority			
Top			
Senior			
Middle			
	Local	Regional	Global

Geographic Responsibility

Figure 9.1. Research Participant's Positions in a Global Matrix

This two-dimensional approach enables us to explore the differences between geographic and management hierarchies. As it turns out, this is vital to understanding our remarkable tolerance for pervasive dysfunction.

The findings of the study are presented with an objective eye on their statistical robustness. The base size of the study is more than acceptable. However, dissecting this group into nine separate populations can create problems with accuracy. So, where necessary, these groups are aggregated to ensure confidence in the findings. Fortunately, there is a strong similarity in respondents' answers to many of the quantitative survey questions. For clarity, suppositions from the qualitative interviews are presented as such.

The geographic location of the participants has a Western bias, but there is no meaningful difference in responses between leaders based on their country of origin or the location of their current assignment. Other factors, such as company size also appear to be inconsequential above 250 employees, which was a criterion for inclusion. All companies are multiregional, doing business in at least two regions within North America, South America, Europe, the Middle East and Africa, and Asia Pacific, which for this study includes Australia and New Zealand.

Statistical accuracy is important. However, this study is for the most part intended as a provocation for exploration and discussion. Each global company is unique and these aggregated findings will only suggest some of the dynamics that fuel or degrade its global effectiveness. So, please treat this work as an invitation to self-reflection and continued improvement. This is not an attempt to define everyone's reality. Rather, it is a stimulus to start a journey that is long overdue.

In the following pages, we will review a variety of findings presented under the broad themes of *Process* and *People*. In a summary of implications, we will combine what we have seen and assemble the not-so-pretty picture that they create.

10. Symptoms: Process

Alternate Realities

Global, regional, and local leaders develop separate strategies. Each strategy describes how its owner believes that they should contend with their opportunities and challenges. These different strategies often have different priorities from one another and, if there is not much overlap, then with fixed resources they can't coexist. Nobody wants to deviate from the strategy they developed. Each claim that only they have the correct answer.

It is no surprise to learn that global, regional, and local leaders consider global, regional, and local strategy, respectively, to have the most value. Leaders of each geographic team prize their strategy the most. It is also not surprising to find that most local leaders agree that regional strategy is more valuable to them than global strategy. However, it is disturbing to learn that only a third of regional leaders, and a quarter of local leaders, agree that global strategy is valuable at all.

All the study participants describe these strategies, particularly global and regional strategies, as separate and with different directions and priorities, and also with little coherence. The implication here is that these different geographic strategies can't coexist. If you adopt one, then you must reject the other. Most global leaders reveal that they are aware of this tense misalignment. Yet, their consensus is that regional leaders cause this fracture when they refuse to consider the opportunities on offer. Global leaders consider their strategy to be the most important and believe that everyone else should as well.

It is not a stretch to conclude that regional and local leaders' low awareness of—and limited role in—creating global strategy contribute to their opinion that it is not a good fit for them. Yet, global leaders say that they don't see this. Instead, they describe regional dissension as a poor or uninformed choice. Meanwhile, their strong belief in the value of global strategy is disconnected from that of their broader organization. Indeed, we find that many global leaders see themselves as benevolent authorities. They are promoting mutuality and interdependence on their mission to improve company performance. However, in many organizations, *global* is simply the identity of another corporate department with its own set of discrete objectives. If you are a regional or local leader, then this group exists outside of your formal management hierarchy. Its involvement in your day-to-day activity is easy to interpret as inappropriate and overreaching.

When regional and local leaders are transparent in their efforts to disagree and disengage, many top global leaders push harder for compliance with their global strategy. In interviews, they describe wanting to prove their naysayers wrong, or at least to demonstrate that they have more expertise when it comes to applying company strategy.

Most top-level global leaders believe that their regional colleagues are not rejecting global strategy on its merits but, instead, rejecting a process that challenges regional autonomy and authority. Even so, the global leaders' response is not to adapt or improve the process but to attempt to resolve the misalignment by forcing their point of view.

Meanwhile, regional leaders see themselves as the true experts with the ideal perspective to be both strategic and tactically relevant.

All parties are entrenched. Each group holds tightly to its preferred understanding of reality. There is also contempt as each one rejects any critique or alternative and claims that only they have the right answer.

Siloed Development

Global leaders create global strategy in a silo. Regional and local leaders prefer to pursue their own strategies and so avoid participating. Both these actions jeopardize the global strategy: It becomes less relevant to current opportunities and challenges and, tragically, achieves little advocacy among its potential executors.

It is common practice for global leaders to be the exclusive owners of the work to develop a new global strategy. Meanwhile, regional and local leaders rarely contribute. In most cases, creating a global strategy is an important objective for one group only, which leads to global leaders developing the strategy by themselves.

Top-level regional leadership may become involved once a global strategy is drafted. However, less than half of this group claim to participate in developing it. Meanwhile, only a small minority of them agree that they have the formal ability to approve or change global strategy.

Most regional and local leaders agree that a global strategy is conceived and developed in a silo without their input and expertise. Many consider this activity wasteful, and they describe the global strategy that results from it as unsuitable and unreliable. For example, they assert that global leaders are missing vital perspective and market-level experience. Meanwhile, global leaders describe their regional and local counterparts as unwilling players who are not interested in the overall perspective.

While global leaders may own the deliverable, this does not mean that they need to work alone or restart from the beginning. However, global teams often find it easier to source information from existing regional and local strategy documents rather than engage with their counterparts face-to-face. They justify this by pointing to resistance and rejection from regional and local leaders.

When teams are not inclined to collaborate, it is typically because they don't share a common need that is compelling and requires them to work together. This seems to fit the situation well as regional and local leaders, who have been left out of the development process, believe that a global strategy is not going to deliver sufficient value. After all, these leaders already have their strategies and, unless they need additional resources to achieve them, they are unlikely to ask for global support or, indeed, any involvement at all.

Understanding this strategy-in-a-silo dynamic is very useful because it highlights a fundamental flaw that can cause major problems right at the outset. If global teams are being asked to play an important role in leading the worldwide growth of their company, then let's agree that this is not "leading." After all, you can't acquire followers from inside a silo.

Political Performance

For many regional and local leaders, a global strategy is a distraction: It is a political performance rather than a driver of business performance. Yet, they choose this by falsely representing their engagement. Meanwhile, top-level global executives are more likely to describe the development and implementation of their global strategy as collaborative and committed.

Many senior and mid-level global leaders agree that developing a global strategy is a political rather than a practical exercise. In interviews, they note that the request for a new global strategy is most likely to come from global executives, not from any other business leaders including themselves. As a result, the new strategy tends to be built with global executives as the customers. So, to obtain approval, the focus is on meeting their expectations, preferences, and biases.

Most regional and local leaders agree that the only way for them to influence global strategy is through their top regional leaders. Sometimes, this leads to high-level top-to-top conversations, but sometimes there is no engagement at all.

Almost half of the regional leaders interviewed believe that it is more important to be seen to participate in global strategy than to deliver it. Meanwhile, many local leaders describe a global strategy as rarely or never useful—and often a distraction.

Both regional and local leaders explain their lack of commitment or engagement by pointing to their limited role in developing and, for most of them, approving global strategy. Global strategy is somebody else's work outside of their management hierarchy, which means that their participation is not required.

At the same time, and curiously, among all nine segments of our 3×3 array of participants, it is the top-level global leaders more than anyone else who describe a company in which there is more harmony, collaboration, and commitment to global strategy. They claim to be least aware of political games. What should we make of this when we consider that a new global strategy is typically requested by these same top-level global leaders? Is this wishful thinking? A blind spot? A smoke screen?

Competing For Control

Global and regional leaders view their respective strategies as superior and the other as competitive and inappropriate. Yet, this divisive competition doesn't seem to be driven so much by the strategies themselves. Most research participants describe personal power struggles rather than reasoned debates about opportunities and priorities. The competition for preeminence is dressed up in the considerations of the business, but it is really about personal power.

All the segments confirmed that it is common practice to have global and regional strategies created separately, at different times, and by separate teams in separate geographical hierarchies. Given this disconnected approach, it is never automatic that regional and global strategies are coherent. Indeed, when asked if global and regional strategies are complementary, very few regional leaders agree that this is likely. Most respond that the potential for overlap is neutral or unlikely, and they describe global strategy using words like *distraction* and *compromise*.

To quote a European country manager, 'If I don't hit my number, then someone else will be sitting in this chair in six months. I know what I need to do and I don't have time for this.'

Most global strategists feel that it is unlikely that regional teams will change their priorities because global priorities are different. Only a minority are optimistic that it is likely that regional and country resources will be reallocated. They have confidence that their global strategy will drive change whether their regional counterparts want it or not.

At the same time, the participants describe the competition between these strategies as a conflict of egos. Each senior leader wants to make the important decisions for their business. Yet, the conflict seems to be less about the decisions themselves and more about who gets to make them.

This internal competition feels like a symptom of something larger and more serious. While it makes sense that, geographically, there are different definitions of success, why are we pitting one strategy against the other? Why do we allow teams in the same organization to try to defeat and subjugate one another? The tension is painfully real. Certainly, ego, power, and desire for autonomy and authority play a role. Believe me, I have seen these leaders red-faced and barking at each other like bull seals. Yet, is there a reason why global and regional stakeholders can't *both* win?

Unreliable Gatekeepers

Regional executives are the most influential gatekeepers of global strategy. They can be the most powerful advocates or detractors. Most will say that they personally support global strategy, but that it is hard to accept this when their organizations as a whole don't.

Almost all top regional leaders (for example, the head of Europe or South America), agree that they are aware of their company's global strategy. Yet, only half of the regions' senior leaders, who would be their direct reports, say that they too are aware of the global strategy. Likewise, only half of the senior local leaders, who are the country department heads such as for sales or marketing, claim to be aware.

All of this suggests that, while top-level regional and local leaders might be aware of their company's global strategy, many of them are not sharing it with their organizations. At the same time, while awareness of *global* strategy is inconsistent, all regional leaders and local leaders agree that they are aware of their applicable *regional* strategy.

Most top-level regional leaders also say that they are committed to delivering global strategy, even though only a third of them agree that it is valuable. Yet, it is hard to rely on these claims when the senior and middle managers of their own organizations are not committed. How is it possible that they are not transferring their commitment to their people?

In interviews, most top regional leaders agree that it is important to have control and authorship of the strategy that they are leading. They consider this essential to their role, and appropriate given their seniority and expertise. They also point out that regional strategy features country-level expertise, which they believe promotes more relevant and usable decisions.

This dynamic reveals a fractured system in which these critical gatekeepers are put in a position that they don't want to accept. With little ability to steer the global strategy, they resort to what some of them describe as *damage control* and which their global counterparts describe as *playing games*.

In discussion, regional leaders deny that they see global strategy as a threat to their autonomy and control. At the same time, they agree that they do not need a global strategy to tell them what to do: 'Who is this for? It is not for my business. They don't know my business.'

Also, many describe global strategy as too academic—for example, describing market segments rather than individual customers, while their business problems are specific and nuanced. Global strategy, they say, is not written for them but for talking to the Chief Executive Officer or the board of directors.

No Accountability

Nobody wants to be liable for the results of a new global strategy—not even the global team responsible for writing it. Many people know this. It is not a blind spot: It is a deliberate choice. Of course, without accountability, the strategy may never be more than a statement of intent.

Even though they developed the strategy, less than half of global leaders agree that they are accountable for its results.

During interviews, the most common explanation presented by global leaders is that accountability for the results belongs to those who execute the strategy. These global leaders cite their limited control over execution and determine that under such circumstances it is not appropriate to hold them accountable. They also describe their role as big picture, or high level, making decisions and adding value, or identifying insights from their unique perspective. Some also point out that the strategy will outlast their tenure as a global leader, which means that they will probably have moved on before the results are in.

Perhaps not surprisingly, while half of global leaders want their local colleagues to be accountable for the results of global strategy, fewer than 1 in 20 local leaders agree with this. Many regional and local leaders assume that global teams are accountable for global strategy. Those who believe that global teams are not accountable refuse to be accountable themselves.

Of course, by not holding local and regional leaders accountable, we inevitably leave in place their existing accountabilities to local and regional strategies. Indeed, most local leaders claim that their annual targets rarely or never change as a result of a new global strategy.

Forgotten Strategy

Only a few global and regional leaders remember their company's last global strategy. Most don't think it was very important. Only a minority can remember details.

When asked if they have visibility to the full journey of a global strategy, from creation through approval, rollout, and implementation, nearly all global, regional, and local leaders say no. Top and senior global leaders are more likely to claim some visibility. However, only a third of them do so.

When asked if it is their role to shepherd the global strategy through all of its phases, most global leaders disagree. In discussion, they suggest that their focus is strategy development and, for most, their responsibility ends with a hand-off to regional and local counterparts. In their justification, they also revisit the point that their tenure as a global leader is shorter than the time frame of the strategy.

Of course, this approach only works if the hand-off is successful. So, it is fascinating to hear that most global leaders do not trust their regional and local colleagues to fully execute the strategy. Top-level leaders are more trusting. However, three-quarters of all senior and mid-level global leaders have low expectations of compliance for anything beyond simple and short-term directives, particularly without oversight.

So, in summary, most global leaders agree that their role is just to develop strategy. They are the owners of the strategy but then they stop and give it up because many of them are unconvinced that their regional and local counterparts will execute it. Meanwhile, nobody is keeping track.

With such entrenched and combative stakeholders, it seems it would be a fantasy to imagine a strategy that the entire organization wants to execute. The typical global company machine and our common ways of working seem tragically unable to achieve this.

As a consequence, when asked about their company's last global strategy, only some global and regional leaders remember it. They are most likely to recall the strategy if it was launched within the past two years. However, while they may remember its name—for example, "Vision 2020" was a common and well-recalled label—only a third of these leaders recall enough detail to discuss it. Most can only provide one or two details. One in five reports that they don't remember what the strategy's objectives were.

When asked about the importance of the last global strategy, most leaders—global, regional, and local—rate the strategy's importance as neutral or lower after two years.

This is not working.

11. Symptoms: People

Confused

Local and global leaders pursue different objectives and have different measures of success. These objectives are developed and assigned separately. They are not shared and compared, showing little thought to their coherence. Many local leaders say that their global colleagues are not contributing to their success and so interactions with them are a distraction.

While almost two-thirds of local leaders agree that regional leaders are committed to their success, fewer than one in four agree that global leaders show the same commitment. Some local leaders go so far as to question whether their global colleagues are even able to support them in a meaningful way.

Perhaps, as a result, many local leaders say that they are not looking for global support. Some suggest that global leaders do not know what their markets need. To that point, almost half agree that global colleagues often push them to pursue an agenda that is outside their immediate objectives. Their sense is, quite rightly, that global leaders pursue different objectives and have different measures of success. The failures in mutual support and collaboration arise when local and global objectives are developed and assigned separately, and not shared or compared, showing little thought to their coherence.

Local expectations of global collaboration are low. Global teams, people say, like to talk rather than listen. This comment from a country manager in Eastern Europe gives us one take on the incoherence: 'They [the global team] come here. We have a meeting. They make a presentation and then they leave. It makes no difference.'

It seems that local and global teams struggle to come together effectively. However, there are exceptions to this—for example, if there is no regional team and local leaders interact directly with global leaders with whom they seem to collaborate well.

Another exception occurs when new products are developed globally. In this instance, although it is not without tension, local leaders often welcome the support, which can provide a valuable opportunity for incremental local growth. As with most global—local conversations, there needs to be a discussion of relevance and local leaders will question whether the planned new products are a fit with their customers' needs. Local leaders report that it is not unusual, when innovation is managed globally, that they will be asked to launch new products that are a better fit in other markets.

Misunderstood

Global leaders claim that local leaders are not strategic enough. Meanwhile, local leaders assert that global teams are disconnected from execution and operational priorities. Both global and local leaders

see their regional colleagues as possible intermediaries. However, regional leaders also want to lead and set direction.

Comparing interviews between global and local leaders, we see each group defining the other's role in terms of their own, and so misunderstanding their competence and contribution. This is basic tribal behavior in which we define value based on what our group considers important. So, strategic global leaders tend to claim that the more operational local leaders are not strategic enough. Meanwhile, local leaders assert that global teams are disconnected or abstracted from execution and operational priorities.

US-based global strategists have commented as follows:
- Country managers don't call us "global." They call us "corporate." It's a message. They are close to customers and we are bureaucrats from headquarters. We can't possibly have something intelligent to say. And if we weren't from headquarters, we'd get even less respect.
- My (global) VP has a mantra: 'Help the markets win,' and the response from the regions is 'That's my job.'

In contrast, European middle and senior regional managers have commented as follows:
- I have a strategy to grow my sales. The (global) group has their strategy but I don't have time for that. I know my business and what it needs.
- If I show them around the country and visit customers … they will tell me how to do my job.

These groups do not seem to agree on their counterparts' roles: One pushes for authority and influence, while the other resists or dissembles to protect its autonomy. There is mistrust between both groups. Questioning competence is a common symptom.

Most country leaders have a direct reporting relationship with regional leaders and so they are obliged to follow their direction. This is preferred less than autonomous self-rule, but it is more focused, relevant, and supportive than a partnership with global teams would ever be.

Global teams would like their regional colleagues to support global strategy and guide the translation of global priorities into local business plans. However, many regional leaders prefer to define and lead their own strategies. So, global leaders often remain frustrated outsiders. This seems to be a place where almost everyone struggles. There is no common approach to guide global and regional leaders to work together and complement each other in an additive way. Without this, they misidentify their roles, compete for authority, and create a confusing overlap. Both groups seem to believe that it is their role to set strategy and each is sure that its members are the best suited to do it.

Disrespected

Local and global leaders question each other's competence and value, often to the extent that they are disrespectful. Local leaders, in particular, will stonewall. Both parties are united in avoiding a rational discussion and debate. Each maligns the other for challenging their tribal self-rule, authority, and inflexible worldview.

Only a quarter of local leaders agree that their global colleagues are knowledgeable about local business.

In discussions, we find that many local and regional leaders believe that global teams think that they know more than they do. For example, they cite global leaders' tendency to minimize the importance of local market differences as an example of their ignorance and arrogance. This criticism is not specific to an individual: The entire global team is considered to have the same faults.

This is important because it is often contemptuous and disrespectful, which in turn points to a problem with trust. This also reinforces just how challenging it is for a global leader to engage with their regional and local colleagues because they must first overcome this negative reputation.

Conversely, global teams agree that their local counterparts don't understand the company's business globally and the strategic decisions to be made. They complain that regional and local leaders wield the idea of being closer to customers, and that competition is a trump card proving that only they have the necessary knowledge and expertise to have a valid opinion.

This explanation from a vice president (VP) of global marketing illustrates the point:

- The VP of sales told me that the only way to understand the business is to visit Thailand and spend time with her customers. What she is saying is that her perspective is the only perspective. She's playing the customer-is-king card because she knows that she owns that expertise. She wants control. But I am not trying to get an order. I want to know if we should invest to grow in Thailand.

Another VP, this time of global strategy, offers this:

- I was a region head and so I know this game. I will tell you (global) that I want to help but I am not sure if my customers will go for it. You (global) have no idea.

Ignored

Global, regional, and local leaders interpret information through their separate understandings and viewpoints. Each is entrenched and global leaders, in particular, are not listening or being heard. Regional and local leaders report that their global counterparts will push a solution before exploring the needs and pain points of their business.

While local and regional leaders agree that they are listening to each other often or always, it appears that communication breaks down with the global team. Many of these same leaders claim that their global colleagues rarely or never listen to them. Meanwhile, almost half of the global leaders in the survey said that their regional and local counterparts rarely or never listened to them.

While it is hard to extract the tribal animus from the conversations, the participants identify two areas where the failure to listen causes a major impact. The first is what we might call the establishing conversation in which the separate stakeholders discuss why they are collaborating. While local and regional leaders wish to explore the need, its urgency, and its importance relative to their existing priorities, many global leaders omit this step. Local and regional leaders are looking for the trigger or tipping point that justifies a change and a reason to work together. Global leaders believe that their direction is always necessary and valuable. Too often, this conversation ends with one party thinking, 'Why do they insist? Can't they see that I don't need their help?' and the other thinking, 'Why do they resist? Can't they see that they need my help?'

The second example occurs when there is a disagreement. Many global leaders report being blindsided by the unraveling of what they understood was a firm commitment. They are convinced that regional and local leaders have agreed to something, but it turns out that this is not true. Some global leaders confess that they may be too quick to convince themselves that they hear what they want to hear. Others feel deceived and manipulated. When this scenario is described to regional leaders, they resent the idea that they dupe their colleagues, claiming that they never agreed or firmly committed to anything.

Many conversations between global and regional or local leaders seem to be one way. Perhaps each group simply presents to the other. When all groups are asked how often they receive questions, the best that they can report is "sometimes." Less than one in five agree that their counterparts are curious.

Independent

Regional leaders with low authority tend to function as negotiating representatives between global and local groups. With high authority, they express independence, choosing to stymie global influence and direct local leaders themselves.

Regional leaders are seen as effective connectors across their organizations and are often the best equipped to get things done in a global matrix. However, the nature of their role changes dramatically based on the strength of their decision-making authority. This authority can be derived from many sources although typically more authority comes with a larger business.

With low authority, regional leaders tend to function as negotiating representatives between global and local groups. They can serve as a valuable bridge between geographies making the case for each and building mutual understanding. However, with high authority, they tend to stymie global influence and are directive with local leaders.

This dynamic is easy to observe. For example, contrast the authority of the regional leaders for North America with those of Central Europe or Australasia. Based on the size of their respective businesses, they often have very different relationships with their global counterparts.

All else being equal, the leaders of large regions show a bias toward independence. Indeed, a large regional business may fit the definition of a cash cow but don't be surprised to see its leaders reinvest their income with self-interest—the geographic portfolio be damned! This behavior is so common that the idea of the profits from a large but lower-growth region fueling a rapid expansion in new or emerging markets elsewhere seems almost naive.

The greater the authority, the more important it appears to be to express it. In a meeting of region heads, we often see the executives with higher authority make a point of clarifying their status in the hierarchy.

Demotivated

Global leadership teams are demotivating their organizations by being too exclusive and not sharing their agendas or decisions.

While there are many ways to construct a global leadership team, most are comprised of the company's most senior leaders in global, regional, and sometimes local roles. They constitute the primary authority that comes together to make consequential strategic decisions.

Each meeting of this team is a big deal. These are the company's movers and shakers. However, half of senior and mid-level global leaders report that they are unaware of the decisions that their global leadership team makes. Senior and mid-level leaders in regions and markets are even less informed.

Not surprisingly, when decisions are not shared, these leaders feel disconnected and even question the importance of their work. To quote one senior global leader, 'What are they working on? I guess we don't need to know.' Disengagement follows. After all, there is an expectation of being led and we don't follow those who leave us feeling undervalued or insignificant.

In discussion, many of the top-level leaders who participate in global leadership teams describe the environment as either negatively charged or falsely harmonious, often ego-driven and political, and with low trust between the participants. Given all of this tension, it is a good thing that these top leaders are connecting. Unfortunately, a significant number of their colleagues find these high-profile, yet exclusive and unforthcoming, meetings to be demotivating.

Misaligned

Most global and top-level leaders claim that there is worldwide alignment on company business priorities. Many senior and mid-level leaders in regions and countries disagree. It appears that many deciders are naive to the limits of their authority and may be disconnected from operations and their execution.

Most participants share the same opinion that global, regional, and local leaders can't agree on what is best for the business. However, most top-level leaders, particularly those in global roles, say that there is agreement. Senior and mid-level leaders in their organizations disagree.

There seems to be a strong confirmation bias that has global and top-level leaders more prone to believe, or at least to claim, that there is broad alignment on business priorities. However, it speaks volumes that mid-level leaders disagree. It is not good news that many local leaders, who are the ones executing these priorities, also disagree. This suggests that there is a real disconnect between top-level leadership and the front lines of the business. Not only do the front lines not agree on where to focus but those at the top appear to be unaware that they are alone in their opinion.

This insight suggests that a company's global and top-level leaders, those most involved with making broad strategic choices, may believe that their organizations are aligned with their key priorities when that is not true. This lack of awareness infers a serious process malfunction. Are top-level leaders too insulated from candid feedback? Are they accepting inaccurate messages of alignment? Are they not hearing valuable operational feedback?

12. Implications

Our report card for global effectiveness is far from satisfactory. Indeed, when we itemize a list of possible dysfunctions, it is quite a shock. Wherever we sit in our organization, it forces us to accept that the status quo is not working. Where we may have been complacent in the past, allowing our systems, structures, philosophies, and behaviors to fragment our global potential, faced with a catalog of embarrassing home goals, it becomes much harder to allow this to continue. This is not least because, as we have explored these challenges, their causes and symptoms, fresh ideas start to percolate. With careful thought and insight, we can unravel this mess.

Yet, before we turn the corner and focus on our opportunities, let's summarize the implications of the reported symptoms that we have just been discussing. We need to be crystal clear about the complexity and the intransigence of our situation.

Consider this depressing scenario. A global strategy is created in a silo by a team that is disconnected from the operational business. Senior leadership approves the strategy, which is then presented to an organization that didn't ask for it, has not been involved, and questions its relevance and value. At this point, the global team walks away, job done. Nobody owns the strategy now. It has no advocate. Nobody is accountable for the results and so nobody measures its impact. Smaller regions may work to secure incremental resources, while the leaders of larger regions comply for a while. Nothing changes and, in a couple of years, the global strategy is mostly forgotten. In time, perhaps when the global strategy is embarrassingly divergent from local and regional priorities, we start the exercise all over again.

This is horrific—so much so that it is tempting to deny how real and common it is. However, some or all of that scenario happens regularly and, even worse, the cycle repeats. Many of us are in denial, which is why we are not learning. It is why we are stuck. Indeed, the overwhelming themes across all of the interviews in the study were a combined sense of frustration, impotence, and resignation to a system so complex and messed up that its stakeholders couldn't fix it.

Let's bring these symptoms of fragmentation together in a more coherent story. Here are some implications that are important to highlight from the research.

Strategy versus Execution

Strategy is simple. It is just a set of choices that we decide to make, and that we are willing and able to achieve. This is not so complicated that we need a specialized team to create it. Yet this siloed practice, in which global teams develop a strategy for all, but behind closed doors, sets up the fundamental and perhaps most universal risk of fracture in all strategies. It separates those who set direction from those who execute. This creates room for all of the nonsense that you read or hear when we talk about strategy and execution as separate things that are somehow in competition. The reason that this is such a fatuous fallacy is that it is a proxy war for separate tribal silos. Success requires both. Doing the wrong things well is not clever. Our real challenge is that strategy and execution have different owners in a system that encourages them to be independent and disrespectful of each other.

No Common Purpose

A global strategy is often rejected or avoided when it is not created in response to a business need that is real and relevant to all stakeholders. Local and regional leaders tell us that it needs to solve a problem that could not be tackled otherwise. These stakeholders can appreciate the global strategy's value when it brings important change and is not contrary or distracting to what already exists. This is easy to imagine if the strategy changes a company's focus, adding or subtracting markets, capabilities, products, services, or customer segments. However, this does not guarantee engagement because perceptions of value will vary based on local needs and conditions.

Many regional and local respondents in the study question the purpose of global strategy. They seem predisposed to resent and circumvent it. Meanwhile, global leaders tend to find it more expeditious to ignore this tension and, by avoiding it, to develop a strategy in isolation. This brings us back to a revealing question. Who are we creating the global strategy for? Remember that there are two sets of approvers: Corporate and operational leaders. Both sets have distinct needs that must be addressed. The most common misstep here is to focus on satisfying the C-suite alone. When we do this, the goal shifts from achieving a strategy to simply producing it.

Strategy Clash

Both global and regional leaders want to set strategy and both are capable. Study participants share that a common sticking point is the competitive clash of these strategies. Each player seems to want to usurp the other's role and, what is more, they claim that they can do the job better. Meanwhile, their counterpart thinks that is ridiculous. Of course, the appropriate solution would be to develop complementary global and regional strategies that are focused on different things yet are still aligned and mutually supportive. However, such collaborative development is rare. For one thing, these strategies are not developed together, and so one of them—let's say the regional strategy—will already exist and its owners will be likely to resist change or incremental objectives.

Without the clarity of the unique value that each stakeholder brings to the table, this competition for authority and preeminence seems unavoidable.

No Follow Through

When a new global strategy is introduced, regional and local strategies already exist. Local leaders, in particular, who inevitably execute all strategies, are going to view a new and separate global strategy as less important than their existing plans. Never forget that they are held accountable to these existing plans, and only these.

Global leaders know that any new strategy that they bring forward will face this inertia. Why then is it so common for global teams to step back and delegate the deployment of global strategy to the very people who don't want it? This takes us back to the question of whether achieving the strategy is important to the global team. This common behavior of delegating and handing off ownership and accountability suggests that deployment and results are a lot less important to global leaders than the act of publishing the strategy, which is a clear and finite deliverable that is much faster and easier.

Regional Royalty

Regional leaders often act as gatekeepers to the distribution of a global strategy through the company. However, many of them view it as inferior to their regional strategy and an affront to their seniority, autonomy, and expertise. Overly authoritative regional leaders will assure the Chief Executive Officer (CEO) of their commitment and at the same time stymie the influence of global leadership to maintain control. They create separateness from the global whole, and coach their regional and local managers to reject the global strategy in favor of their own plans.

On its face, this behavior is duplicitous. However, it is not all that surprising for executives who have the power of a de facto CEO when they are not visiting their company's global headquarters. While we can condemn the ego-fueled passive-aggressive shenanigans that go on, let's not forget that their behavior follows their incentives. This subversion is rewarded.

At the same time, region heads have a most insightful and valuable perspective. They understand strategy, they know the local business, and they are committed to its success. They are also influential and better than most at getting things done in a global matrix.

These players are a fuse in the machine that can blow and bring everything to a stop. For success, the global team needs their involvement as consultants or even architects of global strategy. Yet, in all probability they don't want to play. Participation, if achieved, is on their terms.

Disconnected Leaders

Intra-company connectivity in a global operation is hard to gauge. Technology notwithstanding, with increased scale and sprawl comes greater disconnection. While this has important consequences for trust, it also means that contrary perspectives and operational differences grow in the dark.

Let's start with top leadership. We have heard that the emperor is stark naked, and yet top-level leaders are either unaware, in denial, or complicit—happy to play the theatrical game. An experienced CEO knows that their region heads exercise some optionality when it comes to global strategy. There is nothing wrong with that, although it would be better done out in the open. Yet, at the same time, with plenty of evidence of past failures, how does the CEO justify repeating the same mistakes?

At the core of the challenge is a large gap in perspective. In the 3×3 matrix of participants, the largest differences are, not surprisingly, between top-level global and mid-level local leaders: The generals in headquarters and the soldiers on the front lines. The generals believe that strategy is their purview, and they favor a naive and militaristic view of the effectiveness of top-down orders and their deployment. Meanwhile, the soldiers believe that the generals are uninformed and so out of touch that their decisions don't seem relevant. Each needs the other. Each can learn from the other. However, unless the company is small, this is unlikely.

Many companies' top-level leaders, including the global leadership team, tend to believe that global, regional, and local leaders mostly agree on what is best for the business. However, mid-level leaders, whether they are in global, regional, or local roles, disagree with this statement and believe the opposite. So, in discussions of intent, which happen at higher levels in a hierarchy, alignment is expressed. However, when it comes to taking action, which is the specialty of our mid-level leaders, that alignment is nowhere to be found.

Once again, we see global strategy as a theatrical performance, a presentation of intent that is not realized. Top-level leaders are either overstating their coherence and effectiveness or they are tragically unaware.

How can we make progress with all of the different perspectives and agendas? How can we find clarity with all of the complexity and opacity of a global matrix organization? With all of the potential for dysfunction, we need to find a more objective understanding of the unique dynamics in our company. We need a way to investigate and decode what is going on.

In the next section, you will find a suite of diagnostic tools, designed to help you discover and assess your risk.

Diagnosing the Dysfunction

Honest argument is merely a process
of mutually picking the beams and motes
out of each other's eyes
so both can see clearly.

Wilbur Wright

As we explored the fundamental and ever-present forces that work to derail global collaboration, and as we have heard from a large and diverse group of stakeholders, we are dealing with compounded dysfunctions caused by complex and often mutually reinforcing causes. This should be challenging enough. However, these stresses create a high-pressure crucible that tests our character, and we have learned that those who stumble are tempted to respond with deception and theater. So, now we have seemingly insoluble obstacles that some of us ignore or pretend not to see. How do we tackle these? How can we open the door to acknowledging the dysfunctions and start a conversation that can lead to remediation?

The following chapters contains several diagnostic tools for you to use to identify, locate, describe, and even diffuse some of the causes behind the symptoms of dysfunction that you may be observing. Each tool enables you to lead a company self-assessment and produce findings that can fuel an informed and meaningful conversation. The diagnoses are mostly qualitative, but often that is all that you need. Just a sprinkle of accountability can be very powerful. In many cases, all it takes is a little data and insight to start a conversation, and bring the clarity and awareness that we need to trigger change.

Experience with these tools tells us that we don't have to diagnose or tackle the whole problem. Don't try to solve it all. That's almost impossible. Start small. The dysfunction can feel like a huge Gordian Knot but just pull gently on one small string to start the unraveling.

How your findings will affect your company's global effectiveness will be dictated by your leaders, your culture, and your operating model. Knowing this, each tool is designed for simplicity, ease of communication, and customization. In each case, you will find an explanation of the methodology and advice on how best to approach the diagnosis and any action steps.

Don't be an auditor. Invite your stakeholders in. Engage those who are willing. It is important to approach this work with sensitivity. This is a soft skills challenge that is not for the faint-hearted. Be warned. The findings can be embarrassing and sometimes expose behaviors that were deliberately obscured. Senior leaders in your company may be complicit and yet it is possible they are unaware of this. There are many reasons why global collaboration becomes fragmented and strategy diluted. So, as you approach these diagnoses, it helps to be as objective as possible. None of these tools are about finding fault or identifying a saboteur to global unity. Rather, they are intended to help expose some hard-to-see dysfunction that is caused by common imperfections in an incredibly complex system.

A more light-hearted way to approach these diagnoses is to acknowledge that every global organization needs maintenance and a tune-up, particularly if we are looking for high performance.

Here are some tools for the job.

13. Decision Effectiveness

How do you assess whether your global company is dysfunctional? Are there certain behaviors that you have noticed? Do you suspect that these might be the symptoms of something deeper and possibly systemic? If so, then what can you do to shed some light on these and learn more? You don't want to overreact but, at the same time, you can't afford to ignore this situation. So, what is the best way to start a conversation and lay the groundwork for any appropriate remediation? How can you uncover some meaningful evidence and do it quickly without any fuss?

In this chapter, you will find a simple assessment tool that is designed as a perfect first step to investigate dysfunction in your global company. It is intended to be fast and light, and yet still to deliver findings with enough insight and substance to start a real conversation about global performance.

Picture a doctor holding a patient's wrist to take their pulse. It is a classic medical image. This simple examination is one of the first things that a healthcare professional will do to assess a patient. It gives a sense of how well the heart is working and if it is pumping enough blood. An irregular pulse is an immediate warning sign. Even if there are no obvious injuries, this simple test can reveal the dysfunction caused by a plethora of hidden problems.

The human cardiovascular system is a useful metaphor for company decision-making and, in particular, the healthy flow of decisions from the corporate center to the extremities of the global matrix. This model works well. After all, decision effectiveness is truly the lifeblood of global performance.

Effective decision-making and implementation are basic indicators of a well-functioning global organization. For a shot at a competitive advantage, we need good decisions to be carried out and transmitted quickly all over the world. Yet, we know that the forces of fragmentation will continually push back to derail this potential. So, when global performance is compromised, we can expect to find that decisions do not flow quickly to where they need to go and they are not implemented as intended.

Let's take the pulse of our patient, the global organization, with a similarly simple technique that exposes dysfunction. To do this, all we need to do is to assess how well decisions are made and then follow them through the matrix to see how well they travel and whether they are implemented.

It is time to play detective and gather the evidence.

In this chapter, we will review a *Decision Effectiveness* assessment tool. It is simple to use and provides a qualitative snapshot of decision performance across your matrix organization. In effect, it takes the pulse of your global company to detect signs of dysfunction. This is not a deep-dive analysis to root out problems. However, it is powerful because, when you use this technique, you will capture a picture of matrix performance that will reveal where you may have opportunities to improve decision-making, flow, and execution.

The assessment starts with a very short customized survey. The survey responses are then collated and presented in a unique format that simplifies the interpretation of your findings. This tool makes it easy to identify where there are opportunities to improve decision effectiveness. It also highlights where expectations of global operations may not be met.

Just like taking a patient's pulse, this is only a tool to detect dysfunction. The root cause(s) is often complex and requires additional work to decode and defeat.

Decision Effectiveness

Our first step is to dissect decision effectiveness into a checklist of its component parts.

Table 13.1 A Decision Effectiveness Checklist

Accountability:	Who is making the decisions?
Process:	How are the decisions made?
Flow:	How do decisions travel through the organization?
Speed:	Once made, are decisions implemented quickly?
Commitment:	Are those who will execute aware and engaged?
Results:	Do decisions generate the appropriate actions?
Feedback:	Is there an approach to learn and improve?

The checklist in Table 13.1 is neither definitive nor exhaustive. Please feel free to adapt it for a better fit with your company and culture. However, be sure to include several attributes that drive decision effectiveness across the global matrix. We will be asking questions to understand what is going on in each of these areas.

This is such a straightforward tool to use because we already know the ideal performance that we want to see. So, take each attribute of decision effectiveness and describe briefly what it would look like in a best-case scenario. These are your ideal performance targets.

Table 13.2 A Decision Effectiveness Checklist—Performance Targets

Accountability	Decision-making is pushed down as far as possible
Process	A small number of deciders follow a consistent process
Flow	There are no revisions or reprioritizations
Speed	Timing of intended results is set and tracked
Commitment	Executors are architects or influencers
Results	Yes! Decisions achieve the desired action
Feedback	A commitment to improve decision effectiveness

As above, please feel free to develop your own definitions. Use Table 13.2 as a stimulus if it helps. What is important is that you have a description of the ideal performance for each attribute. We will use these expectations to benchmark decision effectiveness across your organization.

Methodology

At this point, you may be impatient to start interviewing your suspects. However, we need to be disciplined. To detect how decisions are working in your company's global matrix, we must understand the whole picture. Otherwise, our conclusions will be based on incomplete information. A thorough investigation means that we need to learn from all of the different parts of the global organization. It is not enough to know *whether* the matrix is misfiring. We also need to know *where* it is misfiring.

This is why decision effectiveness is such a great lens to look through. As decisions flow through an organization, they reveal the interdependence of everyone involved from the decider to the final actor.

The global matrix is a complex network where geographic and functional organizations overlap and interact. So, who do we interview? How do we identify the right candidates?

Figure 13.1 below shows a simple 3×3 array that describes the matrix in a general sense. This is the same array that we used in the research study. While it is certainly an oversimplification, it allows us to identify candidates to interview according to two important dimensions: Geographic responsibility and management seniority.

Here we have nine groups made up of decision-makers, stakeholders, and executors from top global leaders to local middle managers. For a comprehensive and company-wide review of decision effectiveness, we want to interview all nine groups if that is possible.

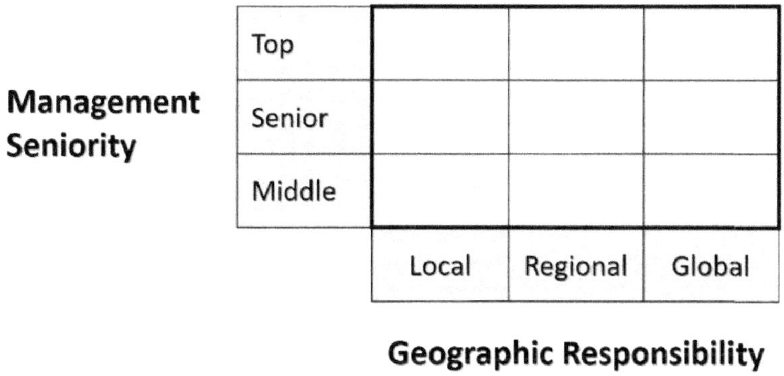

Management Seniority	Top			
	Senior			
	Middle			
		Local	Regional	Global

Geographic Responsibility

Figure 13.1 A Simple 3×3 Model of a Global Matrix

Most decisions don't flow through the full matrix. So, when we are working in the context of a discrete project, initiative, or team, we may be tempted to reduce the scope of our investigation. For example, a leadership team of top managers may only be interested in the flow of decisions between their global, regional, and local members. This may seem to be the appropriate scope. However, while it feels like extra work, it pays to cover all of the bases. There will be prime suspects–those who appear to be more likely to derail decision effectiveness but try to stay objective and do the due diligence. The full picture may reveal some surprising information and your objective fairness will certainly smooth the presentation of findings later on.

You will also need to decide which countries to include in the aggregated local group. You may want to keep some countries as separate targets. In practice, to keep this manageable, it helps to choose key countries of focus or to create clusters.

Also, before you go any further, it is important to ensure that top management agrees with the definitions of performance targets for decision effectiveness. These are ideal descriptors and they don't have to be current practice. Yet, they do need to be locked down or you risk debating these targets after the fact.

Survey Interviews

We are going to quiz each target group using the Decision Effectiveness Checklist. For example, we will ask local senior leaders about each of the seven attributes relative to their ideal performance targets. We want to capture their perceptions of decision-making for decisions that typically affect them. This is important. We are not asking how they manage decisions themselves: We want to know how the decisions that affect them are managed.

You can do this in person, by email, or by survey. Reach as many people as possible in each target group. This will also help you manage cultural differences by giving criticism. We ask all target groups the same questions and ask for responses on a five-point Likert scale. Table 13.3 shows an example questionnaire.

The beauty of this approach is that each target group creates a self-diagnosis of their experience. It is not your opinion—it is theirs. This lends credibility to your findings, which is useful when there are contrasting results.

Remember, this is not a rigorous statistical analysis. It is designed to inform a conversation. We are just checking the pulse with a simple tool to spot whether there is a problem. So, now we need to explain our findings intuitively and powerfully. To that end, the next step is to translate the scores that you received on the five-point scale into green, yellow, and red traffic lights. Traffic lights? Don't think for a second that this is frivolous. If you have not used this technique before, you will be amazed at its impact. In my experience, you can't overestimate the power of a red traffic light to get attention and drive change!

Table 13.3. Example Survey Questionnaire

Question: For decisions that typically affect you, do you agree with the following?

1 = strongly disagree, 2 = disagree, 3 = neither agree nor disagree, 4 = agree, 5 = strongly agree

	1	2	3	4	5
a) Decision-making is pushed down as far as possible					
b) A small number of deciders follow a consistent process					
c) There are no revisions or reprioritizations of decisions					
d) Timing of intended results is set and tracked					
e) Executors are architects or influencers of the decision					
f) Yes! Decisions achieve the desired action					
g) We are committed to improving decision effectiveness					

Average scores for each target group and assign traffic lights as follows:

Green: An average score above 4.0

Yellow: An average score above 3 up to and including 4.0

Red: An average score of 3.0 and below

We assign a red light to any decision attribute when, overall, there is no positive agreement with the performance target.

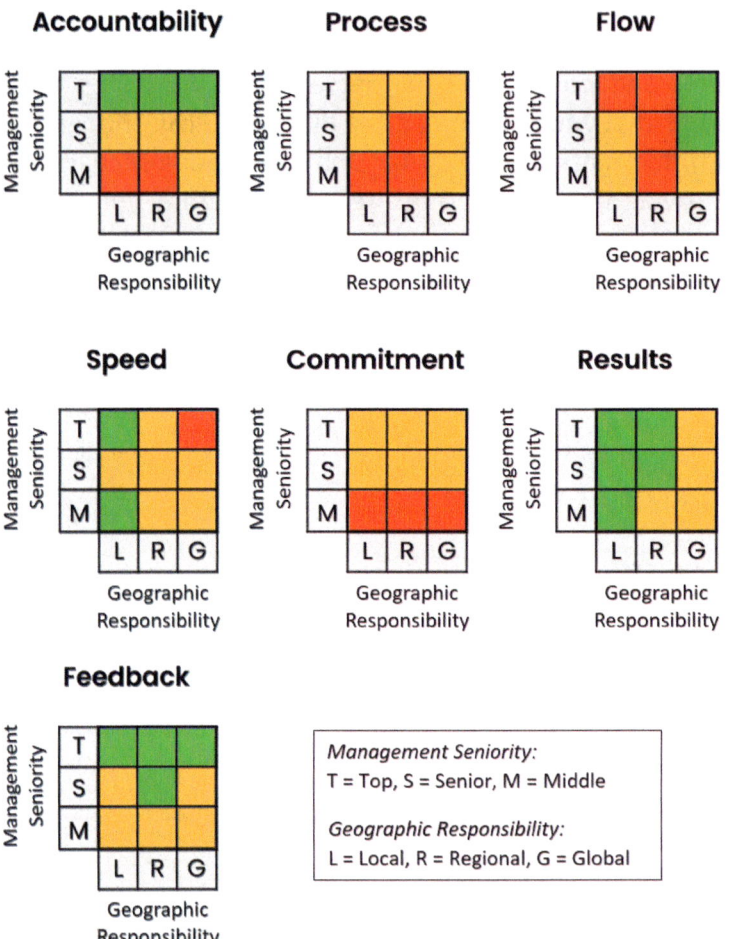

Figure 13.2 Example Performance Ratings for Decision Effectiveness

Take the ratings, translate the average into traffic lights, and map them against each separate decision attribute. You will create a colorful self-diagnosis similar to the one shown in Figure 13.2.

Diagnosis

For each decision attribute, you will have a colorful array that tells a story. Remember, that unless you have interviewed very large numbers of people, this is not a quantitative analysis: It is a quick and rudimentary inspection.

Also, it is important to remember that we are taking the pulse of how the global matrix is performing but not why it performs that way. It is tempting to begin to solve each red light immediately. Don't. Stay in detective mode. The ratings may trigger some action among the target groups. That is great. Let them follow up. We are still studying our heat map of decision effectiveness. We want to find contrasting experiences because these are more likely to indicate real systemic dysfunction.

The ratings for each target group become more significant when we find inconsistencies or contrasts versus other target groups. Look at the groups within the same area of geographic responsibility or management seniority by comparing across rows or down columns in the 3×3 array. Compare these similar hierarchical groups and look for opposing reds and greens.

Management Seniority (horizontal)

Consider top, senior, and mid-level leaders separately, and within each group compare the responses between local, regional, and global stakeholders.

Local and regional hierarchies are typically connected by a direct reporting structure. This should promote some agreement between them. Not always. There is a large gap, physically and in terms of business objectives, between local and global leaders. So, look for the opportunity here.

Geographic Responsibility (vertical)

Consider local, regional, and global stakeholders separately, and within each group compare the responses between middle, senior, or top-level leaders.

Typically, decisions flow better within geographic hierarchies because there are more direct managerial relationships, which means more cohesion and less ambiguity. So, if you do find contrary views, tread lightly. The dysfunction that you find may have nothing to do with the global matrix.

You may detect that senior or top-level leaders do not want to rock the boat. They may feel that this is not the most productive way for them to raise concerns with their peers. If so, then you will not see contrasting assessments when you scan vertically. That is OK.

We are most likely to find the prime suspects of our investigation by comparing scores across the diagonals in the 3×3 array. This is where the largest gaps exist. These groups may have little or no direct interaction. Also, you can often count on middle managers for their candor and their knowledge of how the company really works.

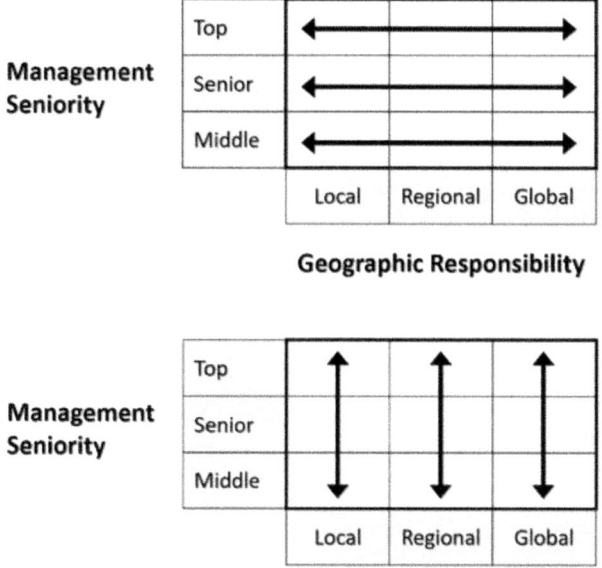

Figure 13.3 Compare and Contrast Target Groups Within Hierarchies

Local Middle and Global Top

Ironically, these groups can be so separate and yet so interdependent at the same time. After all, most top-level global business decisions are not realized without local execution.

If you find large differences between local mid-level managers and global top-level leaders and their perceptions of decision effectiveness, you are absolutely on to something. Global top-level leaders rely on others to manage the flow of their decisions. Think about the decision path. It probably flows from Global Top –> Regional Top –> Local Top –> Local Senior –> Local Middle. A disconnect between the global top and local middle means there is dysfunction at one or more links in this chain.

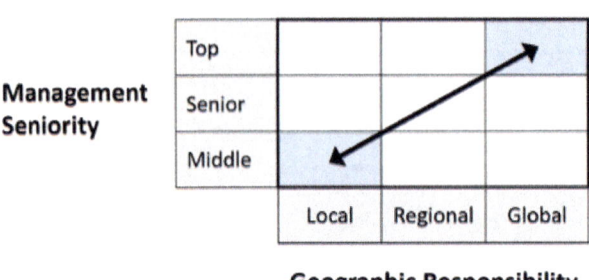

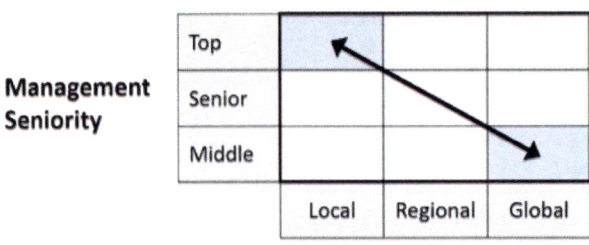

Figure 13.4 Compare and Contrast the Least Adjacent Target Groups

Local Top and Global Middle

These two groups are the least likely to overlap in terms of decision flow. They have no solid or dotted line connections. In fact, they have the weakest level of interdependence of all the groups we have identified. It is unlikely that contrasts in their views on decision effectiveness have the same root cause.

Action

So, you interviewed the suspects, you gathered the evidence, and created a colorful map of self-defined performance ratings that describe decision effectiveness across your company's global matrix. Congratulations!

Now, let's discuss how best to use the information from your decision effectiveness assessment. Here are some best practices for communicating what you have learned.

First, remember that you have only taken the pulse of the global matrix. The purpose of this tool is to detect the presence and likely location of misfires. It is not designed to fully diagnose the root causes and certainly not to recommend a course of remediation. Don't try to converge on any action steps unless this is to do a deeper diagnosis.

If that is disappointing and you are looking for immediate action, I will tell you from experience that meaningful organizational change does not happen as the result of a single simple study. It can be surprisingly powerful if you do nothing more than introduce the idea of global performance as measured by decision effectiveness. Putting a name to complex challenges means that they can't hide so easily and it will be harder to ignore them from now on. If you can introduce a shared language, and perhaps reveal a little tension and opportunity, then you have opened a door that is hard to close.

Any group of stakeholders who have self-diagnosed a red traffic light will probably want to take immediate action. They have acknowledged that there is a problem and they may be very pleased that you have provided a forum where their concern can be heard. While we have not identified root causes and so the appropriate action is not yet clear, you may not be able to slow their enthusiasm to find a fix. For example, when an organization learns that decisions are being revisited multiple times, they are probably going to take steps to prevent this. After all, this describes a confused collision of multiple stakeholders who all want ownership of the same decisions, while the inefficiency, particularly to top-level leaders, will be unacceptable.

There may be a common response from top and senior leaders to challenge or downplay red traffic lights or misfires that their direct report middle managers have identified. Of course, this is because the top and senior managers feel responsible and they may think that a poor performance rating reflects on them. If this happens, don't be concerned. You might remind them that the findings reflect a self-diagnosis, but don't push it. Remember, you are sowing a few seeds and starting a new conversation.

At the end of your investigation, remember that nobody gets indicted. No offenders are brought to justice. The decision effectiveness assessment starts a conversation by finding indications that your matrix is misfiring. It is designed to detect whether the matrix is working, not to identify fault. There may be none. Remember that each separate hierarchy in the matrix has its own business objectives. So, a breakdown in decision effectiveness can happen simply because some decisions do not fit the strategic intent of more than one group. Prosecute the system and not the individuals within it.

An Example

Let's use the findings that we showed earlier to illustrate how the decision effectiveness assessment might play out. The traffic light summary is repeated below in Figure 13.5.

Management Seniority (horizontal)

First, we compare the findings within groups of top, senior, and mid-level leaders, and, immediately, we see some interesting contrasts. When considering both decision flow and speed, top-level global leaders have a different opinion of performance from their top local and top regional counterparts.

Top-level global leaders report that there are minimal revisions, revisits, or reprioritization of decisions. However, top-level local and regional leaders do not agree. Is this a blind-spot? Do top-level global leaders mistakenly believe that decisions flow down through the organization unchanged?

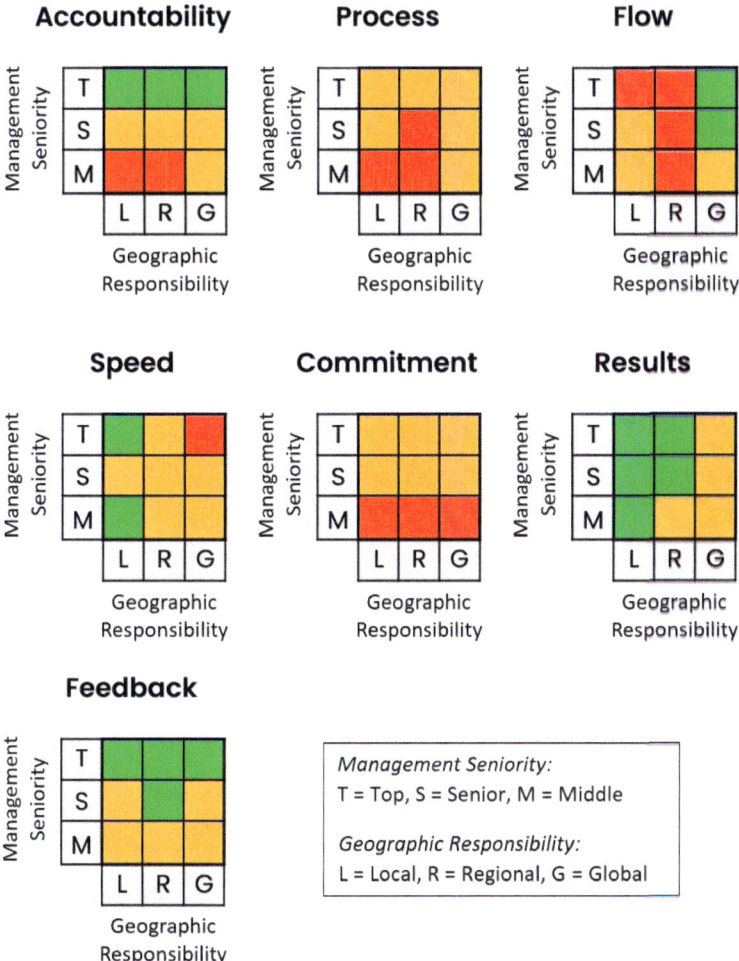

Figure 13.5 Example Performance Ratings for Decision Effectiveness

At the same time, these top-level global leaders note that decisions are not implemented quickly. Could this issue be related to decision flow? It is worth checking out. It may be useful to go back to some of the top-level leaders to find out what happened with some recent global decisions.

In your search for dysfunction, don't forget to highlight what is working well. In this example, all top-level leaders want to push decision-making down into the organization and they are committed to improving decision effectiveness overall.

Geographic Responsibility (vertical)

The second step in the diagnosis is to look separately at the groups of local, regional, and global stakeholders. A lot is going on here too.

To begin with, there is quite a difference of opinion on whether accountability for decisions is pushed down in the organization. Local and regional top-level leaders all agree that decisions are pushed down but local and regional mid-level leaders say the opposite! They also say that the decision-making process is not consistent or well-understood. There is also some valuable feedback on decision commitment as local, regional and even global middle managers indicate that they are not involved in decisions that they will execute. There is a clear issue here because these managers might be frustrated and disengaged.

Local Middle and Global Top

Finally, we look at the differences between these interdependent yet very separate groups. Not surprisingly, there are many contrasting opinions. In particular, we see that these two groups are poles apart when it comes to who is making the decisions, how they travel through the organization, and how quickly they are implemented. It is so dangerous for top-level global leaders to have such a different understanding of how their decisions are disseminated from the group that would inevitably execute them.

You may have suspicions about where these breakdowns occur. Again, don't rush to answer this question. The decision effectiveness assessment has shown that there is some dysfunction. Your global matrix is misfiring in some places, but you don't have the data yet to understand the root causes.

In this example, we will have shown top-level leaders that their understanding of their decision-making does not hold across the global matrix. That insight alone can be game-changing. However, the answer is not to revamp decision-making across the company. Indeed, decision effectiveness is a bellwether, a symptomatic indicator of deeper dysfunction. What is needed now is further work to reveal the full scope of the dysfunction and why it happens where it does.

14. The Value of Strategy

What is the one thing that global strategy needs above everything else? What is more important than great leadership, more valuable than superior insights, more essential even than having perfect coherence between the company's capabilities and the objectives that it desires?

The correct answer is always going to be that an effective and successful strategy must have the energy and the engagement of its executors— that is, if it is ever to be more than just a statement of intent. Indeed, a thought-provoking definition is that strategy is simply directional preparation for what the people on the front lines may encounter. Abstracted, this seems to be such a straightforward riddle. Strategy is both the deciding and the doing. Yet, we know that it is the act of bridging these two where so many organizations run into trouble. This takes us back to the fallacy of one-size-fits-all strategies, the disconnecting effect of tribalism, and the flawed matrix that rewards separateness. In particular, this reminds us why it is so important that the executors of global strategy feel that they own it and that they see important value in pursuing it.

For the global team, most of a strategy's executors are thousands of miles away. It may be impossible to engage with them all directly. Instead, it is common organizational behavioral practice to have a chain of stakeholders linking the most senior global leaders to those on the front lines. Each strategic decision is passed like a baton down the chain.

In a perfect system, each stakeholder would pass along the same global priorities to the next one in the chain. However, the real world is not like that. As we discussed, in a global matrix, each stakeholder has separate and defined objectives, different pressures, and—because they work within different hierarchies—different reward systems. So, even in the most coherent organizations, it is more than likely that each stakeholder in the chain will apply some of their own considerations and biases, making small but cumulative changes to decisions, objectives, and priorities. A chain, as the adage goes, is only as strong as its weakest link. Unfortunately, for global strategy, the inconsistencies in every link of the stakeholder chain are compounded. As the changes pile up, they dilute the strategy's intent and modify the actions that will be taken.

While these changes to the strategy can water down or derail its purpose and impact, the greater risk from the chain is that it enables stakeholders to become gatekeepers to the strategy. Global leaders have little or no visibility down the chain. So, if some stakeholders object or opt to play theater, then the chain can break without the global team even being aware: they may have no clear signal that something has gone wrong.

A linear chain of authority is more suited to command and control of a singular hierarchy. We use this stakeholder chain approach in the global matrix because it is familiar, but it doesn't work. So, what if we bypassed this stepwise stakeholder chain approach? What if we engaged with all of the stakeholders at the same time? This sounds very straightforward and a breeze to execute, and it is. The tool that we will discuss in this chapter is as simple as it is powerful. That it is not standard practice is a curious puzzle.

Purpose

A *Strategy Value* assessment is a powerful addition to every global and regional business strategy. The concept is simple: To allow every stakeholder, every link in the chain, to rate the value, to them, of the strategy. While this is no replacement for true collaboration, it offers a rudimentary indication of worldwide fit and the risk of disengagement.

This assessment ensures, with transparency, that everyone understands where the strategy is likely to deliver value and where it is not. It is also a gentle way of encouraging collaboration. For the strategy's authors, it is a test of its relevance. For its potential executors, it provides a means for high-level feedback. For both, this tool encourages a discussion of the strategy based on its merits. Having a conversation about what it can achieve is one step closer to discussing how each stakeholder might bring the strategy to life.

Remember that universal and equivalent value for every stakeholder Is likely to be impossible. There is no failure if some countries or regions see less value in the proposed strategy. That is normal. "Global" rarely means "everywhere." Consider, for example, that many strategies focus on trends that are present in some countries but not in others. However, by acknowledging where the value lies, and also where it does not, the stakeholders can start a conversation about participation, prioritization, and commitment.

This assessment can also highlight opportunities to improve the value of the strategy that may have been missed. Indeed, it can be a good idea to use this tool iteratively as strategy takes shape, such as for quick feedback on an early prototype.

The strategy value assessment combats several fragmenting forces at once. It reveals how a single strategy does not benefit all stakeholders in the same way and to the same degree. In turn, this ensures that strategy is not rolled out blindly. Also, the feedback from regions and countries is likely to expose any misrepresentations in the strategy, such as inappropriate over-simplification. Chief Executive Officers and company executives can be reassured that the strategy is not created in a vacuum. Indeed, positive ratings from region and country leaders are a de facto endorsement.

If this simple assessment were a requirement of every global strategy presentation to senior executives, we would dramatically reduce the theatrics and the waste.

Methodology

The strategy value assessment takes the form of a short and simple questionnaire that we ask local leaders to complete. We present the findings for each region or market cluster in Table 14.1. In this example, we show survey responses from five markets, A1 to A5, all within a single region, Region A.

Table 14.1. Strategy Value Assessment

Region A	Value 1	Value 2	Value 3	Resources
Market A1	◯	◯	◯	◯
Market A2	◯	◯	◯	◯
Market A3	◯	◯	◯	◯
Market A4	◯	◯	◯	◯
Market A5	◯	◯	◯	◯

Top-level country leaders are the appropriate respondents for the assessment, given that they are setting priorities for local execution. This is empowering and engaging because it allows these mission-critical stakeholders to lead a 'What's-in-it-for-me?' conversation.

Table 14.2 below shows the structure of a short survey that uses a five-point Likert scale to query each respondent's agreement with a set of value statements. It is important to create specific statements that capture the priorities of your strategy, such that they are not open to different interpretations. Use explicit statements of value to ensure that everyone understands them in the same way—for example, gaining market share, investing in a certain segment, prioritizing growth in a certain channel, closing the gap versus a competitor. If you write strategies that feature specific multinational initiatives, then include a statement for each one.

Table 14.2 Example Strategy Value Survey

Question: Do you agree with the following statement?

1 = strongly disagree, 2 = disagree, 3 = neither agree nor disagree, 4 = agree, 5 = strongly agree

Execution of this strategy will deliver meaningful financial value or build important new capabilities for the business that I am responsible for.	1	2	3	4	5
a) Invest ahead of demand and expand portfolio into a premium segment with at least one new product launch in the next 12 months.					
b) Strengthen the core business by realigning the business model to new channel dynamics, including e-commerce.					
c) Increase scale among smaller customers to 20% of total revenue, offering competitive financial terms and greater service.					
d) The organization that I am responsible for has the resources and capabilities necessary to execute this strategy.					

Note the important language in these value statements: '... *for the business that I am responsible for.*' So, your colleague Dirk, who is the country manager for Austria, is only answering for his business in Austria.

Add a time frame to each value statement as appropriate. Do not exceed 24 months. Future returns become increasingly less valuable and our respondents are encouraged to focus on relatively short-term targets.

The final statement in Table 14.2, which confirms resources and capabilities, is not about the strategy's value. However, this is the perfect place to include this. It allows local leaders to identify challenges to the execution. In particular, it encourages a discussion of prioritization. After all, for local leaders, it is not unusual for a global strategy to seem incremental to all of their ongoing objectives. It is a new priority to add to all of the priorities that they already have. This gives them the room to highlight any concerns that they may have about their ability to execute all that they may now have to deal with.

It is perfectly acceptable and probably appropriate to ask the regional leaders to administer the survey to their direct reports. They may even influence the results in their favor and that is fine. Be sensitive to tribal authority.

Traffic Lights

Once the responses are received, the next step, which may be familiar by now, is to translate the findings into green, yellow, and red traffic lights. Assign the colors based on the responses, as follows:

Green: Strongly Agree
Yellow: Agree
Red: Neither Agree or Disagree, Disagree or Strongly Disagree

It is important to assign a red light to any response that indicates that a local leader does not find meaningful value in the strategy.

Once you have translated the survey responses into traffic light colors, then you can populate the assessment as in Table 14.3.

Table 14.3 Example Strategy Value Assessment

Region A	Value 1	Value 2	Value 3	Resources
Market A1	🟢	🟢	🟡	🟢
Market A2	🟢	🟡	🟢	🟢
Market A3	🟢	🟡	🟡	🔴
Market A4	🟡	🟡	🔴	🔴
Market A5	🟢	🟢	🟡	🟡

Diagnosis

The assessment provides a lot of information about a strategy's perceived value in a visually intuitive way. It is not a rigorous analysis, but it is an important first impression and this feedback can be very useful. That said, don't be tempted to tackle any red lights straightaway. The ratings are not decisions. Each one opens the door for a conversation that starts to link decisions to action. The feedback is a gift: It is not a fault-finding critique.

As per Table 14.4 below, stay at a high level and scan vertically up and down the assessment responses. Start by reviewing the collective response for each value statement. If you see a lot of green and yellow lights, then you know that part of the strategy has traction. For a global strategy, start by comparing the responses to each value statement between regions. Do some regions anticipate greater value from the strategy than others? Remember, global strategy doesn't need to be executed identically everywhere. Perhaps your strategy is right for some regions but less appropriate for others. Maybe. Don't draw strong conclusions. Think of the red traffic lights simply as warning lights not to proceed without further discussion.

Table 14.4 Review Strategy Value and Market Engagement

Region A	Value 1	Value 2	Value 3	Resources
Market A1				
Market A2				
Market A3				
Market A4				
Market A5				

Region A	Value 1	Value 2	Value 3	Resources
Market A1				
Market A2				
Market A3				
Market A4				
Market A5				

The contrasts between country managers' responses can be instructive. Mine the differences where one country manager sees opportunity and another does not. You may help uncover the possibility to turn a red light to yellow or green.

Looking horizontally across the assessment gives us a sense of each market's overall engagement with the strategy. It can be useful to know each market's prospects and growth forecast when looking at this. For example, is a market that finds little value in any part of the global strategy on a positive trajectory? What makes it different? What insights can you draw? A wholesale deviation from global strategy by one or more markets should trigger a valuable conversation.

Action

With your assessment in hand, the first step is to understand the feedback and to ensure that those giving feedback feel understood as fully as possible. Ideally, talk to each country leader individually. As a rule, asking people to defend an opinion in public encourages them to fortify their position. That is unhelpful at this stage. So, meet with them one-on-one. Dispel any tension with gratitude and focus on hearing them out. Have no other agenda other than soaking up their market knowledge and expertise. Also, be clear that nobody is making a decision. This is true because the strategy is not final. The trick to making these conversations work is not to be wedded to a certain outcome.

Begin with markets that identify the most value in the strategy and learn why. This is good news but does the strategy give too much away? Ask local leaders to tell you what they need to commit to this strategy. Use these insights to develop an action plan to improve the value scores, to turn yellows into greens. This can be powerful. Simply asking the question creates goodwill. However, don't expect common themes among their requests although, of course, that makes the job easier. Respect the differences.

This information gives you a useful contrast when speaking with country managers who identified omissions, challenges, or barriers to the value that you may have thought the strategy promises. Understand from these stakeholders how their current objectives compare and contrast with the global strategy. Also, learn from those markets that claim insufficient resources to execute it. Are these findings surprising? Are they acceptable? Are there remedies that would change the ratings? What are the local leaders asking for? Look for patterns.

Now, armed with your assessment and a "straight-from-the-horse's-mouth" explanation for each rating, hold a session for understanding with regional leaders. As tribal chieftains and odds-on strategy gatekeepers, these stakeholders are critical to the success of the global strategy. They may wish the steer their country managers' feedback. That is their prerogative. As before, be clear that this conversation is for input and learning. The strategy is not final and no decisions or commitments are being made.

This assessment, and the subsequent exploration offer an opportunity to improve the reach and impact of the global strategy. Nevertheless, some markets may not be a good fit. Again, this is not a failure: A rising tide does not lift all boats equally.

Each red traffic light is a valuable warning. The low-value rating was always there but now it is in the open and we can talk about it. We are in a much stronger position if we want the global strategy to have an impact. Yet, some global leaders find this experience to be an unpleasant surprise. Despite all of the evidence to the contrary, it can be a reality shock to learn that global strategy is not a magic trump card that elicits compliance. With little accountability, and in a global matrix that hides their defiance, most regional and country leaders have the informal power to silently opt in or out. Let's choose to collaborate. Without question, the feedback in this assessment requires global teams to respond. Building a strategy that is both the deciding and the doing is hard work.

Finally, enjoy the insight and authority that this simple tool offers. Continue to invest in the connections you build.

An Example

Let's look at an example to see how this strategy value assessment can work. We will use Table 14.2 again.

Table 14.2 Example Strategy Value Survey

Question: Do you agree with the following statement?

1 = strongly disagree, 2 = disagree, 3 = neither agree nor disagree, 4 = agree, 5 = strongly agree

Execution of this strategy will deliver meaningful financial value or build important new capabilities for the business that I am responsible for.	1	2	3	4	5
a) Invest ahead of demand and expand portfolio into a premium segment with at least 1 new product launch in the next 12 months.					
b) Strengthen the core business by realigning the business model to new channel dynamics, including e-commerce.					
c) Increase scale among smaller customers to 20% of total revenue, offering competitive financial terms and greater service.					
d) The organization that I am responsible for has the resources and capabilities necessary to execute this strategy.					

In Table 14.5 below, we can see the separate assessments provided by three regions: A, B and C.

Overall, the feedback is very positive. Most markets agree to see value in the strategy and there are only two red warning lights across all three value statements.

We start by exploring with country managers how they might turn their agreement into strong agreement. This may not be possible. The example strategy value statements in Table 14.2 illustrate this point as they are going to be more relevant and therefore more valuable depending upon the market-level opportunities in the "premium segment," "e-commerce," or with "smaller customers." Indeed, we should expect variability.

Table 14.5 Example Strategy Value Assessments: Regions A, B and C

Region A	Value 1	Value 2	Value 3	Resources
Market A1	🟢	🟢	🟡	🟢
Market A2	🟢	🟡	🟢	🟢
Market A3	🟢	🟡	🟡	🔴
Market A4	🟡	🟡	🔴	🔴
Market A5	🟢	🟢	🟡	🟡

Region B	Value 1	Value 2	Value 3	Resources
Market B1	🟢	🟢	🟡	🔴
Market B2	🟡	🟢	🟡	🟡
Market B3	🟢	🟡	🟡	🟡
Market B4	🔴	🟢	🟡	🔴

Region C	Value 1	Value 2	Value 3	Resources
Market C1	🟢	🟡	🟡	🟢
Market C2	🟢	🟢	🟡	🟡

In this example, most markets appear to be quite engaged with the strategy overall. That said, there are a few managers who see value but claim not to have the resources to act. This offers another good learning opportunity.

You can see how quickly this strategy value assessment enables us a) to interrogate the strategy for fit, and b) to gauge the reactions of critical stakeholders to each of its components. It makes you wonder about global strategies that are approved and implemented without this perspective.

15. Global Connectivity

In Chapter 5, The Incoherent Matrix, we discussed how common it is to unwisely assume that our organization is set up to support a global strategy. We are making many assumptions when we do this but, just looking at one dimension—connectivity—we find that very few stakeholders agree to adopt practices that connect the separate parts of their organization. It seems clear that, beyond perhaps an annual gathering of senior leaders, international connectedness is not often promoted even though it is an essential enabling part of any international strategy.

In practice, different parts of an organization tend to connect differently. More dependent parties want more access. Others, who prefer their autonomy and independence, resist connecting for fear of forced compromise. Meanwhile, no one has a clear understanding of how well or how poorly their matrix organization links together.

Imagine a map of the world. Now, mentally superimpose a network of glowing lines that link all the people who collaborate across your organization. The number and the strength of these links describe the active and interdependent behavior of these people and their teams across the globe. Energy to do work flows in both directions along these lines. The more connecting lines there are, the more people are interacting. The links become stronger as the parties collaborate more in support of one another.

In each country, the density of these links will be high. It is easier to form a large number of strong connections with people who are nearby. Between different countries, there will be fewer connections and then even fewer between regions. Also, the density of these links may not be the same everywhere. Some parts of your company will simply connect more. Sometimes geography, language, or culture play a role and sometimes there are global functions that are simply more connected than others.

In each multinational organization, we experience a unique connectivity map. This map describes if and where we have trust, effective decision flow, and collaboration. Are we aware of it? Are we conscious of the weak or missing links in our global matrix? Very few companies actively monitor matrix performance. This is a fundamental capability, but there is not even a language to talk about it. Yet, without strong connections in all the right places, competitive global performance will be out of reach.

We are aware of our immediate connections. Beyond that, we need to do more than hope for the best. In this chapter, you will discover a tool to assess the connectivity within your global company. This is a powerful and eye-opening diagnosis. The work will promote global connectivity as a vital strategy enabler and also trigger meaningful and lasting change if there are gaps.

Purpose

Let's define the term *globalization* as the things that we do within our company so that we are more likely to succeed as a global business. Here, we are going to explore different *degrees of globalization* following the logic that a more globalized company will be more effective in pursuing global goals.

Globalization is not static: It evolves, and sometimes devolves, over time. There are changes with new leaders, new strategies, shifts in culture, and new technology that help us to connect and collaborate. Globalization is also not the same across a company. Typically, an organizational matrix will show a range of degrees of globalization within it.

Globalization is not a measure of geographic scope and scale. It is also not about how many countries or regions of operation there are. This is a measure of your company's ability and commitment to operate globally. When you can measure this, you will learn the extent to which your organization is ready, or not ready, to support and deliver a multinational business strategy.

Two drivers of globalization are easy to diagnose: *connectivity* and *engagement*. Global connectivity is a measure of capability. When we count the connections throughout the global matrix, we are assessing only whether the ability to collaborate exists. Global engagement, which we will cover in the next chapter, completes the picture by telling us how invested we are to use these connections to trust, trade, and collaborate in pursuit of mutual benefit. Alone, each driver is important and understanding how we are performing will reveal some valuable insight. Together, they can provide a prescriptive analysis that answers the question, 'Are we set up for global success?'

So, in this chapter, we focus on connectivity, which describes the number and strength of international company connections. Think again of that imaginary network of glowing lines that link your company across geographies. This tool, which we call the "connectivity map", will help you to understand the number of lines and their thickness. It will enable you to chart that critical part of your company's ability to operate globally.

As you will see, this is a simple and powerful diagnosis that also serves as a gap analysis to improve.

The Connectivity Map

To begin, let's revisit our 3×3 model of a global matrix, as shown below in Figure 15.1.

This simple model is useful to illustrate the overlap of management and geographic hierarchies. We used it before to identify the different types of stakeholders in a global matrix. This time, we need to identify all the separate local and regional stakeholders so we can explore the connections between them. This means that our model needs to become more complex. We need a way to view each connection from global to all regions, between regions, and key countries, while also including separate management hierarchies.

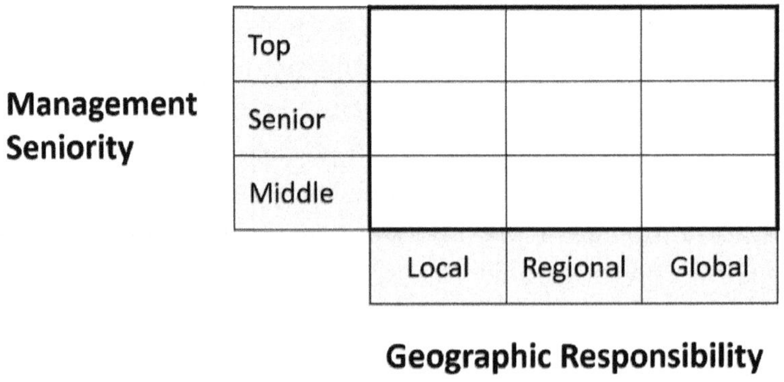

		Local	Regional	Global
Management Seniority	Top			
	Senior			
	Middle			

Geographic Responsibility

Figure 15.1 A 3×3 Model of a Global Matrix

The full global matrix model is three-dimensional and so complex that it is not useful as a diagnostic tool. Fortunately, there are several shortcuts to keep it simple and to speed up the assessment. That said, it is useful to visualize a global matrix in all its complex glory. Figure 15.2 shows an example of this, featuring four regions, each with three priority local markets.

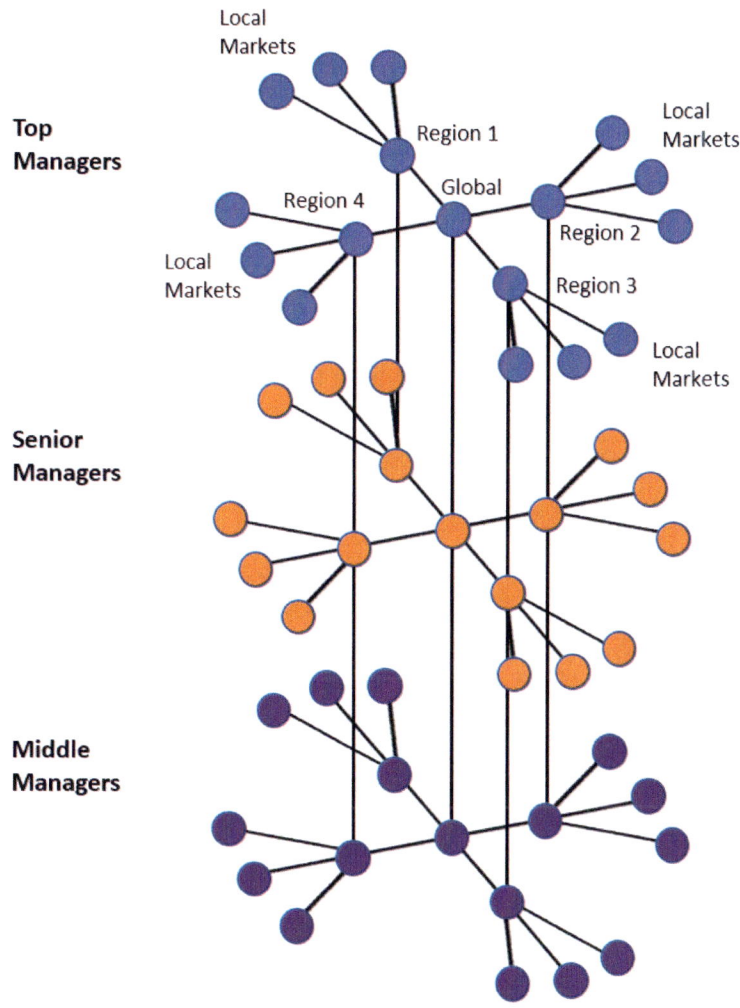

Figure 15.2 Global Matrix Connections—Full Model

Rather than wrestle with this complex model, we can simplify our analysis considerably because not all connections are equally important.

The connections between top, senior, and middle managers within global, regional, or local groups, are often strong. This makes sense because they are reinforced by proximity and a direct reporting structure. So, we can ignore these direct reporting connections in our diagnosis. Any connections that are not between peer groups are less important to matrix performance, but they are not unimportant. However, it is the connections, often informal, between peers and across geographies that can make or break matrix performance.

As we analyze global connectivity, we find most insight by isolating the connections between geographic groups and we look at this within each management level. Inspired by Table 15.2, we break the work down into three separate diagnoses, one for each peer group. That is, we build a separate connectivity map for top, senior, and middle managers.

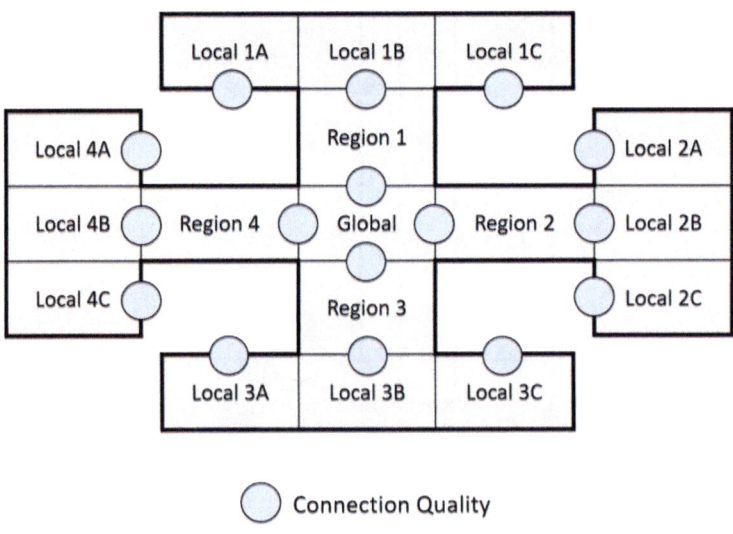

Figure 15.3 A Peer-Level Connectivity Map

Figure 15.3 shows an example of a peer-level connectivity map. In this case, we show four regions and three local countries for each. In the diagram, the circles between the stakeholders will be used to indicate the quality of their connections. The way that we gather the necessary information and then diagnose this capability is explained in the next section.

Methodology

The first step to building the connectivity map is to collect some objective information. As you will see, this means that we don't need to talk to both connecting parties to assess their connection. A short conversation with top, senior, and mid-level regional managers is often enough to map all of the connections across the matrix.

The assessment focuses on three variables: Frequency, duration, and the intimacy of each connection. For simplicity, we grade the responses to build a Connection Quality Assessment using the framework in Figure 15.4:

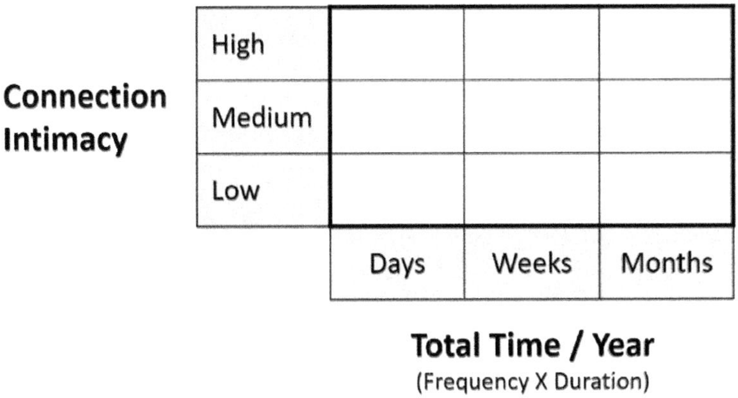

		Days	Weeks	Months
Connection Intimacy	High			
	Medium			
	Low			

Total Time / Year
(Frequency X Duration)

Figure 15.4 Connection Quality Assessment

Total Time / Year

For each pair of stakeholders, we need to understand how often they connect and for how long during the year. If there are weekly calls, a recurring monthly meeting, or perhaps an annual summit, add up all of the time spent. Assume eight-hour workdays and convert your total into an aggregated number of days.

For example, let's say regional and global senior leaders meet once a year for three days of annual planning, a 1-day monthly innovation update, and that between scheduled project meetings and ad hoc calls they connect for a further 48 hours, which is 6 more working days. This adds up to a total of 21 days in the year, which would qualify for the *Weeks* column in the assessment.

Connection Intimacy

We objectively define connection intimacy based on how the connection happens. This is an important variable because, of course, the more intimate the connection, the stronger it is:

High Intimacy:	Face-to-face, a two-way discussion, social interaction.
Medium Intimacy:	Face-to-face one-way presentations, video calls.
Low Intimacy:	Remote presentations, email or phone calls.

It is important to favor real, live, and face-to-face connections ahead of other interactions. This is inarguable when you consider that at least 65% of human communication is non-verbal. Even with video, we struggle to gauge a person's real reactions or emotional state. For group calls, the communication difficulties are even greater. This is not to say that digital communication is ineffective. Just the opposite. For example, video calls improve connection quality overall by replacing low-intimacy technologies, such as email and phone calls. However, to build rapport and trust we, as a human species, do considerably better when we connect in person.

When our connection counterpart is from another country and culture, we need to do a lot more work to build a strong connection. Each party has more to learn and the journey to build trust is longer. Sometimes this can't be done without time spent face-to-face. Often, a meal, a glass of wine, or an embarrassing karaoke performance is necessary as a catalyst for trust.

So, make a note of how the different stakeholders connect and capture the information as shown in Figure 15.5. This example describes the overall connection quality between regional senior managers and their global and local counterparts in markets A, B, and C.

Connection Intimacy				
High			Local A	
Medium			Global	Local B
Low		Local C		
		Days	Weeks	Months

Total Time / Year
(Frequency X Duration)

Figure 15.5 Example Assessment for Regional Senior Managers

We create more of these assessment tables until we have captured all of the connections in the connectivity map and at each peer group level (Figure 15.2).

The next step is to grade and color-code the connection quality assessment tables. Again, we will use the tried and trusted traffic-light approach. Green indicates a high connection quality, which reflects higher intimacy over a longer period. Red indicates lower intimacy and less time to connect. Yellow lives between the two, indicating medium quality, which has room for improvement. Figure15.6 shows how it is done for our example.

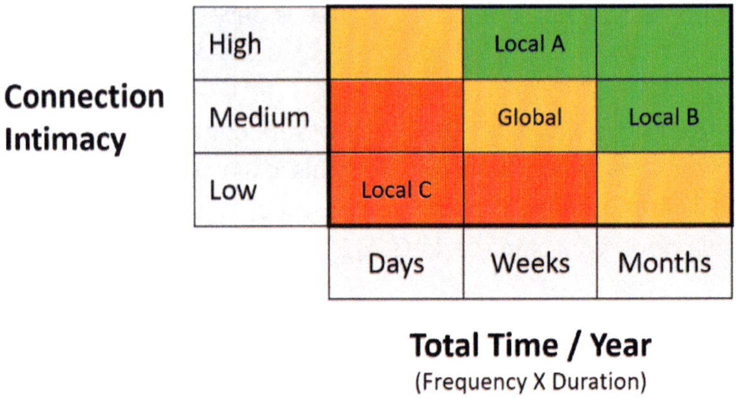

Connection Intimacy				
High			Local A	
Medium			Global	Local B
Low	Local C			
	Days	Weeks	Months	

Total Time / Year
(Frequency X Duration)

Figure 15.6 Completed Example Assessment

Diagnosis

Once the connection quality assessments are done, you can apply the color coding to a connectivity map and create one for each peer group of top, senior, and mid-level managers. Figure 15.7 shows an example with four regions, each of which features three markets. Once again, we have a simple yet powerful and visually intuitive diagnosis. We can see connection quality at a glance and immediately understand where there are gaps and whether there may be serious consequences.

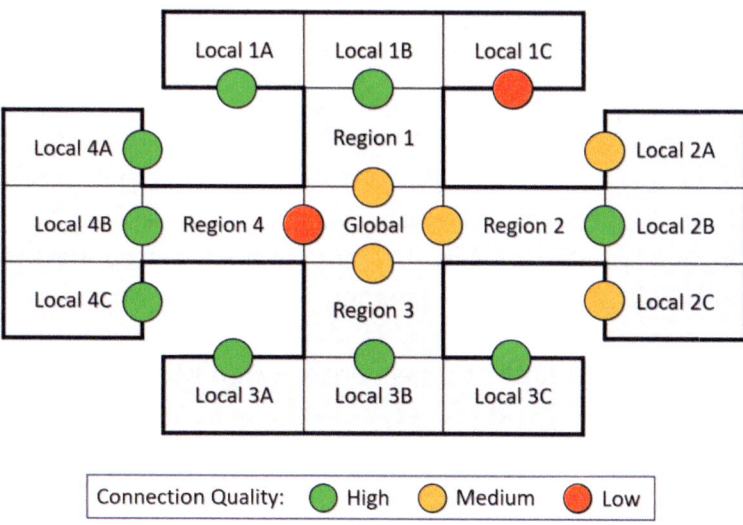

Figure 15.7 Example: A Peer-Level Connectivity Map showing Connection Quality

This is self-reported and objective behavioral information that reflects how—and how often— company stakeholders connect. It is not a blame game. We have not collected any data on stakeholders' willingness to connect.

Use the connectivity map to highlight connections that would benefit from improved investment. For example, in Figure 15.3, it is easy to see that the connections between global and regional managers can be improved. In particular, the connection between managers of Global and Region 4 may need attention.

Red traffic lights appear dramatic, but the cause can be very ordinary. For example, the region furthest from your company headquarters, and with the greatest time zone difference, often has strong internal connections but the link to headquarters is weaker than it is for other regions. Don't assume that low connection quality is deliberate.

Look into the green traffic lights too. Do you have best practices that can be adopted more broadly?

The most effective way to use the connectivity map is to look for contrasting differences. Try to understand why connections that should be equivalent in quality are not. Why are some local—regional connections better than others? Why are some regions less connected to global than others? We want to understand why.

It is also very useful to contrast the connections at different management levels. This will show where good connections may be happening within a geographic group. It is not always necessary to have high-quality connections at all levels. For example, if top-level managers are struggling to commit a lot of time to connecting, then their senior managers can sometimes pick up the slack. However, if these senior managers show the same low levels of connection quality, then you may have found a more profound breakdown in connecting behavior.

You will often find the strongest and greenest connectivity map among senior managers. Typically, they have more time to connect than their top-level managers and they are more accessible. They also have the authority to launch and lead international collaboration, which makes them a valuable partner.

There is no single best global connectivity map. It doesn't need to be all green. Where your company invests in building connections should depend on its international strategy. Connectivity is an enabling capability, and it will wax and wane to reflect geographic priorities and the need for collaboration to get things done.

Here are some questions to help guide your diagnosis:

- What are the connecting practices that generate red traffic lights? (e.g. Are there too few in-person interactions, presentations but no debate?)

- Is connection quality specific to one layer of management or more? (e.g. Are top-level managers modeling a behavior that senior managers are following?)

- Is connection quality common to other similar geographic groups? (e.g. Is one local market uniquely disconnected?)

- What are the connecting practices that generate green traffic lights? (e.g. Are there frequent collaborative workshops?)

Action

While there are global companies that view their internal connectivity as a competitive advantage, most organizations will treat connectivity as an enabler to a planned collaboration. If this describes your organization, then this means that an assessment of global connectivity probably needs a context, a cross-matrix collaboration that depends on interpersonal relationships and trust between the stakeholders. This can take many forms, from a new global strategy or multinational initiative to a new structure and new leadership teams.

It can also be appropriate to frame this assessment as a search for best practices.

We have discussed how top-level regional leaders are powerful gatekeepers to global collaboration and, in this regard, they are not often held to account. So, go slowly if you experience resistance from top-level regional leaders. They may be concerned that this objective assessment will show less connectivity with the global team than they portray. Imagine a regional president who has assured their Chief Executive Officer that a global initiative has their full support. Too many instances of low connection quality may call this assurance into question.

This is a great tool to clarify whether an organization that claims to be collaborative across hierarchies and geographies is acting accordingly.

It is also useful to understand whether global functional teams are biased in their support of regions and markets. For example, are Research and Development supporting the region where they are located to the detriment of others?

An Example

Figure 15.8 shows a global connectivity map for all three management levels: Top, Senior, and Middle. In addition to assessing connection quality within each peer group, we can also look for repeating patterns.

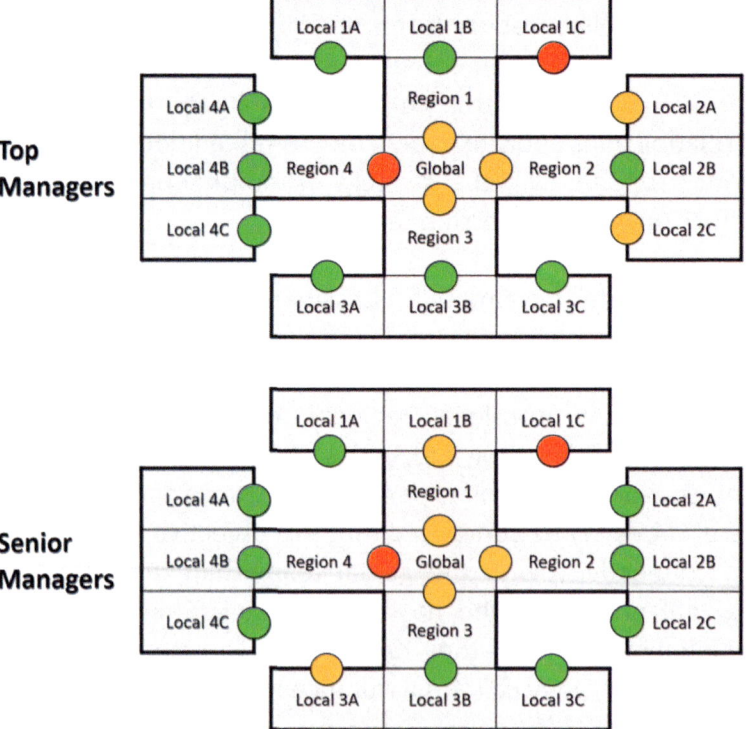

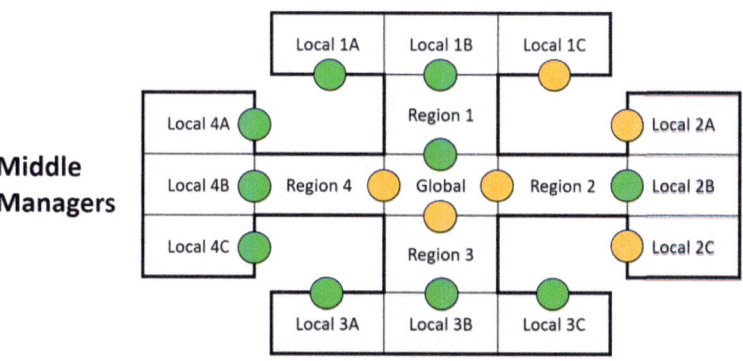

Figure 15.8 Example of a Full Connectivity Map

Overall, this example describes a locally connected organization. The map indicates several gaps in behavior, the most notable being that there is opportunity to improve connection quality between the global team and every region. This is underscored by the similar pattern we can see in all three peer groups. Why are the global leaders staying at home? There is not enough interaction and face-to-face collaboration. Sometimes these connection challenges are created by policy or culture. Yet, whatever the reason, a global team needs to be well-connected or it is going to have a tough time creating value. There is a link between connection quality and focus, and this organization is not focused on global considerations.

In addition, Region 4 is well-connected locally but the relationship with global stakeholders appears to be weak. There is also Market 1C, which has low connection quality with its parent region. The assessment does not tell us why—simply that the desired behavior is not there. Typically, these specific and isolated cases are no surprise.

16. Global Engagement

Global strategy feels unnatural to many participants. After all, collaborating in a matrix and across geographic lines is not the norm. The structure of these relationships can be unfamiliar and it is not unusual for people to feel uncomfortable, particularly when expectations of their performance are uncertain. Individual objectives make sense, but shared objectives can be confusing and may not fit with other responsibilities. For some, to support a global initiative means working outside of their traditional job function and it may not be clear whether this is important or even a priority. Indeed, both reasons for commitment and measures of success are often less clear when we are asked to operate in a matrix.

So, how do you know whether your organization is really committed to delivering a global strategy? Perhaps some stakeholders are on board but is everyone whom you need in the boat? How can you tell? It is not easy, particularly if you want to be proactive and avoid potential disappointment. Also, a lack of engagement is not always deliberate. Factors such as structure, leader behaviors, cultural barriers, and even our propensity to avoid conflict can easily erode our desire to engage.

In this chapter, we break down global engagement into its primary drivers. Knowing what to look for, we can build upon the connectivity map in the last chapter to show not only where our organization has the ability to collaborate but also whether it is motivated to trust, trade, and collaborate.

Purpose

Thinking about connectivity, we previously imagined a map with glowing lines connecting the people who collaborate across our global organization. These lines represent active and interdependent behavior, which is vital to support any global strategy. These connections are critically important and, typically, the more of them there are the stronger your company's global capabilities will be.

Now, imagine that each glowing line or connection has its own dimmer switch. If one or both of the connected stakeholders is not fully engaged, then the glowing line dims as their connection weakens. The capability to connect may be strong but the connecting parties must both want to achieve it. As we know, there are many forces of fragmentation that can cause the most committed stakeholder to disengage. In the end, a global organization is a human network and, at all levels, an Individual's desire to support global strategy should never be taken for granted.

Global engagement is a difficult nut to crack. It is proven through action and performance, but we can't afford to wait and see. Hope, as they say, is not a strategy. So, how do we diagnose engagement across our organization? How do you assess whether people are likely to trust, trade, and collaborate outside of their solid reporting lines?

Also, how can we probe commitment positively and not offend? The answer lies in an essential distinction: Engagement is not the same as willingness. This is important and we need to be careful with the language. Many external factors affect engagement. Often these drivers are beyond an individual's control and, therefore, the resulting behavior is not always a reflection of their personal choice. When you consider that low engagement can have serious and negative implications, it never pays to form a hasty ad hominem opinion and ignore the context.

As before, to avoid this distraction, we stick to a process that will allow all parties to create their self-assessments. Even so, the findings of this diagnosis can be sensitive. We will return to this point later with advice.

We defined *globalization* as the things that we do, our actions, and our attitudes so that we are more likely to succeed as a global business. Indeed, in the previous chapter, we explored *connectivity*, which is a company's ability to connect and a key driver of globalization. This is an objective proficiency and we assess it using a connectivity map. A second driver is *engagement*, which is a measure of how much each stakeholder will invest of themselves in international collaboration. Together, these drivers of globalization describe our ability and our desire to come together across the matrix.

We will break down global engagement into measurable parts so that we can understand the degree to which different stakeholders will commit. We will then combine this information with the connectivity map to create a complete picture, a map of our company's globalization.

The Globalization Map

This tool builds upon the connectivity map that was introduced in the last chapter.

In Figure 16.1, you can see a peer-level map showing four regions and three local countries for each one. The circles that we previously used to indicate connection quality are now split in two to show both connection quality and engagement between each pair of stakeholders.

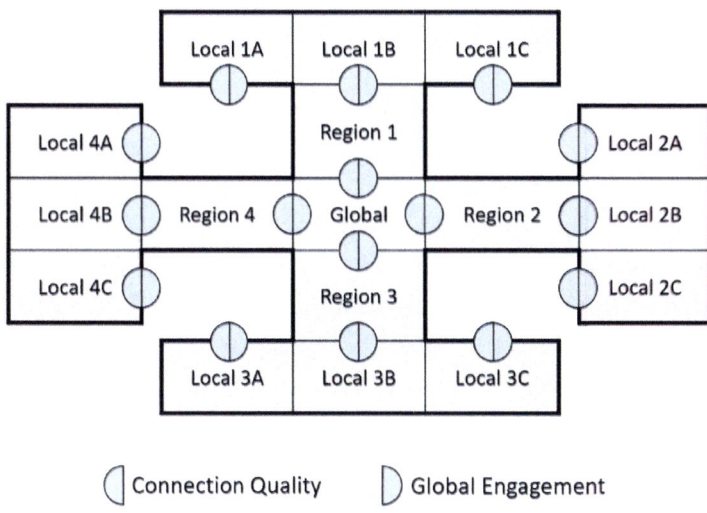

Local 1A	Local 1B	Local 1C
Local 4A	Region 1	Local 2A
Local 4B	Region 4	Global	Region 2	Local 2B
Local 4C	Region 3	Local 2C
Local 3A	Local 3B	Local 3C

Connection Quality   Global Engagement

Figure 16.1 Peer-Level Globalization Map showing Connectivity and Engagement

The map is starting to look a little complicated. However, once we have populated it with connection quality and engagement information, it becomes intuitive and very powerful.

Connectivity and engagement are not independent. For example, you can imagine a situation whereby two stakeholders rarely connect because they have little desire to collaborate. Conversely, we can recognize that, without access to frequent quality interactions, it is hard to build a level of trust that is necessary to offer a strong commitment. Indeed, it is rare to see high levels of engagement without strong connection quality.

We can learn a lot by observing changes in the relationship between connection capability and engagement. By comparing the two, seeing which is stronger, and then contrasting this with other peers, we can quickly build a picture of what is going on.

Methodology

Employee engagement is a top priority in every company, given its impact on performance and well-being. The same is true for global engagement if the company aspires to international success. Broad factors that improve engagement, such as career development, compensation, and equal opportunity, all still apply. However, we are most interested in a short list of drivers that have the most influence on global engagement. For these purposes, we need to focus on a smaller subset of engagement drivers. Specifically, we want to understand the factors that encourage trusting, trading, and collaborating between geographies and outside of solid reporting lines. These are the motivators that fuel active interdependence between connected global stakeholders. As you will see, these drivers highlight some of the toughest challenges of matrix operation.

For simplicity and utility, the list of drivers detailed below is condensed into as short a list as possible. These key drivers represent the most motivating factors that concentrate or dilute engagement. They are also very actionable if remediation is indicated.

Emotional Drivers

These fuel the personal desire of stakeholders to collaborate in a global matrix:

Fairness: Objectives and expectations are defined, agreed, and clearly communicated.

Significance: Participants know that their opinions and expertise matter.

Recognition: Participants know that their contributions will be valued and rewarded.

Rational Drivers

These provide rational motivation to unlock commitment:

Clarity: Objectives and expectations are defined, agreed, and clearly communicated.

Resources: Participants have what they need to get the job done.

Hierarchy: At least two levels of management are committed to the global work.

As with employee engagement in general, you can see from these drivers that top- and senior-level leaders have enormous influence. Global engagement starts at the top. Indeed, if top-level managers are not engaged, it is unusual to see a strong commitment from their direct reports.

In keeping with our mantra of simplicity, we investigate global engagement by asking a short set of questions about these drivers and by recording responses on a five-point Likert scale.

Table 16.1 Global Engagement Drivers Questionnaire

Question: For global initiatives in which you participate, do you agree with the following statements?

1 = strongly disagree, 2 = disagree, 3 = neither agree nor disagree, 4 = agree, 5 = strongly agree

	1	2	3	4	5
a) You receive fair value in exchange for your contribution.					
b) You are involved in decision-making about global work.					
c) Your contribution is valued and recognized.					
d) Your objectives and expectations are agreed and clear.					
e) You have what you need to get the job done.					
f) Two levels of management are committed to global work.					

As this is a measure of engagement, then, if there is a stronger agreement to these questions for other work, we can expect that work to take precedence.

When we were exploring connectivity, it was only necessary to talk to one party in a connected pair to understand if they were connecting. To assess engagement, we talk to the stakeholders who are closest to a strategy's execution.

As global strategy is pushed out from the center, we can expect engagement to decline the further away from global headquarters that you go. It is useful, therefore, to interview the least engaged party in a collaborating pair because, regardless of the other party, this is their maximum level of engagement. This means that, for a local—regional collaboration, we interview the local stakeholder. For a regional—global collaboration, we interview the regional stakeholder.

Traffic Lights

To translate the responses into green, yellow, and red traffic lights use the following formula: Average the scores for each target group and assign traffic lights as follows:

Green: An average score above 4.0

Yellow: An average score above 3 up to and including 4.0

Red: An average score of 3.0 and below

Achieving yellow or green is a high hurdle. This reflects just how difficult and uncommon it is to observe high levels of engagement across a global matrix. There is almost always room for improvement.
A red light means that, overall, your respondents did not agree that these key drivers of global engagement were present.

Diagnosis

Once you have completed the traffic light color-coding to rate global engagement for a peer group of either top-, senior-, or mid-level managers, then you can create your first Globalization Map. Figure 16.2A shows an example and then Figure 16.2B shows how this might evolve when you add the engagement ratings.

In Figure 16.2B, our understanding of the potential for global collaboration is much richer. There is a lot of information to sort through.

Figure 16.2A Example of a Peer-Group Connectivity Map

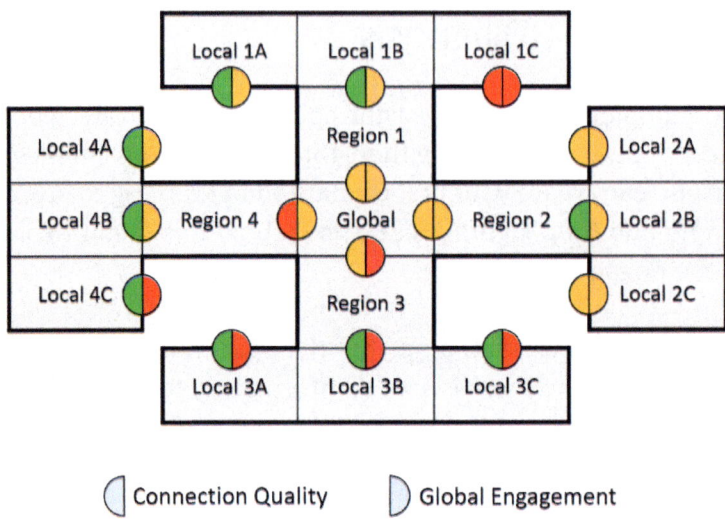

Figure 16.2B. Example of a Peer-Group Globalization Map

Top-Level Managers

Within the top-level manager peer group, you have country managers reporting directly to regional presidents. These titles may vary but the relationship is there. As you might imagine, the practices and attitudes that drive both connecting behavior and global engagement are often set at the top. It may also be easier to change them from the top.

In Figure 16.2B, the head of Region 3 is probably crucial to improve global engagement across the region. Meanwhile, local market 1C shows a low level of globalization that is not present in the rest of Region 1. There is an opportunity here for the head of Region 1 to facilitate change.

These regional—local direct reporting relationships do not exist between senior or middle manager peers because each group reports upward within its hierarchy. So, when comparing these peer groups' Globalization Maps, look for similarities in connection quality and engagement among geographic groups—for example, regional managers. Are these practices and attitudes set at the top?

Global—Regional Collaboration

As we have discussed many times, region heads are critical gatekeepers to the success of global strategy. A Globalization Map is a powerful tool to help them understand how they are leading and enabling the global effort. This conversation can fuel best practice sharing and reveal unknown gaps.

Engagement Over Connectivity

The connection quality between stakeholders is a snapshot of their current behavior. If quality is low, it is not hard to improve things. Take a look at the frequency, duration, and intimacy of their connecting behavior, and close the gaps. However, if engagement is low, the root cause can be complex and the solution is likely to be more difficult. For example, you may be dealing with structural challenges, specific leader behaviors, or entrenched cultural barriers. None of these are quick and easy fixes.

In the example, based on connectivity alone, Region 3 was not a concern. Now, we can see that engagement throughout the region is low and that this is the case regardless of connection quality. This finding is probably the most serious risk to global performance among this peer group.

Action

It can be surprising how a simple tool like this engagement map can reveal on so many things from leader behaviors or strategic alignment to deeper dysfunction in your company's operating model, such as biases toward geographic independence. And, sometimes, awareness really is half the battle. This mapping exercise reveals how and where your company is global-ready. It is a powerful instrument.

Telling Truth to Power

The traffic light scoring system is simple and effective. Expect your stakeholders to respond to their ratings. In particular, don't be surprised when they push back against the red lights. Be prepared to be challenged, even though this is a self-assessment and you are simply showing your colleagues what they told you. Some managers, especially top-level and regional managers, may interpret the findings as a negative critique and reject what they don't like. Let them rubbish the tool or the methodology. An emotional rejection of the analysis says that you have evoked a strong (negative) reaction. Focus on listening to understand and start a conversation. Remember, a red light that indicates that engagement is low is not a judgment. After all, the emotional drivers of engagement have systemic roots. For example, it is perfectly reasonable to expect low engagement if participation in global strategy is not rewarded or participants feel ignored. Be careful how you socialize the findings. Embarrassing your colleagues is an own goal, no matter how intractable they may be or how satisfying it might feel. Focus on starting an important conversation and bringing attention to critical opportunities or issues.

By performing this diagnosis, you have sent a message: Connecting behaviors and engagement are no longer invisible. However, don't think of this as a tool to drive accountability—it is much better to position the findings as an invitation. The solutions will require all stakeholders to adapt.

Action Plans

As this diagnosis was generated from self-assessments, it follows that any remedial action needs to be in the hands of each stakeholder.

However, engagement is a two-way street and so both parties in a connection should work together. They have a lot of information now. So, to improve engagement scores, each stakeholder can develop an action plan to address any gaps in emotional and rational engagement drivers.

While it is valuable to develop remediation plans within each peer group, it will be most effective and probably save a lot of time if top-level managers lead this undertaking.

Changing Red Lights to Yellow

When you are starting from a low globalization score, it is unlikely that your matrix can be improved by a gradual evolution. In all likelihood, there needs to be a deliberate and disruptive intervention to step-change connectivity or to elevate the engaged participation of colleagues and stakeholders. Global readiness is unlikely to improve without a strong impetus for change.

Fairness

Not all engagement drivers are equal. An indicator that you have a real challenge on your hands is a low score for the engagement driver *fairness*. This reveals that your multinational business strategy may not appeal to enough of the people who will be executing it. If so, then the first step must be to revisit the strategy, which currently offers little value to its stakeholders. Only then can you improve the global matrix that will support and enable it.

An Example

Figure 16.3 below shows a full Globalization Map diagnosis featuring all three management levels. It looks like a lot is going on here but, if we follow the diagnosis guidelines, we can quickly unravel the true situation.

For a first impression, we start with the top-level managers and the global—regional connections within that group. So, focusing on the center of the diagram for top-level managers, we see yellow and red lights that tell us that connection quality is medium except between Global and Region 4, where it is low. We also see that engagement is medium between Global and all regions except Region 3. Indeed, engagement is low in all three local markets of Region 3.

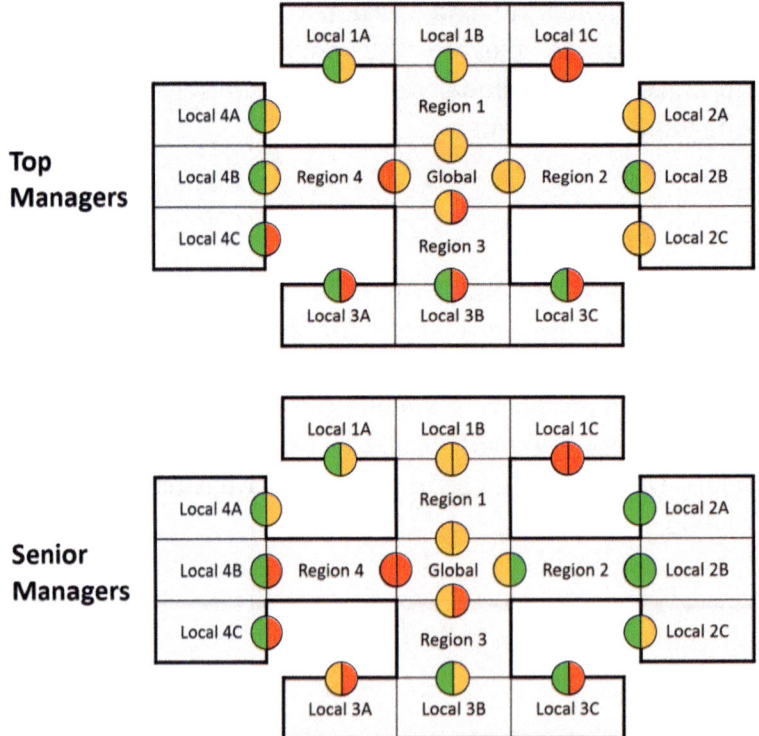

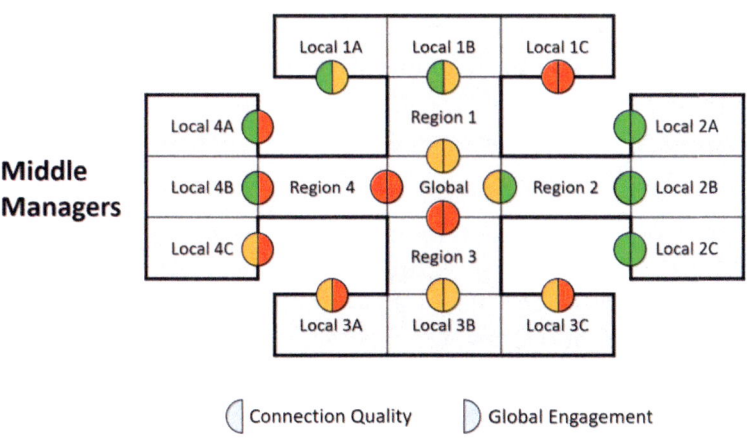

Figure 16.3 Example of a Full Globalization Map

The next step is to go region-by-region down through the hierarchy. So, let's look at Region 3. At the top level, while there seems to be good connection quality, engagement is low between all stakeholders. This is not good. When connection quality is high but engagement low, we waste a lot of time and energy coming together, but we are neither committing nor engaging. Imagine global and regional summits full of presentations but with no true collaboration and generating nothing new. Looking down the map through senior and mid-level managers, we can see more examples of poor engagement. With these findings, it makes sense to revisit the self-assessments of rational and emotional drivers of engagement and to look for patterns. The extent of disengagement puts the regional leaders in the spotlight because they are the common element in all the relationships. The overall impression is of a region that is disconnected.

Looking at Region 4, we can see that the poor connection quality between global and regional top-level leaders is replicated down through the map with senior and mid-level managers. These groups are disconnected. Meanwhile, the region has good connection quality with its local markets. Yet, despite this behavior, engagement between the region and the local markets at senior- and mid-levels is poor. Here we see more examples of high connectivity but low engagement. Again, we can look at the driver data to try to understand why these connections are widely ineffective. The answer may not always be there but now we know there is a missed opportunity that we can explore further and turn around.

The stakeholders in Regions 1 and 2 appear to be well-connected and engaged with one another except for market 1C, which is either deliberately separated or subversively seceding.

Positive Principles

Competition has been shown to be useful
up to a certain point and no further,
but cooperation, which is the thing we must strive for today,
begins where competition leaves off.

Franklin D. Roosevelt

As you have worked through the book to reach this point, you will have built a broad understanding of the many challenges that we face to be effective in global strategy and leadership. Perhaps you are already thinking about using one or two of the assessment tools to detect and decode some of the fragmentation that is holding your company back. Well, in these final chapters, we are going to build on this growing awareness by offering some additional guiding principles that you can use to either preempt or manage that dysfunction.

Global fragmentation is very probable, but the extent of its damage is not preordained. There are constant turning points and forks in the road that offer different outcomes. Even the ability to recognize mistakes as we make them is a massive step forward. Among your competitors, unconscious incompetence in terms of global effectiveness is typically the norm, but we are leaving that world of unknown unknowns behind.

The insights and advice to follow are hard-won. Some are well road-tested and, where appropriate, they have also been reviewed and ratified by research participants. As every organization has its unique advantages and its special baggage, these suggestions are presented as high-level guiding principles so that you can take the core concepts and apply them to your company, your culture, and the way that you and your colleagues work together. You might not always find the perfect answer in these practices but, building on the critical awareness you have already developed, they present insights and solutions that could save you much time and frustration.

From feedback, it can be useful to contrast your own behavior, or that of your company, with these ideas and provocations, and to explore the differences and their implications. In the end, you will need to create your own formula, including your own approach to engaging your organization. Take everything here as raw material. Weigh it, test it, and use it to lead change.

17. Globalization

Global collaboration can be incredibly powerful. It is entirely true that the whole can be greater than the sum of its parts. But how? Well, remember our discussion of globalism in Chapter 3? What if we flip globalism on its head? This would create a system in which the power comes from meaningful diversity rather than forced consistency.

Let's consider the world of difference between globalism and globalization.

While globalism falsely claims that compliance with a one-size-fits-all strategy is better for everyone, globalization describes what happens when we increase and strengthen the connections and interdependencies between geographies. As these bridges are built and reinforced, we unlock more and more opportunities. The benefits of globalization are far-reaching and can include increased trust, communication, collaboration, engagement, exchange of ideas, best practices, access to talent and functional expertise, career mobility and retention, greater efficiencies, speed to market, access to innovation, and improved product or service quality—to name just a few! Indeed, globalization can be an unparalleled source of competitive advantage.

Unlike globalism, globalization focuses on stronger connectivity and integration within an organization, which improves the flow of and access to knowledge, assets, and capabilities worldwide. This integration does not mean harmonization. Globalization creates opportunities as a result of local or regional differences. For example, it generates value by distributing discrete yet superior capabilities and by closing gaps.

So, if we can learn to globalize, then we could be on to something. Yet, as it happens, too few companies choose to invest in worldwide connectivity as an objective unto itself. Instead, globalization is often an incomplete by-product of global strategy. For example, let's imagine our company wants to roll out an innovation process worldwide. To achieve this, we build international teams of stakeholders and we get to work. Unfortunately, after the work is done, the connections that we had created atrophy. It takes a deliberate, concerted, and ongoing effort to maintain meaningful connections between worldwide stakeholders.

The struggle to prioritize globalization is not unusual even though the barriers to connection are lower than they have ever been. It seems that it is easier to categorize the process of improving a company's worldwide connective tissue as a useful enabler of a specific objective. So, for many, this is not an operational imperative or a source of competitive advantage—rather, it is an activity that supports a separate purpose or outcome(s).

Globalization is the process of increasing a company's worldwide potential. Is there a better role for global leaders than to promote this? Interestingly, while globalism encourages global leaders to sponsor authority and dominance, globalization offers them a role much closer to servant leadership. It is a mission to harness a company's multiplicity of knowledge and experience, to make it work for everyone.

18. Culture and Strategy

Steering the Ship

How many times have you heard "culture eats strategy for breakfast" repeated as an axiom of deep insight? This language is frequently misattributed to the management consultant Peter Drucker, and it is offered as the astute answer to an important riddle that has escaped and stymied so many strategists. Well, let's unpack this idea because I want you to know how stupid it is.

Edgar Schein, the father of organizational behavior, defined company culture as a shared pattern of basic assumptions, which colleagues acquire over time as they learn to cope with internal and external problems. As connected employees, these are the attitudes and practices that we assume. They are our norms, our formal ways of working, and the implicit demands that we are obliged to accommodate. It is how we feel about the work that we do and how we go about it. We have all felt the tide of organizational culture. In large companies, it can feel like a living thing.

As all stakeholders contribute to it, culture is much bigger than any one person. For company leaders, this is not something that they can dictate or flick a switch to change. However, it is something for which they are accountable. This brings us to the negligent stupidity of setting culture and strategy in competition with one another. Why on earth would anyone want to have an organizational culture that does not support and advance the company's objectives and strategies? Why would it ever be beneficial to permit a common set of assumptions, attitudes, and behaviors if they don't serve one's business needs?

The word *culture* comes from the same linguistic origin as *cultivate*. It is something that we nurture, tend, and grow. This is not a mystical energy field that surrounds and penetrates all living things. Culture originates with the company's board, with the chief executive officer (CEO), and with their management team.

That doesn't mean that culture is easy to shape and influence. This is a key reason why better leaders are paid the big bucks. Think about a new CEO brought in to captain a turnaround or a change of direction. In this scenario, many behavioral norms will need to change. The company machine needs rewiring and maybe some new parts must be swapped out before it can operate differently. This is hard work that requires uncommon expertise.

Conversely, think about all those management consultants or change agents brought in to identify and lead new opportunities. So many times, they find that the comfort of today's status quo, or the fear of losing what is familiar, is stronger than the perceived value of their recommendations. The world is full of struggling companies whose CEOs look ahead and see the need for different results but are not prepared to change, or do not even consider changing, the attitudes and practices that comprise their organizational culture. Typically, these companies go on to experience more pain, or a change in leadership, before they eventually commit to a new strategy and develop the necessary culture to support it. In these common situations, it may be tempting to view culture and strategy as opponents when they are not coherent. However, if we are honest about this, we all know that what is happening is a failure of leadership. How else would you describe a captain who refuses to steer the ship?

Will the Past Eat the Future for Breakfast?

Cultural change is not easy—not least because much of a company's culture is implicit. Shared attitudes and behaviors formed over time may be understood but they are not always expressed or explained. In this scenario, companies are like the proverbial iceberg. The larger it is, the less you can see. So, it is easy to understand how a new strategy, with new choices and decisions made, can run afoul of incoherence that is hidden beneath the surface.

This illustrates an underlying truth and tension, which is that culture is an artifact of a company's history while strategy captures a set of decisions with future-facing implications. This means that, if we are serious about the success of any new direction or process, we must assess it against the culture that was built before it existed. This is where we often find ourselves stuck because it is difficult to abandon practices that have made us successful in the past. It feels risky to change our habits. It is so much easier to hope that we can "rinse and repeat." Yet, it is not the purpose of company culture to be a comfort blanket of continuity and familiarity. The courageous and far better alternative is to diagnose the coherence of how we used to operate with what we now want to achieve.

Global Sub-Cultures

Now, let's extrapolate this into a global company. The geographic matrix with its quasi-independent players means that we don't have just one organizational culture but many. These sub-cultures may have common attributes if there is enough connectivity and interdependent behavior. However, to the CEO, most of this is too hard to see. It is certainly unmanageable without regional and local leaders doing their part to cultivate coherence.

This is where things become tricky because you want and need geographic cultural differences. These are important strengths for doing business, managing people, and competing locally. So, for a global strategy, the challenge to ensure that strategy and culture are coherent plays out across a set of stakeholders who are by necessity more culturally diverse.

Coherence is hard to get right domestically. Indeed, it is no mean feat to ensure that just one organizational machine operates in a way that is truly fit for purpose. Now we need coherence from multiple, and deliberately different, machines. Set aside all of the other challenges of geographic alignment. Assume that all of the macro and more obvious distinctive differences, such as customers, costs, supply, regulations, are not at issue. Even when all of those other planets align, our global ambitions are at risk if we fail to ensure that organizational culture, in all its permutations and at each different location, supports and advances the global strategy.

This highlights why the success of a global strategy is much more likely when we explore and develop the choices to be made inclusively. However, as we learned from the research, such inclusive collaboration is rare. In most multinationals, global strategies are owned by global teams and created by them in a silo. In fact, it is common practice, after dictating a new global strategy, to delegate or simply to assume that regional and local stakeholders will adapt their cultural fit to create the necessary coherence. Effectively, this is asking them to change something that has made them successful in the past to support a future that they were not involved in defining. The result, which we frequently observe, is a broad portfolio of explicit and implicit resistance to cultural change and strategic fit. You can see it coming.

It is a huge mistake to imagine culture and strategy as opposing combatants because this suggests that company leaders have no agency. The same individuals who are responsible for making strategic decisions are equally responsible for leading and cultivating organizational culture. To succeed, every strategy requires a conversation and even a plan for cultural engineering. What attitudes and practices do we need to achieve our new objective? To what extent do our current behaviors need to adapt, start, stop, or continue?

Success requires that we craft a company culture that is purposeful and proactive.

19. The Magnificent Middle

The Abused Middle

Increasingly, we hear the concept of strategy and its implementation neatly summarized as decisions by top executives that flow through an organization to be executed at the customer-facing front lines. This characterization largely ignores or at least diminishes the value of the organization between those top deciders and the key executors. Indeed, it seems to suggest that those other people are of uncertain consequence. Today, with so many chief executive officers and other senior leaders actively marketing their personal brands and investing in their celebrity on social media, this over-simplified and reality-skipping idea of organizational behavior is gaining more and more traction. It doesn't help that middle managers have a poor reputation. To many, they are synonymous with mediocrity and are believed to have a love for the status quo that is the enemy of innovation and agility. More and more, we hear that it is the leaders' decisions that matter and, of course, execution, execution, execution. Surely, this is where most company value comes from.

So, is everyone in the *bloated middle* a mindless and costly operator of yesterday's company machine? Are they a legitimate impediment to new strategy and direction?

Typically, those in the middle are not involved in developing a new company strategy and, when a new strategy is authored, they receive it as a fait accompli. Most senior leaders do not look for input or advice from this middle zone. They believe that they know better and that they are appropriately equipped to make strategic decisions.

Not only are they not consulted but the inhabitants of this awkward middle are frequently seen as challenging and resistant obstacles. They must be overcome to ensure that decisions flow, that culture adapts, and that change is accepted in the quest to improve company results. Senior leaders and management consultants seeking change often look at this middle zone as a reactive and troublesome entity to be managed. This mindset is fueled by a common view that middle managers are risk-averse and unimaginative. They are saboteurs of strategy and churlish about change.

With these perceptions in mind, consider the inescapable reality that strategy will only happen if it is executable by the company's operating model. Earlier, we defined the operating model as the way the company is run. It describes the main processes that the company follows to create and deliver value. So, guess where in the organization the mastery of these processes lies? The answer, of course, is the abused middle.

The Sweet Spot

It is so myopic to think of this zone of the organization as a no-man's-land. Rather, it can be a sweet spot with the potential for more insight than anywhere else in the company. Consider that stakeholders in this middle zone will always be closer to customers than senior executives. At the same time, as they are close but not on the front lines, those in the middle have perspectives on how the company executes and how it might improve. In fact, they generate more ideas than any other part of the company. Or at least they would if their senior leaders would listen and give them credit for it.

In strategy, an indispensable power of the middle is to act as a buffer and a check for new ideas and strategies that are not coherent with how the company works today and what its capabilities are. If we are not paying attention, this coherence filter can be brutal. After all, this evaluation is unavoidable. Senior leaders may be unaware, but their decisions will be screened and then accepted or rejected, in part or entirely, depending on whether the operating model can adapt.

We can see that the idea of executive decisions flowing straight to the front lines is foolish. The naivety of the concept suggests that the critical contribution that the middle makes is not understood. To treat its constituents as intermediaries with little inherent value is a reliable script for dysfunction to be played out again and again until we learn. The common practice of targeting this group for layoffs has serious consequences for a company's operating model and a direct effect on its ability to support existing and future strategies.

For sure, the organizational middle may contain inefficiencies. However, it is much more helpful to view it as the central hub of the company and to mine its strengths.

The Global Middle

Now, let's translate this dynamic of the organizational middle into a global company. The same principles apply. The middle or middles, as there will be more than one, possess vital operational insights and each will act as a coherence filter to support or oppose new strategy.

Regional teams often serve as this bridge between global decisions and local execution. As they are more distant from execution than their local counterparts, their feedback is more strategic. At the same time, the local middle offers insights on front-line execution and they also screen strategy for operational fit. It is useful to imagine this multi-stage filter when we consider decision flow and the effectiveness of senior global leaders to create lasting impact.

These acts of filtration by middle managers are not mutinous or subversive. Rather, they are a practical and informed response to a critical question: Can our organizational machine do what is being asked of it? In most cases, the answer is not a simple yes or no, and the organization may try to make a new strategy work even if the operational fit is just fair. In less favorable scenarios, success depends on whether the expertise of the middle will be heard. Unfortunately, the research shows that this is unlikely. The majority say that they do not have a voice and that they are not expected to have one.

Senior leaders are not in a position to fully understand the intricate details and variations in their global company's operating model. The larger the organization and the larger its geographical footprint, the more impossible this becomes. Despite this, it is not unusual for global leaders to simply assume that operational coherence or adaptation to support a new strategy is feasible and will happen automatically without adverse effects. They are convinced that the organization will comply with their authority.

This is ironic, perverse, and fascinating. We are desperately looking for a bridge that links decisions and action. It is right in front of us.

Ignoring the power of the middle, either in strategy development or in its validation, can be an expensive game of hit and hope. If we continue to ignore their expertise, we are missing out on vital insights about feasibility as well as a valuable source of ideas for efficiency, innovation, and competitive advantage.

20. Friction Is Fuel

The Magic of Disagreement

One of the secrets to building effective collaboration, and to working with a diverse international group on a common and compelling objective, is to validate the differences between each stakeholder. If we want everyone to agree to a common contract, then we must recognize that every stakeholder starts their journey from a different place. So, one of the worst things that we can do is to sideline, discount, or ignore their individual perspectives, priorities, and expectations.

When we recognize and respect individual differences, we are not only honoring and valuing each contributor but also investing in the health of our shared endeavor. To do this, we need to learn to disagree because it is the magic of that friction that turns suspicion into empathy, blind spots into insights, caution into commitment, and incomplete or imprecise ideas into focused action. Conflict unifies and it helps us to not only reach better decisions but also to reach better decisions that we can all agree to.

However, this is a lot easier said than done. There are so many barriers to healthy disagreement that the personal risk can seem unacceptably high. For just a shot at success, we need to navigate many challenges, such as company politics, cultural differences, tribalism, poor leadership, and, of course, our atavistic fight-or-flight response. We can say that disagreement is a positive and valuable practice, but it can feel like we are putting so much on the line. Logically, we can accept that avoiding conflict will probably lead to failure. However, acting on this knowledge is hard enough for one person and we need all the stakeholders to join in.

Unless we all engage, we will never know whether separate stakeholders are truly and voluntarily committed. While it may feel more harmonious and safer to move ahead hoping that there is full agreement, this creates a dangerously weak foundation. As many global teams have experienced, at a future date, under stress, the collaboration will fracture. Everything that you have built on this foundation can collapse.

Faking Harmony

Learning to disagree and to be disagreed with is a mission-critical skill for successful global collaboration. Yet, we make this so difficult. For one thing, global cooperation requires the involvement of top-level leaders with local, regional, and global responsibilities. However, it is these leaders, executives with the most seniority and authority, who work hardest to maintain the appearance of conflict-free harmony. More than anyone else in the company, top levels of management try to curate an appearance of calm and considered control. Rather than disagree, they prefer to stay silent because many believe that saving face and preserving an image of calm competence are imperative to their identity and their success.

All of us feel a little humiliated when a group of our peers disagrees with us. After all, it is hard to avoid making the classic error of conflating our point of view with our identity. We can feel threatened or shamed. Yet, for executives, used to having their authority and their superior status acknowledged, this experience is even harder to deal with. According to Erving Goffman, one of the most influential American sociologists of the 20th century, it is not unusual in these circumstances to either shut down and conceal our feelings or to try to sabotage the encounter in order to feel better.

So, the challenge for global leadership teams to disagree, debate, and then decide together is hard. Yet, of any groups, these are the ones that must negotiate, agree, and then truly commit to their decisions.

Structured Debate

Disagreements can feel threatening because they are often a surprise and play out unpredictably. Sometimes, if the topic is complex or there are many stakeholders, disagreement can degenerate into an unstructured argument that does little to resolve the concerns or issues. To anticipate this, it can help to manage the debate by breaking it into phases. Allow for a time-bound *diverging phase* to discover and capture all of the challenges to the initial idea or proposal. The key here is to understand the issue raised but not to discuss and resolve it immediately. Next, create a summary assessment of all of the counterpoints and ensure that everyone feels heard. Finally, lead a *converging phase*, in which the team can tackle every contention individually and possibly come together in resolution. This structure improves the quality of the debate by slowing things down and depersonalizing the points of disagreement, which can reduce the tension in the room.

Giving Face

An excellent technique to promote constructive disagreement is a powerful social skill called "giving face." Our face is the image or persona that we want to present to the world. So, giving face is being sensitive to how others wish to be seen, and then accepting and confirming that. In a debate, this helps each partner maintain their sense of personal power and safety.

When we are given face, rather than concentrate on our self-defense, we can now focus on the substance of the disagreement and even look for win-win solutions. The core principle to remember is that the most productive collaboration happens when all of the stakeholders involved feel as secure as possible.

Often, global leadership teams do better when they resolve disputes one-on-one, which allows the disagreement to take place away from an audience. This makes sense because the less people feel compelled to maintain face in front of their peers, the more flexible they can be.

Do not allow there to be winners or losers in a disagreement.

Separate an opinion from the proponent's sense of self. Remove the pronouns. It is not *his* opinion or *her* opinion: It is just *an* opinion. If there is a lot of emotion, then capture the point of view and come back to it later. Ask a neutral third party to re-present it to the group. Also, think about how people can change their minds and look good. Acknowledge that behavior as a rare and valuable achievement. Give them face.

Feeling One-Down

Another powerful technique is to be aware when a colleague sees themselves as "one-down." This term was coined by William Donohue, of the University of Michigan, and Paul Taylor, of Lancaster University, and describes the party, in any kind of negotiation, who feels most insecure about their relative status. Anyone who feels that they are one-down is likely to focus their energy on ways to reassert their power and autonomy. They are not going to work towards a win-win outcome. So, as with giving face, spotting colleagues who may feel one-down and then closing the gap is vital to achieving a positive and reliable agreement.

With this in mind, I am sure you can also imagine the scenario whereby some parties in an international collaboration feel that they are "one-up." As some markets and regions are necessarily more important for sales today or for tomorrow, it is not unusual for their leaders to feel superior and separate from the global whole. Paraphrasing Orwell, everyone is equal, but some are more equal than others. These one-up parties are also less inclined to look for a win-win to resolve a disagreement. They enjoy their sense of power and, while their confidence may lead them to be magnanimous, they are likely to prioritize their independence. This is even more likely if those who feel one-up have less need for cooperation. While it is typical of smaller and less developed markets to seek the benefits of mutual global assistance, larger and more self-sufficient markets tend to see collaboration as a loss of power.

To manage this, the answer is certainly not to try to bring down those parties feeling one-up. Challenging anyone's self-perception of power only creates more risk to the collaboration. Instead, the best approach is to ensure that nobody else is feeling exclusively one-down. There is strength in numbers. Let's say that there are four parties and one sees itself as one-up. If the remaining three are feeling essentially similar about their relative status, then they are unlikely to sabotage the collaboration. Disagreement and debate may still be rocky because the one-up party creates an imbalance. Yet, if you are lucky, you can encourage their magnanimity while you give face to the others.

In summary, assume that any behavior in a debate that does not bring you closer to mutual agreement is tainted by an imbalance in perceived status. This is a powerful idea that encourages you to pay attention to whether the discussion is constructive or not. Remember that all participants need to feel secure and relaxed. So, give face where it is needed and rebalance the group so that nobody feels that they are one-down. Pay attention to how you feel too.

To quote sociologist Morton Deutsch, a pioneer of conflict theory, 'The point is not how to eliminate or prevent conflict but rather how to make it productive.' The way to do this is to lead for a win-win. Conflicts become destructive if participants feel they have lost something, so it is vital that we minimize any sense of loss whether it is real or imaginary.

Towards the Tension

Marcus Aurelius's famous quote is perfect advice to recall when we detect new tension: 'The mind adapts and converts to its own purposes the obstacle to our acting. The impediment to action advances action. What stands in the way becomes the way.' The insight here is that—to solve a hard problem that can degrade global collaboration—we need to focus not on the problem itself but on why the problem is hard. If poor alignment, commitment, and company politics are the obstacles, then that is where we need to start. What stands in the way becomes the way.

More often, we are focused on the deliverable. We herd the cats focused on achieving the outcome despite the cats. We are also reactive in our frustration and just as guilty of ad hominem judgments as any of our colleagues. So, how do we embrace this stoic mental jiu-jitsu and make it a useful habit?

The secret is to flip a mental switch. For global practitioners, the game-changing technique is to assess and course-correct your purpose and therefore your identity, and how you show up. Think of the end deliverable as context and so—rather than drive toward it, which risks ignoring the obstacles in the way—take your time to understand the obstacles and make friends with them. The attitudes and behaviors you encounter are not unwelcome or disappointing: They are expected and become the job.

Be more curious and more courageous. Seek out disagreement and engage with it as constructively as possible. After all, moving toward the tension is not a choice. If you don't take the initiative, then the tension will find you eventually.

Remember, the most productive mindset with which to approach disagreement and debate is to welcome it with curiosity. Invite disagreement as a necessary and valuable path to learn and improve. Remove the ego-driven challenges and conflict simply becomes information, very important information. Build a culture in which objections are understood to be signs of engagement not failure. Don't allow bystanders or spectators. Encourage a rigorous debate to improve the work and to shake loose anything that stands in the way of full commitment.

A last point on this: Try to avoid using responsibility assignment tools that are intended to bring harmony to decision-making by defining stakeholders' roles for different decisions. These tools are a great example of how our desire to avoid tension and disagreement can make us act without real insight. We know that confusion in decision-making is caused by problems with the company's operating model, leadership, strategic priorities, alignment, connectivity, communication, engagement, or commitment. A responsibility assignment tool does nothing to address any of these root causes. Instead, it is a bureaucratic device that forces the appearance of harmonious behavior but ignores what causes the issues in the first place. Inevitably, stakeholders feel unheard, and this creates strain, confusion, and disengagement. Enforced governance does not overcome dysfunction: It is another trigger for global strategy theater.

21. Why You Listen

Listening Behavior

Developing global strategy, or any global collaboration for that matter, is a negotiation. Each party has objectives, critical needs, lines they can't cross, and, hopefully, a ZOPA, their 'zone of possible agreement.' There is personal risk in these negotiations. This is amplified by a destabilizing dynamic, which brings leaders who are used to being the top executives in the building into a situation where the hierarchy of personal power is less clear. So, it is no surprise that leaders are spending a lot of time thinking about themselves, their business, their needs, what they hope to gain, and whether they are being respected as they would prefer. Yet, the path to collaboration requires that we focus our attention on others. We must understand our collaborators if we are going to resolve our differences and come together to find a productive path forward.

All of us can tell when someone is not listening to us. We know because we do it ourselves. We listen for a while, but we are stuck in our heads. We start by listening but then we check out. We think about what we are going to say next. We check out again. We hear something that grabs our attention and check back in. We nod, grunt, or pretend to take notes as if we have been paying attention the whole time. And we keep this up until it is our turn to speak. At this point, ironically, we assume that our counterparts in the conversation will give us their full attention.

Have you ever been on the receiving end of active listening behaviors? The person you are speaking with is working hard to concentrate fully on what you say. They are fighting all of their urges to check out or to be distracted. They express their understanding of the points you make, clarify your insights, and maybe summarize your message. We should applaud their hard work. Yet, there is a basic flaw in this practice. It is just not enough to learn and act out the behaviors of a genuinely interested listener. Most of us can tell the difference here as well. Human communication is mostly non-verbal and no one can hide all of the minutiae that signal whether their actions are authentic or phony. More often than not, pretending and acting out the role of a genuinely interested listener is going to be clumsy with the danger that the recipient can feel more managed than listened to.

Know Why You Listen

If we are genuinely interested to listen and learn, then we are automatically curious and humble. If we care for our colleagues and want to understand them, then we are empathetic to their experience. These are not techniques to be learned. The question to ask is not 'How do I listen?' but 'Why am I listening?'

A global leader has very compelling reasons to listen. As we have discussed, stakeholders start from different places. We need to invest ourselves in their stories and with the patience to ensure that they know it. Successful global collaboration requires that we capture and understand all of the differences between the stakeholders. It is the only way to find a common path forward.

To put this simply, if you want to build commitment to a global outcome, then you need to understand what motivates each stakeholder. A global leader is interested to listen and learn because it is essential to their success.

As you start a collaboration, it can help to set the foundation by defining everyone's needs and concerns. In a group setting, before any debate starts, you want to identify and describe all stakeholders' needs so that everyone can confirm that they feel satisfied that they are understood. During this initial phase, make it everyone's responsibility to help their colleagues to share and express all of their needs and concerns. Ask open-ended questions. Suspend judgment. Nudge people to fill in any gaps. Don't get too lost in learned behaviors. Stay focused on why you are listening and your colleagues will respond.

Self-Disclosure is a Drug

Is there a reason why we are all so bad at listening? Why is what I have to say so interesting?

Many of us love to talk. Not only do we love to be listened to, but we find enormous pleasure in telling others about ourselves. Harvard University's Social Cognitive and Affective Neuroscience Laboratory studied brain activity among people talking about themselves and about other people whom they knew. When the participants talked about themselves, their brains were stimulated to release dopamine, the neurotransmitter associated with pleasure and reward. The researchers concluded that 'self-disclosure produces a burst of activity in neural regions associated with pleasure, motivation, and reward.' Dopamine release leaves us with a strong memory of the pleasure that we felt, which in turn can prompt us to try to experience it again.

Sadly, listening to others talking about themselves has no such neurochemical reward!

However, when we don't allow others to talk about themselves, we deny them their dopamine fix. It is no wonder that they are frustrated. And they may be less likely to listen to us in return. So, listen first.

You Have 30 Seconds

Career coach Marty Nemko has some excellent advice for speakers, which he calls the "Traffic Light Rule." During the first 30 seconds of talking, your light is green. This means that your listener is probably paying attention to you as long as what you are saying is relevant. However, unless you are a magnetic and compelling speaker, you don't have much more than 30 seconds to get your point across. For the second 30 seconds, your light is yellow. This means that the risk of your listener losing interest is rising quickly. At 60 seconds, your light has turned red and it is time to stop. While there may be times when your listener is so engaged that it is safe to "run a red light," this is rarer than any of us want to accept. It is best to assume that, after 30 seconds, once your light is yellow, with every second that passes, while you are still talking, you run the risk of losing your listener. Look for a place to stop. Plan for it. If your listener wants more, they will ask a question.

This rule is a powerful mnemonic to remind us to be concise, to think about what we want to say, and to structure it into digestible segments. It is fascinating to think that by speaking less we can increase our listeners' understanding.

Beware of the Counterfeit *Yes*

Chris Voss, a former FBI negotiator, gave us the insight that a *yes* is a commitment, while a *no* is protection. We see this in disagreement when saying *no* is triggered by loss of face or feeling one-down. The antagonism we may express or experience is not about attaining a specific outcome but protecting status through a demonstration of power. Saying *no* is not just empowering: It makes us feel strong and safe. Meanwhile, saying *yes*, if we mean it, is a promise that can feel risky.

While not every *no* is for protection, not every *yes* is a committed *yes*. There is the conditional *yes* that we say under pressure. There is also the counterfeit *yes* that we say when we feel trapped. This is a *yes* that later turns into a *no*.

To spot a counterfeit *yes*, you can paraphrase the commitment or clarify and confirm the person's position until they have responded a few times, and you will see whether they are consistent. Even more effective is to explore how the commitment would be implemented or executed. A counterfeit *yes* will not stand up to this scrutiny.

This behavior teaches us to grade each collaborator's commitment and to be aware of the circumstances under which they made it. If you give them every chance to opt out and they still opt in, then you know that you are in it together.

22. Architects Are Advocates

Stakeholders—The Clue is in The Name

The phrase "architects are advocates" has become a mantra that I use when coaching leaders to develop global strategy, or, really, any endeavor that needs other people to buy in and invest their energy over time.

For context, it is important to remind ourselves that the stakeholders who will execute a new global strategy need to understand it, to want the results, to know what to do, and to be fully committed to it. If each stakeholder believes, as nearly all of them do, that they have to contend with a set of unique challenges, then they will engage only when these challenges are respected and reflected in the strategy. Furthermore, each stakeholder wants their value and the significance of their expertise to be needed and appreciated. These considerations lead us to the irrefutable conclusion that presenting strategy as a fait accompli to uninvolved stakeholders is a wasteful mistake. However, I have seen global leaders reveal new strategies to geographic and functional stakeholders so many times—as if their audience were just waiting for decisions and directions—while these same leaders chose to be blind to the indignation, annoyance, and resentment in the room.

Global strategy created in a silo will not be executed effectively, if at all. Even when compliance is forced, it will eventually fail. We can rightly assert that such a strategy would be biased, hegemonic, uninformed, and possibly unrealistic. Yet, its deepest flaw is that nobody has a personal commitment to see it succeed.

Let's unpack this architect idea.

An architect has clients and they do not present them with a fait accompli. Their job is to plan, design, and oversee construction, and there are critical steps throughout that process for review and adaptation by a range of stakeholders.

To begin with, an architect is designing for a purpose. Once engaged in a project, they work through a discovery phase to develop a brief, which includes objectives, scope, and a roadmap that describes how the project will unfold. Transpose this onto the global strategy development process in your company. How do you start the work?

The architect analogy offers some powerful lessons. For example, we can unlock surprising potential when we collaborate with stakeholders to develop a strategy's scope. This simple step has stakeholders feeling heard and respected on Day 1. This can reveal tensions early before they have time to fester and grow. It also provides stakeholders with the opportunity to introduce their needs and clarify their priorities. This is exactly the foundation that we need.

Competitive versus Complimentary Overlap

When a global strategy is not developed inclusively and collaboratively, it inevitably leads to competitive tension. Global and regional or local strategies can be incoherent in two ways. First, they can conflict and contradict. In this case, executors need to choose which strategy to ignore and which to follow. Alternatively, they can simply be separate and disconnected. In this case, while the strategies may not clash, they are still competitive in terms of the resources and support that are necessary. Incremental objectives will require existing activities and assignments to change. Something has to give and be deprioritized. And so, again, executors need to choose which strategy to ignore and which to follow.

When regional and local strategies already exist, which is most often the case, it is very easy for a global strategy to fall into this competitive trap. Indeed, many global strategists are guilty of treating regional and local strategies with disdain, as something insufficient that needs to be overwritten. However, it doesn't take a great shift to build strategies that complement. After all, existing regional priorities are ideal input to inform the scope of a global strategy. The shift is simple in concept. We develop a blueprint that articulates where global and regional priorities overlap. To be complementary, either the priorities are separate, in which case neither one should detract or distract from the other, or they fit together and mutually reinforce, offering increased focus and support.

We are the Champions

The power of this approach is for all stakeholders to see themselves as architects of the global strategy. Global teams may lead, facilitate, develop drafts and prototypes, and do as much of the heavy lifting as is needed. Yet, at every step, all stakeholders are working to ensure that the strategy that they design is feasible and can be achieved according to plan.

Of course, the early stages of this collaboration can seem slow and messy. Indeed, there is a lot to work through in the initial discovery phase. However, once regional and local stakeholders realize that their ability to meet their individual objectives is not at risk and that they have a respected seat at the table, then we start to see the power of this concentration of expertise. Patterns and priorities emerge while disagreements and debates reveal barriers and opportunities. Importantly, the scope and value of global strategy relative to regional and local strategies become a lot clearer.

Some global leaders express concern about giving too much power to regional and local stakeholders. There is no doubt that more inclusive collaboration reduces the global team's control over the process of developing the strategy document. However, the dividend is paid out in full during the implementation and execution. To be clear, regional and local stakeholders have tremendous power over global strategy. Indeed, so much of the theatrics and dysfunction that we experience are the games that we play to deny this reality.

If we say upfront that not all of a global strategy is mandatory, then we are doing nothing more daring or progressive than acknowledging what is already true. The upside is that now we are building trust rather than eroding it. We are not challenging autonomy and we have removed the need for pretense. We have a chance now to change intractable adversaries into cautious allies, and all it takes is to respect our stakeholders' knowledge and expertise, and to recognize their needs and concerns. Now, we can invite our stakeholders to put their cards on the table and help us to develop a better strategy.

23. The Right Leader

The Profile of a Global Leader

As we discussed in Chapter 6 *The Wrong Leader*, we need to make large changes to how, why, and whom we select for international leadership. The data is overwhelmingly conclusive. We promote the wrong people eight out of ten times in domestic roles and, when we transpose this weakness to international roles, the result is much worse. If you are curious then to see an example of this fiasco, compare and contrast the job descriptions of a few global leaders. In both small and large multinationals, outside of the functional skills you would expect, you will find hardly any consistency in the capabilities that separate companies identify as important to a role with global scope. Indeed, of the few common requirements, the more typical are along the lines of "partner with regional business leaders," "lead global cross-functional meetings," and "contribute to the global leadership team." Deliverables are conspicuously absent. There is no description of success. Overall, for anyone with meaningful tenure in a global role, it is clear that most of these jobs are not well understood. We are missing clear competencies, a clarity of purpose, and a defined mission.

What are the most valuable strengths that we might look for when selecting for a global role? What are the nice-to-haves and what can we never do without? To explore this, I asked research participants to rank strengths that they considered to be the most important in such a role. A significant number of them were familiar with Gallup's CliftonStrengths assessment and so I asked them to select and prioritize from among Gallup's 34 themes.

A group of 43 respondents representing global, regional, and local management hierarchies chose the following from among Gallup's themes as most important to the best global leaders:

- **Strategic**
  People who create alternative ways to proceed. Faced with any given scenario, they can quickly spot the relevant patterns and issues.

- **Communication**
  People who generally find it easy to put their thoughts into words. They are good conversationalists and presenters.

- **Maximizer**
  People who focus on strengths as a way to stimulate personal and group excellence. They seek to transform something strong into something superb.

These themes describe a leader who can be trusted to pursue the best decisions. This is an individual who can quickly absorb and analyze information, and share their insights clearly. Stakeholders want an effective influencer who can take charge but will also make sure that others are heard.

A second tier of strengths includes the following nice-to-have themes:

- **Learner**
  People who have a great desire to learn and want to continuously improve. The process of learning, rather than the outcome, excites them.

- **Deliberative**
  People who are best described by the serious care they take in making decisions or choices. They anticipate obstacles.

- **Restorative**
  People who are adept at dealing with problems. They are good at figuring out what is wrong and resolving it.

There are advantages to having a global leader who is constantly curious. At the same time, it is valuable to have a leader who is not only quick to identify risks and obstacles, however complex, but is also effective in diagnosing and resolving them.

It is interesting to see in this ranking that relationship-building strengths, such as winning other people over and empathy, are not so important. International stakeholders, it seems, are asking for competence over warmth. They are telling us that the role of a global leader is not easy. They want an effective partner who will do what they say they will do and deliver results.

As a side note, regional leaders were very consistent in their responses, which suggests that their needs are not biased by cultural differences.

Agreed Purpose

While the intent, scope, and objectives of a global role will vary in each company, a common mistake, which can set a new leader up for failure, is to develop the role and then fill it without the express agreement of critical stakeholders. Imagine that you are a regional president and a newly minted global leader explains to you that their objectives will affect your region. How will you feel? What if you disagree? Where does this fit among your priorities?

The new global leader can't succeed without the approval and support of important gatekeepers. They must be advocates. Ideally, we should ask these stakeholders to provide input to shape the role. Unfortunately, this is rare. As a consequence, many global leaders find themselves caught between the ambitions of their superiors and the stone-walling or fake commitments of regional leadership.

Looking at this from the outside, before you take a global leadership role, be sure to interview the gatekeepers and any stakeholders whose goodwill and collaboration you are going to need.

Effective Tenure

No regional or local leader is eager to partner with someone who is in a short-term assignment in a global role. Many international stakeholders agree that their global colleagues are not particularly effective for at least two years. There is so much for them to learn, not just about the business but also about how to operate in the role. It takes time to develop and master the new skill set. Trust, which is in part built on competence, requires this. Such a viewpoint is particularly strong if the new leader comes from a large domestic market and will return there at the end of their global tenure. Such leaders are not considered to be serious. Local leaders call them "tourists." This practice of short-term global assignments creates churn and waste with little to show for it. Companies without a formal global career path create the circumstances for ineffectual global assignments and repeated theater.

24. Pay for Performance

Global Incentives

The root cause of so much of the theatrics that degrades global strategy is our failure to appreciate how structures and processes create conflicting pressures for all of the stakeholders involved. Something has to give when these company leaders are unable or unwilling to pursue all of the objectives that are proposed. A key example of this is when we ask regional or local leaders to invest in global strategy when this has negative consequences for them both personally and professionally. Under these circumstances, global strategy is subtractive. Indeed, we hear from them again and again how global strategy is at best a compromise that dilutes their focus.

Furthermore, we know that the reward systems of multinational companies are inherently local and tribal. This is appropriate for roles with limited scope because it encourages their focus on specific and discrete initiatives. It also introduces a very clear prioritization of well-defined, autonomous, and controlled actions. Global strategy rarely fits this description. When we ask regional and local leaders to integrate global strategy into their workload, they need to be able to translate it into specific and controllable outcomes that can be achieved with their current resources and capabilities. The strategy must also be achievable without compromising their existing measurable performance. If this is not possible, then it is considered to be incoherent and unsuitable. Indeed, these stakeholders are rewarded if they can reject the strategy and avoid it.

We seem to be stuck with the same game playing out in so many multinational companies. Can we break this paradigm? Well, what if we pay for performance? What if implementing a global strategy comes with a bonus payout? What if collaborating with the global team is a path to incremental rewards? Imagine the shift in mindset and what new behavior this might unlock.

We might not like the idea of additional incentives. However, we have diagnosed and discussed in detail how in most global companies there are powerful disincentives to making global strategy work. Indeed, incremental rewards are much less expensive than the cost of all of the dysfunction and failure to implement that is so commonly reported. Yet, it can feel mercenary. In some company cultures, it can be disappointing to realize that the we-are-all-in-this-together ethos is naive and that we are a lot more coin-operated than we want to admit.

Opting In or Out?

With all of this talk of inclusivity and the democratization of global strategy, it might seem reasonable to expect this question: To what extent is global strategy a suggestion rather than a mandatory directive? Should regional and local stakeholders choose whether to engage or not? Many companies try to manage their dysfunction by operating at either end of this continuum. Once their global strategy is unveiled, these companies either assume that the global teams' job is done or they attempt to overwrite all existing strategies and demand compliance from their organization.

In a way, this is a trick question because regional and local leaders already have this power, even though global leaders find that hard to accept. The point that global leaders miss is that each regional or local stakeholder's decision to commit and engage depends on how well the global strategy fits with the performance that is required of them. Regional and local leaders have regional and local deliverables that they are accountable for. A global strategy that detracts from this is unlikely to receive much attention. These stakeholders have the power to manage their engagement with global strategy whether that is recognized formally or not.

We have heard from all sides that a key reason why so many of these strategies don't live long after their presentation is that nobody owns them and nobody wants to take them on. We see all those political games and faux commitments because there is little incentive to engage or to develop plans to execute. If we pay for performance, then this can change. Indeed, now the conversation can shift towards results and metrics, which is exactly what we have been missing. We are no longer discussing whether the strategy is appropriate but how we will implement it. Nothing is perfect. For example, we still need to drag global teams out of their silos. Yet, now we have enhanced the basis for collaboration on a personal level. We have lowered the risk. We have stakeholders with a shared aim, a compelling reason to come together, and a new need for each other.

The Wind Shifts

Paying for global performance promotes an increased focus on results and, in turn, this encourages clearer separation between global, regional, and local strategies. With an incentive to understand what is incremental, global strategy becomes additive. So, where previously, global strategy could exist as an aggregate of regional strategies, this now becomes the starting point for global strategy development.

In addition, regional and local stakeholders see more value and reward in participating in developing global strategy. Regional heads, the most powerful gatekeepers, will still control their region's priorities but many agree that incremental rewards shift their perception of global considerations into a positive light. They are more likely to ask, 'What is possible?', which is a significant improvement on 'How to avoid this?'

Meanwhile, global teams are less likely to be unwelcome pariahs and instead accepted as bearers of opportunity. At the same time, they must adapt to manage a new level of participation. For example, there will be more competition of ideas and pressure to focus on short-term measurable initiatives rather than longer-term plans.

25. We Are All Strategists

Self-Destructive Squabbling

Earlier, we explored some of the tribal dysfunction between leadership and operations. We saw much the same thing between top-level executives and middle managers, and also between global strategists and local executors. It is always the same story—each group seems to be entrenched in their desire for preeminent control and claims superiority in their understanding of the decisions and actions that are needed. What is more, we have learned that this competition is not really a rational debate about what is best for the business: It is a contest between people who prize their autonomy, authority, and need for control.

At the same time, it is obvious that this separation between strategy and execution is a mistake. These capabilities are not duplicative and we plainly need both. Strategy brings us perspective and looks chess moves ahead. Execution focuses on winning in today's reality. Yet, each tribe views the world through the lens of its own faculties, which means that

297

each undervalues the other. Indeed, we have heard how each tribe will frequently disrespect the other and question their competence.

Let's review how this unfolds between global, regional, and local teams. First, we find that global leaders are more isolated as regional and local leaders are closer in the matrix, often sitting in the same management hierarchy with direct reporting relationships. Second, regional teams, who could be bridge-builders, tend to set strategy themselves and often choose to dilute or ignore global strategy to maintain their dominance. This leaves global teams struggling to have influence.

Without a bridge, without the combination, our business is unmistakably disadvantaged. Yet, we seem to be stuck, captive to this self-destructive squabble between interdependent stakeholders who want everyone to believe that they are not.

Is there a key to this behavior? How can we escape this negative paradigm? Forcing compliance doesn't work. Picking a side doesn't work. How might we harness this undeniable force of motivation?

Well, what if we are making a critical mistake by separating strategy and execution? What if we are hurting ourselves when we decree that strategists and executors are so different that they can't do each other's jobs, and when we say that only executives can make decisions and that only local leaders understand in-market performance? Can we fuse the roles of strategist and executor? This would be a major pivot. We are so used to pulling apart the roles of thinkers and doers. Yet, the tension that we are fighting, and we are always fighting this, is created when we try to separate those who can make choices and those who can't. Indeed, the entire matrix is rebelling against this. It is at odds with our human drive for autonomy.

In a 2013 survey of 700 executives across an assortment of industries, Strategy&, the global strategic consulting arm of PwC, asked participants to rate the effectiveness of their company's top leaders at strategy and execution. What they learned was that most of the leaders who were rated good at strategy were also rated good at execution, and vice versa. Only a minority were good at only one or the other.

These findings indicate that most people who are good at either strategy or execution are good at both. Small wonder then that regional and local leaders agitate when others insist on being the masters of strategy, and global leaders fume when they are told that they know nothing about execution. We have designed antagonism and competition into this system, which is why the dynamic that we see so often is confrontation, a battle to claim superior expertise and to demand leadership, or disengagement.

What can we do with this insight? What could this mean for global, regional, and local roles? How does this help us to bridge across the matrix?

Stay in Your Lane

An obvious implication is that we need to recognize that all of our leaders can make strategic choices and act on them. If we accept this, then it leads to an interesting shift in identity for everyone, with global, regional, and local roles defined not by an artificial assignment of responsibilities but more appropriately characterized by the value of their separate perspectives and scope. Now we can focus on which decisions and actions belong where and with whom.

In this new model, we expect global, regional, and local roles to offer unique value, with less overlap and with exclusive contributions shaped by such factors as geographic scope, and timing of impact.

This recasting of roles might help us to avoid a lot of dysfunction and end some of the wasteful theatrical games that result. There would still be a need for negotiation as global, regional, and local strategies will always overlap. The trick is to avoid inappropriate duplication. We need each geographic team to keep to their lane so that we can be clear about why one strategy is global in scope and why another strategy is regional. We haven't removed the need for candid debate to reconcile these strategies, but we have calmed a major cause of resentment and conflict.

Accountability or Nothing

If we allow all stakeholders to lead both strategy and execution, then all strategies need their corresponding plans, and vice versa, with clearly defined pictures of success, each with its measures and targets. Importantly, there must be individuals who are answerable to achieve these. This has particular consequences for global leaders who typically assume that others will execute their strategy and that they will not be held accountable for its success. However, if we are creating global strategies that are not duplicative with regional or local strategies, then global teams must lead them. The metrics to measure the success of global strategies and plans will not be the same as for local strategies and plans. For example, a strategy to bring expanded capabilities to multiple regions might be measured based on an internal assessment or regional feedback. Yet, there must be accountability.

This approach also helps global leaders who typically struggle to understand the value of their contribution. Now they are no longer handing responsibility to others for execution. They are happy to be on the hook and able to point proudly to their own achievements.

Sharing is Power

These findings also invite top executives to change. As we learned in Chapter 7 from the McKinsey study[7], senior executives are spending over half of their time making decisions, and yet they rate only 30% of them as good. While some executives enjoy their decision-making, many are

---

[7] The McKinsey Quarterly 2008. McKinsey & Company, Strategy & Corporate Finance.

frustrated because they know that they are not being as effective as they could be. Well, we have now learned that the ability to make choices is much more broadly distributed, and it is clearly advantageous for executives to fuel this. There will always be vision-setting, tie-breaking, and calls to make as we negotiate between global, regional, and local strategies. What is important is that top executives and global leadership teams don't frustrate or infantilize their subordinates by appropriating their sense of agency. Our strong executors are also strong strategists. Empower them. We have every chance of improving on that disappointing 30%.

In addition, for an organization to make the right choices, it is vital that its leaders, at all levels, are appropriately informed. This means that everyone must have access to information, from big picture stuff, such as the company's next steps for growth and major pain points, to new best practices, successes, and lessons learned. This is a powerful role for executives to ensure that their teams have all the information that they need to make the most informed and effective decisions. Indeed, the same holds for global, regional, and local teams. This is a great case for the connectivity that comes with investing in globalization.

A Last Word

My first intent was to craft a playbook to help others navigate the minefield that is between them and the opportunity to transform their company's global effectiveness. I wanted to offer a manual with instruction to improve how we build and prosecute global strategy. Yet, we are concluding with a clear view of a system that is not really built for purpose. We need to accept that we are going to be working within the minefield and we will never cross all the way to the other side. And so, this playbook offers knowledge, insights, tools, and advice to anticipate and mitigate the risk, the waste, the posturing, and the theatrics that are all but guaranteed by the status quo.

Along the way, and certainly in these final chapters, I have also offered some alternatives. It is not impossible to shape a different kind of global organization and we need to try, knowing the consequences if we don't. For, if we choose not to steer, then we choose to accept a future with too few inspiring leaders, too few good decisions, and far too much theater as we try to force sub-optimal strategy on stakeholders who don't want it.

Disentangling these considerations in order to promote global effectiveness is always going to be a custom project. Every company, every separate part of the same company, has its own hidden code that we need to find if we are to unlock its potential. Yet, now you know how to approach this. You have the mugshots of all the usual suspects. You know how they operate, how they work together, and the mischief that they cause. You know how to walk the crime scene. You also know where to find the perpetrators and how they give themselves away. You are ready to take them down.

My humble request is that you start by looking at your own mugshot. Assess it with objective self-awareness and appreciate your role in the drama. Change is a process and it can start small. Diagnose all the ways that you might contribute to global fragmentation. At the same time, don't be discouraged by the dysfunction that is all around. Accept where you are. Make this the benchmark to improve upon step-by-step. By all means, have a vision of global effectiveness but don't allow the size of the gap and the power of today's inertia to discourage you. All adoption curves start slowly before they accelerate. So, model more effective behaviors, build converts and advocates, and create case studies to persuade. However, pick your battles and be patient when you feel blocked or when you are pushed two steps back. Remember that small changes in a global operating model can be incredibly valuable.

I promised that you would not look at global strategy the same way again. I trust that is true. I hope that, where once you felt trapped in a world of tension, waste, politics, and dysfunction, you now see a way forward. I also wish you the fortitude to follow that path with all of the rewards that it brings.

A Fiction of Unity

Printed in Great Britain
by Amazon